外黒人

GAIKOKUJIN - THE STORY
II

Contributors

Edited by Joshua S. Yeley

Proofreading by Tracy M. Riva

<u>Cover Art</u>

Drawing: Griffin Reid

Calligrapher: Minori Ito

Note: Please make your contribution by leaving a review of the book here:
https://www.amazon.com/review/create-review?asin=B01AQT38V2&ie=UTF*&#

https://www.goodreads.com/book/show/28349177-gaikokujin---the-story

Thank you in advance!

Copyright

Publisher's Cataloging-In-Publication Data
(Prepared by The Donohue Group, Inc.)

Names: Amaru, Takuan.
Title: 外黒人 = Gaikokujin - the story. Book II, Making of a soldier / Takuan Amaru.
Other Titles: Gaikokujin - the story. Book II, Making of a soldier | Making of a soldier

Description: Nagoya, Japan : AfroAsiatic Books, [2016] |
Book II of a trilogy. | Interest age level: 014-030. |
Includes bibliographical references.
Identifiers: ISBN 978-4-908556-07-4 (set) | ISBN 978-4-
908556-03-6 (print) | ISBN 978-4-908556-02-9 (ebook)
Subjects: LCSH: Racially mixed youth--United States--
Fiction. | Basic training (Military education)--United
States--Fiction. | Fathers and sons--Fiction. | Child abuse--
Fiction. | Depression, Mental--Fiction. | American
literature--Japanese American authors. | LCGFT:
Biographical fiction.
Classification: LCC PS3601.M37 G352 2016 (print) | LCC
PS3601.M37 (ebook) | DDC 813/.6 [Fic]--dc23

Published by AfroAsiatic Books
www.afroasiatic.jp
www.gaikokujin-thestory.com

外黒人

GAIKOKUJIN - The Story

Book II: Making of a Soldier

Takuan Amaru

AfroAsiatic Books
Nagoya, Japan

Table of Contents

A Few Notes on my Army Enlistment

"Tre, a black man ain't got no business joining the Army" ~ *Furious Styles, in Boyz 'n the Hood.*

I agree with the advice given by Laurence Fishburne back in 1991. In spite of this, I am very proud to be an American. To some, these may appear to be conflicting statements. I tend to disagree.

In the 21st Century, the policies of the US government have strayed so far from the tenets established by America's founding fathers, they have more in common with Nazi Germany than any "Land of the Free" or "Home of the Brave." I first began to notice discrepancies with the United States' walk and its talk while I was still in high school. Yet, it was only after gaining first-hand experience in "this man's Army" (as the drill sergeants were so fond of saying), when I was able to connect the dots and realize we were just an organized gang. The biggest, baddest gang with the most dangerous weaponry, instead of red or blue, our colors were olive drab / camouflage green. *Therefore, I could never endorse joining the military.*

That said, believe it or not, my time spent in the Army was invaluable to my overall development as a man. Especially in the social arena. In fact, I'll go as far to say I doubt I could've have spent a more productive two-years-and-nine-months anywhere else.

Separate but Equal?

Similar to life in a penal colony, everyone segregated into groups based on ethnicity. The fundamental unwritten law was: when in doubt, seek out folks who look like you. Although everyone knew this, rarely was this peculiar behavior addressed intellectually. At the mere mention of race, many soldiers either walked away, or became nervous and defensive. Well, fortunately everyone did not think in this narrow-minded way. While attending Air-Assault School near the end of my enlistment, I was lucky enough to eat dinner with one such unique soldier.

By the friendly way this Guamanian NCO sat down next to me, a bystander would have never guessed this was our first time meeting each other. For a quick second, I thought he was someone I had met but forgotten. A little shorter than me, he looked like a stoutly built Latino with piercing black eyes and a pock-marked face. After giving me a pound, he wasted little time before explaining the reason for his visit.

"Specialist Amaru," he said after glancing at my chest. "Please, if you would, take a look around the mess hall." Extending his arm with his palm facing upward, he gestured toward our fellow diners.

Glancing around the room, I scrutinized the various groups of soldiers he pointed at. Not seeing anything worth reporting, I looked back at Sgt. Moreno's hawk-like stare.

"What? Don't you see it?" he asked in astonishment, stretching his scarred, coppertone complexion. "There's all blacks to our right, all whites to our left, and the Latinos sit over there," he said pointing a finger at the middle of room towards the back. "Only two of those tables, and the one we're sitting at, show *any* kind of racial diversity whatsoever. But check this out," he said with a grin, "if signs were put up tomorrow that read, 'Blacks only,' 'Whites only,' and 'Latinos only' in those same areas, everyone would shit a brick and be ready to fight. But they segregate themselves anyway, I don't understand." Shrugging both shoulders, the hard-charging sergeant was frustrated with the racially-divided institution he had volunteered to join. "Am I right? Am I right?"

Listening to him repeat his question over-and-over again, I thought he would never stop until I answered. *He was right.*

Fiending to Scheme

In June of 1989, Ft. Bragg shrunk in my rear-view mirror for the last time. Similar to many soldiers who are making the transition from the military back to civilian life, my mind was replaying a summary of my entire term-of-service in flashes. This is when I realized my experience had been nothing more than a a series of dreams woven into a nightmare. Considering how it started, it's mind-boggling I ended my enlistment as a decorated paratrooper with numerous medals of commendation. And an honorable discharge.

From the first day of basic training, I was scheming to manipulate the system. Despite this, I never received *even one blemish* on my military record. Not until I considered writing this book did it occur to me this had little to do with any ingenuity on my part. So what was it? Why was I allowed to bumble along like a sightless Mr. Magoo? Why was I permitted to continue onward unscathed? The only possible answer I could come up with is divine intervention. In other words, for some reason, it was not the time for my negative-karma to play itself out. While other pranksters got arrested, kicked out, or at least demoted, some sort of angelic energy time and time again protected me. These series of events bewildered the minds of jealous haters like Gimenez and Stew.

One night, early-on in basic training, Pvt. Odom and I snuck into an office that someone forgot to lock. Inside, we found a drill sergeant's hat laying on a desk. Seeing this, we looked at each other and grinned. After Odom put the *brown-round* on his head, I walked in the hallway to be the lookout. When four unsuspecting trainees approached, I coughed. This was Odom's signal to go into action.

Charging out of the office, Odom began screaming. *"Amaru drop!"* Then he pointed at the petrified foursome. "What the hell're you maggots looking at? All of you, drop!"

By the time the suckers noticed I was standing next to Odom—*and we were both cracking up at their expense*—they had already knocked out about ten push-ups apiece. From this one observation, I detected a loophole in the Army's system. Nevertheless it took me nearly a year to find the right opportunity to exploit it.

After being transferred out of the rugged Airborne Infantry, I became the sole, PLL clerk in a brand-new aviation unit. Before long, I noticed a few personalities who stood apart from the other soldiers. For some reason they appeared freer, or should I say more relaxed, than everyone else. Determined to figure out why, I decided to spy on them. It took me about a week of snooping around to confirm that these officers and NCO's were either bending the rules, or outright breaking the law. This information encouraged me to put on my thinking-cap. A few days later, I asked my supervisor for permission to take the manuals on my Military Occupational Specialty to the barracks. Because our motor sergeant knew very little about my MOS, he was ecstatic I wanted to do some extra studying to improve my job performance.

Every night, for the next two weeks, I pored over the documents while my roommates snored in their sections of our room. My goal was to engineer a method to make expensive military equipment disappear from the records without a trace. About a month later, I felt ready to start my operation so I visited a slew of pawn shops in Fayetteville. Once I fingered who I thought was the slimiest proprietor of the ten or so shops, I approached him with my crooked business proposal. The balding middle-aged man, who appeared to be from an Arab country, was unshaven and reeked of oregano. Appearing unsurprised, not only did he agree, he informed me the only obstacle in my scheme was obtaining a fake, military ID.

"I'll need a copy of one if you're pawning military equipment," stated the pudgy store owner. "It's just a formality," he added with a smirk. "Frankly, I don't care if there's a white guy in the picture."

In the Army, a person is equivalent to whatever their uniform expresses. Name, rank, accomplishments: it's all on public display. For this reason, if dressed appropriately, it is possible to walk around post in the guise of someone else and never raise an eyebrow.

This being the loophole I detected that night in basic, now I finally had a plan to sift money through it.

Betting everything on this premise, I entered a dilapidated, wooden building with 'Replacement ID' written on a tattered card taped to the door. Just as I figured, with the correct uniform on, no verificative identification was necessary to receive my 'license to loot.' After filling out an application, I affixed magnetized letters spelling "Aaron Johnson" to a black metallic board. Then, I was instructed to sit down in front of a camera and hold the board under my chin. Ten minutes after the mugshot was taken, I claimed my alias. Just like in high school, I reflected with a smug grin, they never conceived anyone being so bold.

The most difficult part of my plan had been getting my hands on the 'correct uniform' the night before. Recognizing "Johnson" to be a popular surname among folks of a darker hue, I visited the resident Johnson in my barracks one evening after dinner. When I realized he was in the shower—and his roommates were not around—I took the liberty of borrowing one of his BDU shirts without his knowledge.

Several months after dedicating my life to Christ, I was chatting with my motorpool buddies while we waited for the after-lunch formation to commence. When four CID[1] officers arrived, everyone got quiet. Following a short conference with our company commander and first-sergeant, they walked over and placed our supply sergeant under arrest.

Like everyone, I was in shock watching Sgt. Simmons being escorted toward their cars with his hands cuffed behind his back. Seeing this, I had a fleeting recollection of the night Sgt. Simmons and I busted each other smuggling equipment from the supply room. Reminiscing thus, I knew I could easily be headed to Ft. Leavenworth right along with the shady sergeant.

---

[1] The meaning of Army Acronyms are listed in the *Glossary of Terms, Historical Figures, and Events*

"Thank you for saving me from a life of sin—*and incarceration,*" I murmured to my maker under my breath.

Almost six months had elapsed since I followed my friend, Che's advice and ritualistically cut my fake ID into nine pieces before burning them in a fire. Even though some people might consider this to be witchcraft, that was the day I knew for sure I was a full-fledged Christian. As I considered Sgt. Simmon's fate, one of the CID officials approached our platoon and stopped in front of *me.* I was aghast when the captain addressed me by name.

"Good afternoon, Specialist Amaru," stated the lanky Caucasian. The tall man had wide-set blue eyes and a flat, broad nose. With his arms folded, he took a few seconds to verify the name and rank stitched on my shirt before he spoke again. "Or should I say, Johnson?"

Although I was *shook-daddy,* I pretended to be clueless. "Excuse me sir?"

Unimpressed, Captain Zealand resumed his indictment. "We wanted to arrest both of you low-lifes together, but your partner was getting too greedy; so we couldn't wait any longer."

"What's he talking about Amaru?" shouted Sgt. Will after he ran over and, following a hurried salute, inserted himself between me and the captain. As my platoon sergeant asked the question, he bulldozed me backward several steps to create some space between us and the CID officer.

"I have no idea Sergeant," I spit the lie out the instant I formed it in my mouth while still in my back pedal.

Once Sgt. Will heard this, he wheeled around to confront the CID officer who was now standing several feet away.

"Sir, the specialist says he doesn't know what you're

xvi

talking about," the NCO bellowed. "Can you please be more specific?"

Ignoring my supervisor, Captain Zealand looked over Sgt. Will's shoulder and spoke to me in a coaxing tone. "Amaru, do yourself a favor," he began. "With Simmons out of the way, we're gonna concentrate on investigating you now. Trust me, we *will* get a conviction. However..." Softening his voice, he smiled before making me a fool's proposition. "If you're smart, you'll confess now. Remember, you're guaranteed a fair trial under Article 15 of the UCMJ..."

'Blah blah blah!' is what I heard. "Pardon me sir," I interrupted him, "but I don't know what you're talking about."

Although the ninth commandment forbids bearing false witness, I figured under the circumstances God would understand. *Plus, I knew my boy, A-Rock would be damn proud!*

"You don't know anything, huh?" the captain replied in a calm tone before pointing at me and raising his voice. "Once a thief, always a liar! You'll steal again Amaru...or Johnson...or whatever the hell your name is! And when you do, I'll be there to take your ass down! Remember my face smart-alec because I have a picture of yours—on a fake ID!"

Even after Sgt. Will pushed me an additional twenty feet, the infuriated captain continued shouting until a group of warrant-officers and NCOs ran over to escort him back to where his fellow cronies had been observing.

In spite of Cpt. Zealand's swagger, considering I was not shackled next to Sgt. Simmons at that moment, I knew someone over there was not as convinced as he claimed to be. Minutes later, as I watched their lime-green cars disappear into the traffic, I exhaled a sigh of relief. *The Billy Bad-Ass*

Era is finally over, I reflected.

"Welcome to Ft. Leonard Wood, Missouri!"

For five days, before any training began, we lived in a neat set of barracks to get sorted out. It was a hectic atmosphere. With hundreds of young men in-processing, the reception station was a whirlwind of paperwork, medical shots, physicals, haircuts, equipment issue, and some very bad attitudes! The process of sapping away our freedom had begun. Even though the NCOs in charge of us were not drill sergeants, they bossed us around to illustrate our indentured-servant status.

"G-I are the initials for 'General Issue!'" yelled one sergeant. "In other words, just like a tank, a jeep, a pair of boots, or a uniform, we're all government property. While this may seem trivial to the uninitiated civilian, next week when boot camp begins, you'll fully understand my meaning!"

Although I imagine our feelings of confinement paled in comparison to my brothers and sisters pinned behind prison walls, those first couple days were traumatizing nonetheless. Due to the stitches in my hands and face, I was almost sent back to Philly shortly after arriving in Missouri.

"Even a blind man can see you're damaged goods!" scoffed one of the doctors checking-in the incoming trainees.

Later the drills were equally baffled I passed the final physical at the airport. "Amaru, you should've been rejected back in Philly!" complained a drill named Sanford. "The first time I saw your sorry ass I noticed your stitches."

When my recruiter spotted my sutures on the morning he picked me up at Herb's house, he almost panicked. Saying little in the presence of my family, after we left, he stopped the car around the corner to inspect my injuries.

"You know you still gotta pass one more physical before you're allowed on that plane, right homeboy?"

"Nah, you ain't say nothing about that before," I protested. "Sarge, I gotta leave no matter what. My pops kicked me out so I ain't got nowhere to live."

Hearing this, Sgt. Thompson playfully punched my arm. "Don't worry," he said with a sly grin, "we gonna get you outta here. Okay, this is what you do..." As he removed my bandages, he explained one MEPS doctor would check groups of four boys simultaneously. Then we got out of the car so I could practice the body movements I had to perform.

"Make sure you're in one of the outside lines—away from the doctor," Sgt. Thompson emphasized. "This is key because he'll walk down the middle row to inspect for obvious injuries like yours. But if you keep your head down, it's hard to see those stitches under your lip."

Once he felt confident I understood the situation, he led me through the body movements I had to perform. After raising my arms, he had me do several squats which I did easily. For the finale, I had to do ten push-ups. Since I could not open my hands, this was the most difficult task. Nevertheless, once I practiced balancing on the ridges of my palms, I had no trouble doing them in front of the doctor.

When a drill sergeant inquired why no one noticed my injuries back in Philly, I played dumb.

"I don't know."

"I don't know, *Drill Sergeant*," the round-hat wearing disciplinarian corrected me.

"Oh yeah, Drill Sergeant."

At the conclusion of the physical and the subsequent

interrogation that followed, the doctor summoned the company commander so he could have the final word on whether or not he wanted to accept me into his unit. Following one look at my face, the CO echoed the sentiments of the others.

"Private, you must've been invisible for them to miss all those train tracks running across your face," he said with a sneering grin. "Consider yourself lucky to be here." Still shaking his head in disbelief, Captain Yates then looked over at a stubby specialist holding a clip-board. "Check Amaru's name off, he's okay," he declared giving me the thumbs-up.

Considering I had devolved to the level of barbarism after only one week in the street, it was crucial that I left on September ninth. To say some structure and a support system was vital for my continued existence, even this might underplay the severity of the situation

"Yo Philly!"

Because all my paperwork read Philadelphia, fellow privates-in-training nicknamed me 'Philly.' In addition, once word hit the grapevine about my stitches, I gained an unmerited reputation as a street-fighter. Not minding any of this free publicity, I was happy to assume the 'Tough Fighter from West Philly' theme.

By the second day, I found myself on the verge of fisticuffs with three, different whiteboys who wanted to test my mettle. Of the three, only one appeared ready to go beyond the talking stage. At that time, even had I known this guy was destined to become my squad leader, it probably would not have changed my shitty attitude. Looking at him, with his dirty-blonde high-and-tight hair cut, I imagined he was one of those crackas posing for a photo next to a lynched negro with a big smile on his face.

On our final morning at the reception station, we stood in formation with our gear piled behind us. Using sign-language and whispers, the four of us made promises to settle the score once boot camp got underway. This is when I realized I had to watch my back for the next eight weeks.

Book II

Chapter 1: First Day

Only five days of in-processing had passed and I was homesick. By the time a fleet of semi-trucks arrived at the reception station to pick us up, I was already having second thoughts about my enlistment. *Could I really deal with this left-right-left bullshit for three years?*

These tractor-trailers were pulling what appeared to be giant, metal iceboxes with tiny windows along the sides. After a second look, I realized they were wheeled cargo-freighters for transporting livestock. "That figures," I murmured under my breath and snickered thinking what could be more appropriate than for us to be delivered across post like a flock of sheep? Even after the cadre barked commands to board the 'cattle trucks,' I continued referring to these vehicles as 'sheep trucks' simply because it was more fitting.

While I contemplated my situation, we were crowded into the cargo holds. Not quite standing-room-only, there was one drill sergeant dressed in his Class A's on each truck. Like everyone, I was eager to get my first look at a genuine, drill sergeant. Portrayed in books and movies as larger-than-life, imposing taskmasters, by the time I put my duffel bags down inside the truck, I was snickering again because the dude riding with us was a little guy. At five-foot-seven, let's just say he was a far cry from the 'big bad' drill sergeant I had in mind.

"My name's Sandoval," said the jovial drill. "Make

yourselves comfortable…the ride's gonna be about fifteen minutes."

As he spoke, I noticed the sharply-dressed instructor's eyes were bloodshot-red. So my first impression of a drill sergeant was they were short, friendly guys who possibly smoked weed. While I considered whether or not he was high, it was difficult to suppress a grin from materializing on my face. At first, I thought Drill Sergeant Sandoval was Latino but later he revealed he was Filipino, like Ant. Because I was standing amongst the herd of privates gawking in his direction, I was surprised when he singled me out of the crowd.

"Where're ya from?" inquired the drill.

Even though I was sure he was talking to me, I feigned uncertainty by hooking a thumb at my chest. Once he nodded, I proclaimed, "Philly!" in a loud, confrontational tone. In addition to broadcasting my urban affiliation–*like that meant I was tough*–I was making it known to my fellow trainees that I was setting-up camp.

"Philadelphia huh?" he replied, ignoring my challenge. "I've never been to the east coast. I'm from LA." Then the easy-going drill fixed his attention on the private to my left. "How about you…where're ya from?"

For the next couple minutes, Sgt. Sandoval engaged in hometown conversations with about a dozen trainees. While he was chuckling at a comment made by a kid from Reno, Nevada, he glanced out a side-window.

Imitating his example, I noticed the trucks were turning down on a street with identical brick-housing units on both sides.

"Welcome to the barracks of Alpha Company, 4th Brigade 3rd Battalion—or the Alpha 4-3 Raiders–Oooah!"

2

boomed Drill Sgt. Sandoval. Using a much stronger voice than just seconds ago, it seemed he was now revealing his true personality.

I was not the only one who was taken aback by his sudden change in demeanor. Before we had a chance to rebound, Sgt. Sandoval addressed us again.

"Everyone!" he bellowed. "Grab one of your duffel bags!" Yelling this, he swiped a bag from the stunned private next to me. "There's a small buttoned-pocket on the side…right here," he said demonstrating which pocket he was referring to. Popping it open, he issued his first command. "Put all thoughts of your civilian life in here and close it." With a wicked grin plastered on his face, the drill finished talking precisely as the cattle truck stopped. "Because it's finished!"

His speech, seeming rehearsed, was synchronized to end when the truck came to a standstill. Proof of this was the vehicle had barely stopped moving when the side-door was viciously thrown open from the outside. *What had been a peaceful ride to this point suddenly became total bedlam.*

Pandemonium erupted when several drills invaded the cargo hold screaming like crazed savages. Charging through the open door, they snatched petrified boys by their arms and began shoving them out of the truck. Although these drill sergeants wore the identically-designed camouflage uniforms we were sporting, somehow their BDUs looked faded-and-seasoned compared to ours, which looked amateurishly new and off-the-rack.

Soon many boys decided it was better to exit on their own rather than being pushed; so they took the initiative and jumped out. However, before their feet touched the ground, they were swiftly met by the outside welcoming committee.

3

Like the other drills, Sgt. Sandoval seemed possessed by a violent-crazed entity as he added to the mayhem of the moment. *"Drop you filthy maggots!"*

We learned the command 'Drop!' meant to get down and do push-ups; and the starting position was called the *front-leaning rest.* For those first, unfortunate privates who did not comprehend the military jargon, they were mercilessly grabbed and thrown to the ground. Needless to say, their example served as an effective demonstration lesson for the entire group.

The chaos continued to escalate as more and more boys exited the truck. Never missing a beat, prior to each frantic youngster's boots touching the pavement, a foul-mouthed drill showed up to greet him. *"Drop!"*

During the panic-stricken exodus, I moved next to the door to avoid getting sucked into the exiting stampede. Seconds later, I looked around and found the entire cargo hold was empty. Everyone had exited the truck. Well, everyone except me. Somehow, I had gotten caught-up watching the drama like it was a television episode of 'Boot Camp—Live.' Once I understood the drills did not suspect anyone remained inside, I decided to stay put. In other words, I was in no hurry to be called nasty names and do push-ups. Unable to see the nearby hostilities from my location, I sat down and listened. Doing so brought to mind being on the porch with Wayne and listening to the Isis vs. Asia battles. By this time, in one way or another, everything reminded me of Asia.

It was the reeking odor of sweat being poured in the autumn sun, that plus the grunts and groans of muscle-fatigued youths gasping for oxygen, which woke me up. Exactly how long I had dozed is uncertain; however, it was clear some time had elapsed. Rising to my feet, it was then I recognized the unique predicament I was in: exactly how did I plan to exit the truck without being seen? Since trouble appeared unavoidable, I decided to milk my hiatus for as long as I could.

Slowly but surely, the round-hat taskmasters herded the trainees onto the sidewalk in front of the barracks. Daring to take a peek, I was horrified seeing these privates dripping with sweat. Once the area in front of the trucks was clear, the drivers revved-up their engines in preparation to leave. It wasn't long before a tall, Caucasian soldier approached the cargo-hold to shut the door.

I had to make a move.

Gingerly stepping through the closing door, I greeted the E-4 with a wink, a cocky grin, and a slight bow of my head. I was pleased to see his startled look of amazement as I jumped down to the ground. Remaining quiet, I then grabbed my duffel bags and began navigating my way through the crowd of dropped privates. While I stepped around several guys struggling in the front-leaning rest position, I checked out all the excitement around me.

Having arrived to the sidewalk, I searched for an area that was clear of bodies. Once I found one, I placed my stuff on the ground and took a seat on one of my duffel bags. By my calm, carefree demeanor, I could have easily been mistaken for a spectator taking in an early-afternoon matinee. All I needed was a box of popcorn.

Although my actions were not premeditated, the drills appeared shock-and-awed by my brashness. Two of the three nearest drills ignored me. I don't know why because I was sure they saw me. But I did notice the one who was paying attention seemed confused about what I was doing. All three

5

of these instructors were Caucasian. Just before I got comfortable, my honeymoon came to a screeching halt.

"What the fuck do you think you're doing?" screamed an irate voice from my blind-side.

Glancing to my left, I focused on the tall, muscular black man. "Good morning, Drill Sergeant Sanford!" I bellowed after reading the name-tag on his chest. With a big *Kool-Aid* grin etched on my face, I enjoyed the dramatization to the end. In all honesty, I was a bit disappointed it had taken so long for someone to address me.

Hearing my sarcastic response, Sgt. Sanford was beside himself with anger. When he reached out to grab me, I stood up and side-stepped away from him. Before he could take another swipe, I jumped down into the front-leaning rest position next to my brothers.

As I cranked out my first push-ups, I heard the privates nearby giggling under their breath. I was delighted my efforts had not gone unappreciated. *Drill's ain't so tough…it's just a bunch of hype like everything else!* I thought to myself, mentally chalking-up one point for the visiting team.

This illustrates how little I had learned in my fight with my father. There I was celebrating a captured pawn while the veterans were focusing three moves ahead—when they planned to have me in-check. When the dust settled, the result of my late-exit bore dire consequences because I had violated one of the cardinal rules of boot-camp. Never draw attention to oneself; it's the absolute worst thing a trainee can do.

During my time serving Uncle Sam, I got over on many supervisors, so I know what I'm talking about when I say it's rare to get away with clowning a drill sergeant.

Unbeknownst to many, drills are some very impressive people. Aside from having mastered the skills of modern warfare, they are intelligent, witty, and well-spoken. Their assignment, which is to transform the 'on the block,' civilian personality into a professional soldier who will not flinch when obeying a dangerous order is no small task. Think about it: exactly how does a person go about teaching others to kill? Or, to obey a command that may get them killed? Of course, this could also be seen as brainwashing because it is undoubtedly necessary to use a form of mind-control to transform kids from all-walks-of-life into one, efficient fighting unit. And all of this occurs within the span of a couple months.

Return of the Beast

Having survived our grand welcome, we were lined up in one of three platoons. I was designated in second platoon. Once the three, 2nd platoon drills introduced themselves, they launched into a bunch of 'hoo-rah' speeches about proper conduct before herding us into another line to receive linen. While collecting our blankets, sheets, and pillows, we were also given room assignments within the barracks.

"Alright," yelled one drill sergeant named Taliaferro in a somewhat surprisingly high-pitched voice. "We're gonna let you bumbling fools into our barracks. Notice I didn't say 'your' barracks. You dumb-ass privates don't own shit, don't have shit, and ain't worth shit…you understand me?" he yelled.

"Clear Drill Sergeant!" Everyone but me responded.

After taking a second to glare at us,the light-skinned drill continued. "You have exactly thirty seconds to report to your assigned rooms. Once you jack-asses get there, you stand at attention next to your bunks. There's no talking…do you understand?"

"Clear Drill Sergeant!" Once again everyone chorused.

"Ready, move!" the round-brown disciplinarian bellowed with a scowl on his face.

On his command, blankets in hand, we were finally permitted enter the hallowed halls. Although this was our home for the next two months, every drill made it vehemently clear the barracks belonged to them. In fact, they claimed to own everything while insisting we privates owned nothing— *not even the shirt on our back!*

Loaded down with our bags and linen, we bumbled up flights of stairs and filed into our rooms filled with excitement. After finding our bunks and laying down our belongings, everyone took a brief second to assess their surroundings. Regardless of race or religion, each young man knew he was looking at his new family. Before we had a chance to greet one another, the booming voices of the drills lashed out again. Their new command required us to move to a designated room for a class on bed-making.

Once my roommates and I assembled in the room next door, Drill Sergeant Sanford demonstrated, in painstaking detail, how to fold the sheets and blankets at a forty-five-degree angle to create hospital corners. Immediately following the lesson, we were tested.

"You have twenty minutes to make your beds in accordance with Army standards…any questions?" Then, without giving anyone time to respond, he released us. "This class is over, you're dismissed!" Sgt. Sanford spoke in wrathful tone.

On his command, everyone scuttled back to their respective rooms. Since the drills would soon be inspecting our beds everyone knew there was no time to waste. However, before getting to work, each private introduced himself with a quick sentence or two. Our room leader spoke up first.

"What's up everybody, just call me Brown. I'm from DC," announced the big athletic brother in a scratchy voice.

"Hi, my name's Jack, Jack Winters," said a lanky white guy, "I'm from Omaha, Nebraska."

"Whattis upu every...one?" It seemed the Korean private was trying to imitate Brown but had forgotten his lines. He soon became conscious he was taking up too much time so he just blurted out his name. "I'm Kim."

I figured this was the best act to follow.

"West Philly's in the muthafuckin house boyeee! Name's Amaru, don't wear it out!" This is what came out of my mouth.

"I'm Bill Arrington…"

Self-introductions completed, I walked toward my area of the room and noticed my bunk-buddy was already there. 'Bunk-buddy' is a label for a pair of privates sharing a set of bunk beds and adjoining wall lockers. My 'buddy' was another big dude from the Washington DC area named Jones.

Private Samuel Jones was a chubby, light-skinned brother who weighed-in at about two-hundred-fifty pounds. He was a little taller than me, maybe about six-foot-one. Although I don't recall hearing his self-intro, everyone already met their bunk-buddies outside while we waited in-line to collect our linen. When I shook his hand he seemed to be a cool guy. Honestly, I was just relieved I was not bunking with a whiteboy—*and I'm sure many of them felt likewise.*

Approaching closer, I saw Jones was already folding his sheet around the mattress on the bottom bunk. This upset me. It did not have anything to do with sleeping on the top bunk. As a child, I shared a bunk bed with Ken and after he left for the Air Force, I took turns sleeping on both bunks. Had Jones expressed he wanted to sleep on the bottom, there would have been no problem. My point is, I wanted to discuss the matter like I saw my roommates were doing. It was about respect.

Since the drills had already demonstrated their tendency to punish us in groups, I knew the failure of one trainee to make his bed would lead to the whole room being dropped. And like everyone, I did not want to be that weak link. With this in mind, I resolved to let the incident go. Nevertheless it seemed I was not the only one in an agitated state of mind that morning. Faced with our first timed task, the room seemed to be heating up as I stopped a few feet shy of our bed.

"Yeah Jones, I see you already got started," I opened up subtly. "Lemme see if I can remember how Sergeant Sanford did this…" Since his back was facing me, I made small-talk to announce my presence. When he ignored me, it was difficult to play down the urgency I felt about being the last private to get started. Seeing he had placed his blankets and pillow on the top bunk while he applied his sheets, I needed them to be moved so I could begin too. "Yo cuz, can you move your stuff?" I spoke louder this time, revealing I was losing patience.

Jones never looked in my direction when he sighed loudly like I was bothering him. Then he snapped at me,

"Bitch, wait a minute! Can't you see I'm busy?"

I was shocked. His rude reply took me off-guard because, like I said, we shook hands thirty minutes earlier and at that time everything seemed cool. There was no way for me to pretend he was not dissing me. But just in case his intention was not clear, he stood up and snatched his pillow from the top bunk—*leaving his blankets there.* Then, he had the nerve to glare at me for a split-second before turning back around to place it on his mattress.

Although I was stunned, when I heard him mumbling "punk" and "bitch"—for a second time—something inside of me snapped. This wasn't about my pride, being cool, or anything trivial like that. Jones had ruptured my Emotional Pain Body, and once this bolt of energized hate was activated, it demanded its release.

The entity I came to regard as 'the Beast' had made its debut at Malik's and returned later the same night in the drunken brawl with the Serpent. What distinguished its third manifestation from the first two was this time the Beast's host—me—was sober. Not to mention I was exhibiting the edginess and paranoia of a withdrawing substance-abuser. Whenever activated, the Beast was single-minded in confronting and destroying its target. Now it had a big target indeed.

Fuck a bed-making drill! This thought activated the release of a warm sensation near my feet. Within seconds, an awesome energy-force was creeping upward through my legs; once it coiled its way up around my spine and reached my face, it incapacitated my ability to speak. Then I felt a throbbing sensation pulsating behind my eyes; it was then I lost all control of my actions. At this point, I instinctively knew it was about pain—mine or somebody else's—it didn't

11

matter. The Beast was not specific about who got hurt, so long as someone did. Even if I took a cruel beat-down—as I did in the fight against my father—this too would satisfy the debt of violence required for summoning this belligerent deity.

Since the Beast would not attack someone from behind, I had to settle for the next-best, aggressive action. Without making a sound, I stepped forward and snatched Jones' blankets off the top bunk. As I proceeded to carry them to the nearest window, I suddenly had Jones' full attention.

"Hey! What the fuck do you think you're doing?" he yelled in a rough voice.

This was the second time that morning I had been asked this exact question.

Nonetheless it was my turn to do the ignoring. Opening one of our second-story windows, I tossed Jones' blankets out before turning to face him. Having walked six paces to reach the window, there was about twenty feet separating us.

"Now what, fat-boy?" I taunted after realizing I had regained the use of my vocal cords.

By this time, every private in the room had paused their frantic bed-making to witness the impending battle. As I stepped in Jones' direction to escalate the confrontation to the physical stage, many expressed their surprise seeing Jones bolt three steps in the opposite direction. I too was taken aback but the Beast's flow was never interrupted. Since Jones was not within reach, I swiped his sheets and pillow off the mattress and returned to the window.

"Come on chubby, whatchu wanna do?" I asked in a threatening tone as I threw them out too.

With the letters *p-u-s-s-y* clearly stamped on his

forehead, it was obvious Jones wanted nothing to do with the Beast. On my third trip to the bunk for his mattress, PFC Brown, along with three others, blocked my path.

"Amaru, chill-out before the drill sergeants come!" a burly, Caucasian pleaded while Brown put his arm around me in big brotherly fashion.

"Yeager's right, Brown agreed before pointing at Jones. "He was acting like a dick-head...everyone here knows he was wrong. But none of that's gonna matter when the drills get here, so you gotta chill!"

Believe me I wanted to, but the Beast hadn't gotten his fill. As my frustration mounted, I again found it impossible to speak. Seeing my path to the bed blocked, I ran straight at Jones while Brown struggled to grab hold of my shirt. Jones sprinted away before I could catch him; however upon reaching the door he veered hard to the left—*in the nick of time to avoid a head-on collision with Drill Sergeant Sanford.*

"At ease!" Jones screamed, appearing frightened all over again.

Hearing this command, every private in the room stood erect and placed his feet shoulder-width apart before neatly folding his hands in the small of his back. This is called the 'parade rest' position, and this is what we had been instructed to do upon the arrival of our masters.

The tall, dark drill's entrance reminded me of an angry *Darth Vader* manifesting amongst his *Storm Troopers.* Sgt. Sanford looked pissed off but remained quiet. After walking to the center of the room in silence, he scanned the semi-circle of men facing him. Considering the circumstances, his opening comments were rather somber.

"Fights are common in boot camp...especially during

13

the first week," he stated. Following one more look around the room, the drill took everyone off-guard by abruptly yelling. *"Jones, what the hell were you doing?"*

"Nothing Drill Sergeant!" Jones shouted his lie in a trembling tone.

"Okay, maybe you weren't *doing* anything. But you certainly were going somewhere. Why, you almost ran me over trying to get out the door. Where were you going?" demanded the drill.

"Nowhere Drill Sergeant."

"Nowhere?" After repeating his reply in a sarcastic tone, Sgt. Sanford stepped closer to stare into Jones' eyes. "Boy, you think I'm stupid?"

"No Drill Sergeant!"

Pausing to 'eye-ball' Jones a second time, the drill decided to dig deeper. "Jones, since you say nothing is going on here, whose blankets just flew out the window? And you better not tell me you don't know!" he said pointing accusingly into Jones' face.

"They were mine, Drill Sergeant."

"Wrong!" The tall drill blasted at an even louder decibal. "Those blankets belong to me. I thought I made it clear you nasty maggots don't own shit around here! You understand me?"

"Yes Drill Sergeant!"

Despite being chastised, Jones sounded more convincing now that he was telling the truth. His voice even projected a military tone.

"Private," the drill continued wearing a puzzled expression. "Help me out here because I'm obviously missing something." Saying this, Sgt. Sanford scratched his chin. "Why did you throw my blankets out the window?"

"I...umm...I d-didn't d-do it on purpose, Drill Sergeant," Jones stuttered his response, trying to stall.

I couldn't just stand there and let him take the blame so I raised my hand to confess but PFC Brown, who was standing next to me, grabbed my arm with one hand and extended his other hand over my mouth to silence me. Once I looked at Brown, he released me and placed his index-finger against his lips, in the classic 'Shh' pose.

Brown and I snapped back to parade-rest a split-second before the drill scanned the room. Since Sgt. Sanford had had his back to Brown and me, he did not see us break our military bearing. On the other hand everyone else, including Jones, saw what had transpired between us.

"Dammit Jones, this is the last time I'll ask," Sgt. Sanford threatened. "Why did you throw my blankets out the window?"

"It was an accident, Drill Sergeant. I was umm, running with the blankets in my hand and umm, I tripped...that's when the blankets flew out the window."

"Boy drop! You *do* think I'm stupid." While Jones got into the front-leaning rest position, the drill continued yelling. "Well, I guess you tripped twice because my equipment flew out the window two different times, son. Get your fuckin' lie together! The truth is, someone deliberately threw my blankets out the window and I'm gonna find who it was. Count out-loud maggot!" he barked after Jones had done three silent reps.

"One, two, three—"

"That's 'One-Drill Sergeant, Two-Drill Sergeant!'" Sgt. Sanford shrieked.

"One-Drill Sergeant—"

"LOUDER!"

15

"One-Drill Sergeant, two-Drill Sergeant, three-Drill Sergeant..."

With Jones on the floor howling like a wounded hound, Sgt. Sanford focused his attention on the rest of us.

"Look around!" he yelled, pointing at the bunks and lockers. "Everything you see belongs to me. And these beds and blankets are GI-government-issued, just like you. You *will* respect my barracks! Do you understand?"

"Yes Drill Sergeant!"

"I can't hear you!" he encouraged us to scream louder.

"Yes Drill Sergeant!" we repeated.

Not satisfied with Jones' flawed confession, Sgt. Sanford then pivoted one-hundred-eighty degrees and menacingly growled, "Private First-Class Brown!"

PFC Douglas Brown was older than most of the privates in Alpha Company. Having recently graduated from a small college in Maryland where he played basketball before joining 'the war,' after Brown and I became tight, he showed me photos of his baby, his wife, and members of his team. When I asked why he had joined the Army—I mean, dude had a four-year degree—Brown chuckled before responding in a sarcastic tone. "Amaru, for a black man, a B.S. degree is exactly that...bullshit! Because you're still unemployed."

Although Sgt. Sanford was smiling when he turned around, it was more like the evil snarl of a Doberman Pinscher. "Brown, now tell me what happened. And I don't wanna hear no bullshit. You understand?"

"Yes Drill Sergeant!" bellowed Brown in his husky, scratchy voice.

"Look at Jones," the drill said, pointing at him on the floor. "He's scared to death. The coward obviously didn't throw the blankets out the window himself. So the only question is: who did?" Following another scan around room, he returned his attention to Brown. "You know what I just noticed?" Before Brown could respond, the drill answered his own question. "You're the only one here bigger than Jones."

As Sgt. Sanford stepped forward to eye-ball the PFC, I felt uncomfortable because Brown was right next to me. In spite of this, the drill's next question almost made me laugh.

"PFC Brown, did you punk my private?"

"No Drill Sergeant, I did not punk Private Jones and I don't know what happened," began Brown. "I was busy making my bed. I didn't see anything."

When Sgt. Sanford started laughing, the incident took on a humorous edge. "Everyone here thinks I'm a fool. Ain't that right, Winters?"

Having given up pressuring Brown, Sgt. Sanford was now stalking the skinny private from Wisconsin.

"No Drill Sergeant!" replied Winters in a loud, high-pitched voice.

When asked to give his version of the incident, Pvt. Winters responded in accordance with the protocol established by our room-leader, PFC Brown.

"Drill Sergeant, I don't know what happened. I was making my bed. I didn't see anything."

My roommates were not going to turn me in.

With the Beast having long since vanished to the netherworld, I was hoping to escape the situation without further incident.

"PFC Brown!" Sgt. Sanford snapped, turning back toward me and Brown. Although the drill's facial expression was serious, he seemed amused. "I know that you know what happened, but since we're in the middle of an inspection, I don't have time to force a confession." Then he pointed

around the room. "And by the looks of these fucked-up beds, you shit-heads need all the time you can get. *Brown!*" he screamed again.

"Yes Drill Sergeant!" Brown yelled back.

"You're the highest-ranking man in this room. Therefore I have decided to leave this situation in your hands. Any more outbreaks will be your responsibility. Do you understand?"

"Yes Drill Sergeant!" shouted Brown.

In spite of all the screaming and yelling back-and-forth, Sgt. Sanford and PFC Brown appeared to be enjoying themselves. While their faces remained stoic, their eyes held a glint of laughter.

"Last question," bellowed the drill. "Were Amaru and Jones fighting?"

"I don't know," Brown replied like a robot. "I was busy—"

"Making your bed, I know, I know," Sgt. Sanford completed Brown's statement with him.

Appearing confident the situation was under control, the drill spun around and returned to the center of the room. *"Alpha Company!"* he boomed to not only us but also to the entire floor. "Anyone caught fighting will be sent back to the block immediately. Is that understood?"

"Yes Drill Sergeant!"

"I can't hear you! Is that understood?"

"Yes Drill Sergeant!"

As we responded, the tall drill pivoted to glare into each private's eyes. When he reached mine, he stopped.

"Amaru, you gottit?"

"Yes Drill Ser—"

"I can't hear you!" he interrupted me.

"Yes Drill Sergeant!" I yelled.

"Jones?"

"Yes Drill Sergeant," he strained to respond through his labored breathing. Jones was still on the floor in the front-leaning-rest position.

"Good!" the disciplinarian emphasized, looking at his watch. "You legless larvae have nine minutes remaining, and there will be no extra time added-on to make up for this distraction. Do you understand?"

"Yes Drill Sergeant!"

"As you were!"

Hearing the command to release us from our spell, everyone rushed back to their beds.

"And you boy!" the drill said looking down at the pathetic figure on the floor. "Recover, and go outside and get my linen. *Move!"*

Jones, well beyond the point of muscle-failure, had stopped doing push-ups long ago. Still on all-fours, he had his butt arched way up in the air. Hearing the drill's command, Jones showed his fatigue when he struggled to get to his feet. This prompted Sgt. Sanford to yell again.

"Boy, you better move faster than that!" he roared.

Once Jones scurried away like a frightened puppy, the drill was almost out the door himself when he stopped and turned back toward us. It seemed he had just remembered something.

"Brown!"

"Yes Drill Sergeant!"

"For the inspection, go ahead and finish making the bed you're working on, but after dinner, I want you and Jones to switch bunks and lockers. Is that clear?"

"Clear Drill Sergeant!" responded Brown.

19

By the time Drill Sergeant Sanford was walking out the door, he was mumbling in a manner which suggested he wanted to be overheard. "It's a damn shame!" he said, shaking his head in disgust. "Big ol' boy like Jones getting chumped by a lightweight like Amaru."

Hearing this, everyone stopped to look at Sgt. Sanford's back as he exited the room. We were shocked to discover he had been playing dumb all along. Minutes later when Jones re-entered the room, he was breathing deeply and his face was flushed with sweat. He was clearly surprised to see me working on the top-bunk instead of the bottom one. I chose to remain on-top to illustrate I did not care which bunk I slept on.

Soon afterward, we heard Sgt. Sanford yelling at a private down the hall. Now certain the tall drill was nowhere near our room, only then did we dare to relax. Looking at each other, everyone busted-out laughing. This prompted Brown to proclaim what was on everyone's mind.

"Yo, Sergeant Sanford ain't no joke!"

Chapter 2: 2nd Platoon Roll Call

From the moment I exited the cattle truck, I noticed it was mainly the responsibility of the melanin-rich drills to discipline the darker-skinned privates. In 2nd platoon, this meant I needed to be wary of Sgt. Sanford. After he identified me as a potential bad apple, not only did he dub me with the nickname "Billy Bad-Ass," he also started referring to the group of brothers I hung-out with as the "City Crew."

The *CC* was comprised of brothers from the major metropolitan centers—plus one frontin' suburbanite. Basically, we were a bunch of dudes who considered ourselves to be 'down by law.' Down by Law was Hip Hop's way to describe being tough or cool in the streets. This idiom was later replaced in the 90s by "Keepin' it Real." Our crew extended throughout the three platoons of Alpha Company, and boasted over twenty privates in all. The members of 2nd platoon were Brown (D.C.), Odom (Brooklyn), Jenkins (Chicago), Colón (Bronx), Dunbar (Oakland), Lonnie (LA), and me. These privates, plus my boy Hawker and a cock-diesel dude named Freeman, were my 'dawgs' in boot camp. Although *Hawk* and *Free* were cool as hell, they were not part of the crew. This was because these two had received more parental guidance than the rest of us, and therefore did not feel the need to be identified with our clique. Plus, they were country boys!

Pvt. Blaine Hawker was blessed with an unusually strong character. Despite our onslaught of jokes about his 'backward' hometown of Alliance, Ohio, he always exuded a calm, steely confidence. A proud young man but not in an arrogant way, Hawker possessed many positive attributes that I lacked. Hence the attraction on my part. In a sense, Blaine was my alter-ego. In fact, I can remember privates claiming we even looked alike—and I'm not talking about white dudes either. Not only did Blaine help me make it through basic, he proved his friendship by saving me from the MP's. *Not once but twice!*

Due to the 'blanket out the window' incident, Brown and Jones had been ordered to switch bunks and wall-lockers. That night, while the rest of us polished our boots or wrote letters to loved-ones, those two moved their personal belongings. With all of our roommates present, Brown let it be known he was far from intimidated by my 'Billy Bad-Ass' attitude.

"Hahahaha! Did y'all see how big Jones' eyeballs got when Philly ran at him? Whew that was funny!" Brown said, clapping his hands together. "I can't believe he's from DC, 'cause I know he ain't from around my way!" Then, looking directly at Jones, he asked him a question. "Jones tell the truth, where're you from?"

"DC," Jones simply replied, saying nothing more.

"Like I said, I don't believe him," Brown spoke like Jones was not in the room. "He's probably really from soft-ass Silver Spring. Or maybe he's one of them white-washed negroes from Columbia? All I know is, I wish some little guy like Amaru would have the nerve to step to me. Hahahaha!"

In the first week Brown amused himself in this way almost every night. Since he was a certified old-head, it never dawned on me to take offense. Honestly, I doubt anyone thought the incident was funnier than I did.

The Pecking Order

In the military, the hierarchy for everyone to follow is known as the 'Chain of Command.' Some people are assigned to positions a little higher-up on the totem pole, thereby granting them the authority to tell others what to do. These perks came with a huge downside: a great deal of responsibility. We, in the City Crew, referred to these special-assistants to the drills as *house niggers.*

One platoon-guide, four squad-leaders, plus the guide-on, the privates for these positions were hand-picked by the drill sergeants. Most of these young men had either taken ROTC classes in high school or attended some college.

Our platoon-guide, which is the head private who reports directly to the drills, was an old-looking dude named Peterson. PFC Peterson, despite barely making the entry cut-off age at thirty-four, looked closer to being sixty-four with his gray hair and wrinkles. A bit too old and too white for me to relate to on a personal level, the only thing I can say about him is he was competent in his position.

Next were the four squad-leaders; one for each line in the platoon.

The 1st squad had a cool brother from Portsmouth, Virginia leading them. Trent Jefferson was one of the guys who had taken ROTC in high school. He will always be remembered for some of his catchy comments. One of his favorites was: "I may not be the most handsome guy in the world, but I'm a smooth-skinned brutha 'cause I use alcohol to clean my pores." This guy practically did commercials for rubbing-alcohol every night in the latrine.

To my dismay, the 2nd squad, which happened to be

my squad, had a *Ku Klux Klansman's* son in charge. Pvt. Kenneth McCormick was one of the guys I was slated to fight once training got underway. Of my three challengers, McCormick was the only one who appeared ready to put-in some work. I'll never forget meeting him at the reception station. He was bragging about his father being a high-ranking member in the Association of Georgia Klans. Ironically, near the end of boot-camp, McCormick and I *almost* became friends. Since everyone, including the drills, was anticipating a showdown between the two of us, the details of how our relationship changed could have been its own chapter.

Following an ominous, first couple weeks, I was trying my damnest to turn over a new leaf. Being my squad leader, McCormick extended a helping hand in my time of need. Once certain of my sincerity, he oft-times assisted me right in front of Gimenez, Jacoby, and some of the other white conservatives in Alpha Company. *I had no choice but to respect that.* Without McCormick's assistance, I never could have made it to graduation. Although we never quite became buddies, a relationship which had hatched out of ignorance concluded with mutual feelings of respect.

I don't have much to say about the guy who assumed control of the 3rd squad. PFC Jeremy Hughes was cool as a fan and never bothered anyone who didn't have it coming to him. This low-key, *flower child* seemed like a guy who preferred to be backstage rather than in the spotlight. All in all, he did a good job while never appearing to enjoy it.

Pvt. Barry Jacoby became the 4th squad's leader by default. In week 3, he was promoted after a PFC was fired. Like McCormick, Jacoby was another Klansman's son. However, unlike my squad-leader, Jacoby lived up to his bigoted father's expectations.

At lunchtime, the day after Jacoby's promotion, Dunbar said Free had requested a meeting with the City Crew. That night, minutes before lights-out, we assembled in Odom's room as planned. After we kicked his roommates out so we could have some privacy, what Freeman told us made our jaws tight.

Jacoby was allegedly penning racist rhetoric in his mail. Freeman claimed Jacoby's bunk-buddy told him Jacoby was writing grandiose lies about being in-charge of a "bunch of stupid niggers." Hearing this, the City Crew decided to check the veracity of this indictment by intercepting a few of his letters. After further investigation, Free's information was proven correct. Jacoby was indeed weaving Tarzan-like tales about dominating a platoon full of "niggers and spics." With nigger-this and spic-that in every other line of his racist propaganda, nobody was surprised when the letters we read from his family and friends turned out to be even worse.

Some of the guys, especially Dunbar, got heated reading Jacoby's letters. Seeing this, I never expressed my feelings. Obviously, I was against any racism against my people but in all honesty I found Jacoby's letters amusing because his embellished stories had much in common with the fables spun by some of my friends who were doing bids up-state. You know what I'm talking about: "Sun, I'm runnin' shit out here…I got everything on lock!"

After reading a couple of his letters aloud, we took a vote and unanimously agreed to revoke Jacoby's mailing privileges. From the next night on, we combined our efforts to destroy any envelopes with his name on it. I seriously doubt Jacoby received a single letter after the first couple weeks. Since two of our crew were guaranteed to pull fireguard every night, it was easy to accomplish our conspiratorial crusade.

Starting the following week, Jacoby complained every day that his mail was being stolen. Weeks later, Drill Sergeant Terrier individually interrogated the entire platoon about it. Afterwards, Jacoby looked surprised when the drill reported that not one man, besides Jacoby himself, had admitted noticing anything strange about the mail. Due to Jacoby's peculiar philosophy, even the white privates seemed okay with the justice being served. With boot camp being such a lonely and depressing place, this punishment proved to be more effective than any black-eye one of us could have administered. Ask anyone who has been through basic training and I'm sure they will agree that besides chow-time, mail-call was the highlight of the day.

Lastly, there was the guide-on. This is the fool who stands in front of the formation carrying the unit colors. I say 'fool' because the drills told us there are actually guide-ons carrying flags in real battles while everyone else is shooting a rifle. And peep this: Sgt. Sanford chose *me* to be that fool. *Well, there was no way in hell I was going to stand in front of our company holding a damn stick with a rag attached to it!*

When I stated I was not interested, Sgt. Sanford separated me from my platoon in order to talk to me. I strained to keep a straight-face listening to him as he explained how much of an honor it was to be chosen as the guide-on. Following this, he emphasized I was the most qualified for a number of reasons. The only one I remember was his claim that I possessed a great deal of "natural discipline," whatever that means. The tall drill even took his exaggerations a step further by saying whenever the company was ordered to stand at attention, more than anyone else, I demonstrated the "wherewithal to stand longer and stronger than the others."

It was difficult, but I patiently waited and said nothing until he was finished coaxing me. When he finally asked for my reply, I wasted no words and outright rejected his assignment.

"Drill Sergeant, I don't think I'm cut-out for such an important role, so I choose to humbly turn-down the post."

Had I known Sgt. Sanford was going to get so angry, I might've accepted it. Nah, on second thought, fuck being the guide-on!

I've never been impressed with big titles and fancy positions, so at eighteen-years-young, doing anything extra was synonymous in my mind with being an Uncle Tom. In my place, ol' punk-ass Jones became the guide-on.

Another Kind of Role Model

Well before arriving at Ft. Leonard Wood, we were warned about the two cardinal rules of boot camp. Number one: never volunteer for anything. And number two: under any circumstances, never stand out as the negative example in the crowd. No one had to tell me not to volunteer because as I've explained this crossed paths with being a sell-out. However I completely dropped the ball on the second axiom, which was probably the more important of the two.

Generally speaking, the not-so-positive archetypes in our company were the members of the City Crew. In addition, there were two Caucasians named Mulholland and Vaughn who also gained a lot of notoriety that autumn back in '86. Private Michael Vaughn was in 1st platoon. Although I

27

barely saw the guy, I heard his name being yelled several times a day. The only thing I knew about this skinny trainee was he didn't have much of an appetite. Once the bigger privates began squabbling over the privilege of sitting next to Vaughn at meals, the drills started cracking jokes hinting at possible, homosexual tendencies. It did not take long for them to realize Vaughn's neighbors were consuming his food because we were not allowed to waste any of it. This led to the lanky private being seated in front of the drill sergeant's table so they could force him to eat.

Pvt. Allen Mulholland was in the 4th squad of my platoon. Mulholland is easily the goofiest, most physically uncoordinated person I have ever come across in my lifetime. A short, chubby dude sporting brown hair and freckles, with his Army-issued glasses tightly strapped to his two-chinned face, Mulholland was well-known for stumbling while we were marching. I'm not talking about tripping over an unseen object on the ground, mind you. This guy would just lose his balance and fall down.

With more than a few disreputable stand-outs spread amongst the three platoons, I had hoped to get lost in the shuffle but that never happened. In fact, it was quite the opposite. Once everyone heard about the 'blanket out the window' episode through the grapevine, I became infamous overnight. I think it's safe to say no one in Alpha Company commanded more day-to-day attention from the drills than yours truly. Trust me when I say, this was *not* by design.

Three conditions appeared with my starring role. First, many privates were clearly intimidated and made every effort to stay out of my path. This was a good thing because I was not looking to make friends outside of the City Crew. Second, the privates who deemed themselves to be tough started greeting me like they had known me for years. Initially, this took me by surprise but once I determined they were showing respect, I thought it was cool. Third, a few privates, especially one guy named Gimenez, were offended by my celebrity status. These individuals openly displayed their disdain any chance they got.

Lyle Gimenez was a mama's boy that made everyone sick for kissing Sgt. Terrier's ass every day. Although I confronted him on more than one occasion, he refused to fight me; he just wanted to spy and snitch like children do. Since Lyle was shook-daddy whenever I stepped to him, I chuckle whenever I think about him. This being said, I have to admit he was correct to condemn me; however it's difficult to respect anyone whose greatest attribute is being a stool pigeon. Well to his dismay, instead of catching me red-handed Gimenez ended up becoming green with envy by the end of boot-camp as my reputation not only grew, it went from negative to positive.

Basic Training Note: The Army's Rainbow Coalition

"Integrate it! We're all green here!"
During the first week, the drills pointed at our uniforms and screamed this each time we entered the cafeteria. To further emphasize their decree, they prohibited soldiers of the same race from sitting next to one other. Since they were uncertain of my ethnicity, I was not permitted to sit near any Asiatics. One afternoon, they even stopped me from sitting next to my roommate, Pvt. Kap Koo Kim, the Korean soldier who had spent time in the ROK Army.

Chapter 3: First Full Week

"If it doesn't kill you, it'll only make you stronger!"

Often recited by coaches, teammates, and even teachers, this quote is useful provided a person can maintain their sanity under pressure. In Week 1, this theory was tested to its limit. In other words, I can't imagine a person being more depressed, angry, and confused than I was in the latter half of September. Every night, movie-like projections of hanging out with my boys—and of course being with Asia—played non-stop. And each morning at four a.m. on the dot, this beautiful dream transformed into a 3D nightmare. But in reality.

It is no secret that boot-camp is designed to be tough. However, the mornings were the worst time of all. For one thing, since we got up before sunrise, it was still dark outside. "Go to bed at night...wake up at night!" This was the phrase many privates cited to express our new lifestyle. When the drills invaded our rooms yelling "First-call ladies!" these assholes would cut on the lights and start snatching privates from their beds. Already fully-dressed, the drills looked like they never went to sleep. This was a part of the mind-game they played well; and truthfully, their barbaric behavior was more than I could handle. My back-at-home dreams being interrupted in this manner brought out my most dysfunctional qualities, especially whenever I thought about how a week ago at this same hour I had been snuggled-up with Asia. To say I felt sorry for myself does not quite describe my misery.

GAIKOKUJIN - The Story

It was a combination of self-pity, selfishness, and an immature, unrealistic view of life.

On one morning in the beginning of Week 2, I woke up a minute before the drills' invasion. Before I was aware of what I was doing, I had already jumped out of bed and scurried into the latrine. There I sat down in a stall, covered my ears, and waited. Once the commotion began, I was pleased to discover the yelling and slamming doors were muffled to an almost-acceptable level. Moreover no drills came in. I also discovered by escaping into the bathroom, this provided me with a head-start on my morning-routine. This meant being able to relieve myself and brush my teeth before the long-lines of privates formed at the toilets and sinks. Incredibly my new habit, which had been dictated by necessity, was my first move in the right direction.

The Making of Billy Bad-Ass

Frustration and loneliness were my constant companions. Emotionally hampered like I was, I needed an outlet to release my anguish but the only physical activity in our daily schedule was our Physical Training, which was called 'PT.' Needless to say, the Beast was dying to resume one of the beefs from the reception station. Yet, even this proved to be difficult because no one wanted to fight a guy who showed so little concern for his own well-being.

I can vividly recall wanting to receive pain more than dish it out. To me, those experiences now seem surreal; but to other privates at the time, they simply thought I was crazy. Big, tough guys, much more physically imposing than my slim, five-foot-eleven, one-hundred-seventy-five-pound frame, would talk all kinds of macho-shit until they got a closer look at the Beast. *Then dudes had a sudden attitude adjustment.*

"Hey Amaru umm, no disrespect intended...we cool?"

"What?" I would reply in confusion. "No, no, we ain't cool!" Then, I always tried to keep the atmosphere of violence alive. Yet, time after time, what had appeared to be a certain fight just seconds ago would gradually dissolve into some kind of truce.

For kids growing up in the hood, one of our childhood challenges is to establish we are not punks. Back in school, after a few bumps and bruises, I learned how to meet this minimum requirement. However, I had never been known as a 'hard-rock.' That role was anchored by the likes of Jo-Jo and a few others. So it was strange to watch trainee after trainee—I'm talking about at least a dozen guys—back down with no embarrassment whatsoever after talking all kinds of shit.

Since the Beast could not whet his fangs in any real battle, *Billy* haphazardly constructed a *very* bad plan to exploit what he considered to be a bunch of cowards. In boot-camp, the list of tasks for trainees to complete is endless; and this burden increases by the day. In addition to making our beds and ensuring our boots were polished, we also had to maintain the common areas. Every morning, the latrine, halls, and stairwells were swept, mopped, and polished to perfection. With this needing to be done in a limited amount of time, it was incumbent all the privates worked together. If any squad failed to complete their assignment, the entire platoon was dropped at formation. Of course, the guilty squad was given the credit; and while this occurred the other platoons watched and waited provided they too were not likewise being punished.

In spite of this, once I noticed the morning routine was being conducted without the supervision of the drills, I equated this with break time. For this reason, when I told Brown, "Fuck the morning duties, I ain't doing shit!" it never occurred to me this would make me the enemy of our entire platoon. Well it did. And, scared of me or not, everyone had their own way of communicating my newest stunt wasn't cool.

Of all the bad decisions I've made in my life, this one's got to be near the top the list. Even now, I wonder how I could have been so stupid. Then I think back to the nightly 'lectures' I attended at the courts.

"Y'all young bloods listen here," Ernie used to say. "Don't ever forget that life's all about getting paid, j'd, and laid!"

While old-school cats passionately discussed the three ghetto-fabulous priorities, beverages like *Olde English 800* and *Coqui 900* quenched our teenage thirst. Sitting back, listening to these diatribes, I concluded they were expressing a particular attitude. And it damn sure ain't have nothing to do with mopping no dirty-ass floors!

Since I was one of the slowest to get into the latrine each morning to begin his morning routine, in the beginning, no one noticed my non-participation. By the time I finished waiting in line at the toilet and sink, many privates were already dressed with a broom in their hands. However, after my wake-up early revelation, I was done with the latrine before most privates took their first piss of the day. By the middle of the second week, I was completely dressed, bed made, and boots polished before half of my company.

When my roommates rushed back into our room, they

would catch a glimpse of me lounging on the floor, taking a nap. Because my bed was already impeccably made, I was careful not to lie on it. Not only did I never consider grabbing a mop, I was surprised to see other members of the City Crew doing their part. Following twenty minutes of counting sheep—while everyone else worked their tails off—the commotion would die down, indicating the indentured servants were finished with *their* tasks. At that time, I'd sit up, rub my eyes, and yawn before donning my headgear and strolling outside for formation.

It took me a week to figure-out why my roommates were giving me the cold shoulder. Due to my friendships within the CC, I barely noticed other guys in my platoon were not talking to me either. Once I did, I had no idea why everyone was so angry. This type of naïve-ignorance can only develop if boys don't spend quality-time with men who impart life's lessons. My bunk-buddy, Brown, was probably the only person who sensed and understood my confusion. Thank god, he took time to shed some light into the murky haze surrounding my dome.

"Amaru, have you noticed I usually get the nine to ten o'clock fireguard watch?"

"Hell yeah!" I replied with emphasis. "I've also noticed that I *always* get it at two in the damn morning! What the fuck's up with that? I need to have a talk with the platoon-guide," I voiced with concern.

"What're you bitchin' about Billy?" Brown asked, enjoying a chuckle at saying the nickname Sgt. Sanford used for me. "That's the price you pay for being a bad-ass!"

According to Brown, our platoon-guide gave him the easiest time-slot because he was my bunk-buddy. He claimed this was Peterson's indirect way to inform me that my predawn assignments were far from a random coincidence. At first, I didn't buy into Brown's theory; that is until I confronted the platoon-guide in private. After listening to my inquiry, I remember Peterson glaring at me coldly before creasing his lips into a fake smile. "There's nothing I can do about it." Saying this, Peterson seemed pleased his targeting efforts had not gone unnoticed.

Under the circumstances, Peterson had every right to do what he did. Actually, it is incredible I did not receive even more negative backlash from the platoon. I guess this was just another case of God taking care of old folks and fools. Overall, it was my dawgs which allowed me any chance to recover from my social faux pas. As can be imagined, a group of black and brown men bound-together by something deeper than Army green were not to be taken lightly by the masses. Not only did the CC have my back, they had *juice!*

A known fact, which is mentioned less-and-less these days, is how melanin-rich folks feel a kinship toward each other by nature. In other words, functioning as an extended family unit is our normal state-of-mind. However, in order to achieve success in "the System," we are required to abandon this way of thinking.

Following Brown's counseling and my talk with Peterson, I decided to change my ways. But before I could earn my peer's respect, I had to be forgiven first. Clearing this hurdle was not as easy as putting on a sad face and saying "I'm sorry." This is because I had insulted the entire platoon, and other than our formations, where the drills were also present, there was no place where everyone was assembled together for such an opportunity. Believe me, I wish I could've apologized to everyone at the same time; however, this was something I had to demonstrate little by little through my attitude and actions. "Words are cheap; it's the actions of man which define him," I remember Mr. Davis preaching to me. Even though I was skeptical, I humbled myself only because I knew it was the right thing to do, and to my surprise, once I and started working alongside the other privates in the morning, I felt such a relief. It was refreshing to release the burden of the 'tough guy' chip on my shoulder. Day after day, I continued doing my part, and soon the icy detached atmosphere in my room began to thaw.

I scored high on every test in boot-camp, but in my opinion, reconciling with my peers was my most significant achievement along the road to graduation. Still, being on an emotional roller coaster from start to finish, this feat could easily have been overlooked or forgotten. Although nothing could be done about my fireguard slot, it was clearly a case of being blessed with the lesser of two evils. This cannot be emphasized enough because in the Army, to be ostracized from the platoon is very close to death itself. And actually, this is the next step all-too-often for any unfortunate soldier who has been isolated from the group.

Check out the suicide and accidental-death statistics in the military and imagine that most of those ill-fated folks could not, for any variety of reasons, conform to the required standard. Perhaps they had difficulty doing push-ups; or maybe they failed to earn enough points for their next promotion. Or whatever. This level of societal pressure to fit-in is insane. The only other culture I've experienced which can compare to the stress of a GI's world is the life of an average citizen in Japan. With Japanese being required to live by the motto: "The nail that sticks out gets hammered down[2]," it becomes necessary to all but surrender their individual personality in order to mindlessly accept roles dictated by class expectations. If they cannot, or will not, they risk being rejected by the society. Hence, the incredulous suicide rate.

From this experience, I learned it's the dynamics governing a group of individuals which distinguishes a genuine community from an assembly of heathens who happen to be coexisting in the same area. In other words, consciously aware of it or not, each of us is our own brother's keeper. Now, imagine if this was the 'science' old-heads were dropping at the courts!

---

[2] [出る釘は打たれる]

Chapter 4: The Drills

I am a Drill Sergeant.

I will assist each individual in their effort to become a highly motivated, well disciplined, physically and mentally fit soldier, capable of defeating any enemy on today's modern battlefield. I will instill pride in all I train, pride in self, in the Army, and in country. I will insist that each soldier meets and maintains the Army's standard of military bearing and courtesy, consistent with the highest traditions of the US Army. I will lead by example, never requiring a soldier to attempt any task I would not do myself.

But first, last, and always, I am an American soldier, sworn to defend the Constitution of the United States against all enemies, both foreign and domestic. I AM A DRILL SERGEANT...THIS WE'LL DEFEND!

- Drill Sergeant's Creed

There were three drills assigned to 2nd platoon. The most imposing, and only melanin-rich instructor of the trio, was Sgt. Sanford. As mentioned, he was the drill who dubbed me 'Billy Bad-Ass.' This occurred one afternoon when he caught me cutting in line. From witnessing one dirty look I gave a private as I shoved him out of my way, Sgt. Sanford deciphered much about my character.

Sgt. Terrier, on the other hand, was a skinny redneck from Mississippi. Although some of his policies may have been less than ethical, he was a better drill sergeant than I gave him credit for back then. In other words, I can see why he believed resorting to deceitful measures was the right thing to do. The final drill in the tandem was a stout New England man who possessed a decent voice for singing Army-cadence songs. All in all Sgt. Lavendar, with his dark hair and Mediterranean features, seemed too nice to be a drill sergeant. Although the two, Caucasian drills were proficient in their duties, to me, they registered as regular 'ol whiteboys—i.e. suckers. In layman's terms, not only did I think I could outwit them, I also believed I could whip them in a fight too. In many cases, this is the only way kids from the street know how to evaluate people.

Of the threesome, the guy in my face from day one had been Sgt. Sanford. Once I understood he was watching me closely, I likewise began to monitor his movements. For this reason, the news he was leaving came as a shock. It was a cold, rainy morning when the tall drill announced his father had died the previous evening. Following the sullen news, he apologized for having to miss part of our training to oversee the funeral and grieve with his family.

That night, in the barracks, the CC planned to have some fun in Sgt. Sanford's absence. Beyond merely calculating his loss would leave our platoon understaffed, we drooled at the prospect of clowning the two whiteboys. Well it never happened. *Not even for one minute of one day!* Any mature person can look back into their past and see vulnerable moments where death, pain, or failure seemed imminent. Sometimes fate and circumstance shake up our fragile existence to where the least likely person becomes a significant part of our life.

The next morning, when a short drill with flaming eyes invaded our space, he definitely got our attention. More than a tad interested in me, he made it clear there would be no uprising on his watch. We were surprised a drill sergeant from *another platoon* would take it upon himself to plug the gap created from Sgt. Sanford's departure by visiting us so often. For the remainder of basic, Brown, Dunbar, and other members of the City Crew heralded the drill I met in the back of the cattle truck as "Amaru's personal drill." They thought it was hilarious how Sgt. Sandoval was on my case all day long.

Perhaps it was the "Asian connection" he used to joke about. To this day, I'm not sure. Of course, it never dawned on my immature mind that Sgt. Sandoval was risking his career with his move against the established protocol. Nor, that his extra effort was largely why I did not end up on a bus back to Philly. With more than a hint of brotherly love in his mannerisms, my personal drill was a cool cat. In fact, he even smoked *Kool* brand cigarettes. Like Ant, Sgt. Sandoval was short; he was about the average height for the Philippine ethnicity he wore as proudly as his brown-round. Something else I recall about my private drill was he claimed to be a mind-reader.

"You don't believe me do ya, Private?"

"No Drill Sergeant." I boldly replied when he stepped closer to eye-ball me.

"No?" he asked with a smirk. "Then tell me this: how do I know that you're wondering why my eyes are always red like this?"

Hearing his words, I almost became a believer.

"That's right Philly, my eyes are always like this. It's because ever since I was a baby, I been spittin' fire!" Sgt. Sandoval bellowed in his confident tone. "But don't confuse my flame-throwers with no red-eyes from smoking pot,

41

homie, 'cause I don't need nothing to get me high…I'm high on soldiering!" Then, he breathed his final warning into my neck. "They may be red, but they're as sharp as an eagle's…you remember that!"

Day 3

One night early on in basic, the temperature suddenly plummeted from the Indian summer heat we had been experiencing. When I woke up not only was my nose stuffed up, there was frost glistening on the grass; so I'd say it was beyond chilly. In spite of the frigid conditions, we were *not* permitted to wear our field jackets.

The 'correct uniform' was announced each evening so privates could have the proper equipment ready the next morning. However, on some occasions, it was altered due to unanticipated factors such as inclement weather. For example, in the case of rain, our wet-weather gear would be added. Because our uniform included both equipment and clothing variations, the possible combinations for the next day's uniform were endless. Easily this was the most popular discussion at dinner until the following morning. The point is, we were never allowed to think independently at all.

I despised how every detail of our existence was dictated to us. So when I woke up in my normal pissed-off mood and saw the frost, I took it upon myself to be "out of uniform." More than feeling cold, I had a need to exercise my human right to make a decision. Keenly aware of the risk but enjoying the cat-mouse game, I concluded that since my BDU shirt and field-jacket were the same color and design, it would be impossible to distinguish if I was wearing my jacket so early in the morning.

And just like I imagined, I made it through the first formation because it was still dark; so naturally, I thought I was hot shit. My gamble relied heavily on our company following the previous day's pattern of being sent back inside the barracks after the formation. On the day before, there were so many gigs in our clean-up routine, after several rounds of push-ups in the dark, we were sent back inside to clean again. It was reasonable to believe something had to be out-of-order today as well, so I planned on taking off my jacket after we re-entered the barracks. By that time, I'd be nice and warm from the push-ups. I had it all figured out!

And just like I thought, all three platoons got scolded again for our lack of hygiene. As we cranked-out our push-ups, I noticed the sky was getting bright; so when we were commanded to recover, I stood up feeling a sense of relief.

"You nasty-ass heathens still ain't learned how to GI my barracks!" yelled Sgt. Lavendar. "But we ain't got time for remedial-cleaning before breakfast this morning because we gotta date with destiny!"

"Company!" boomed Sgt. Sanford from somewhere in the dark.

"Platoon!" yelled three other drills.

Attention!" commanded the tall drill. Right face! Forward…march! Left, left, left-right…"

"Alpha!" the trainees chorused as we were required to do whenever 'right' was mentioned in the drills' cadence.

As we departed our company area, I could hear Brown snickering over his shoulder at me. *Oh shit!* I thought, realizing this morning's 'date with destiny' was not part of my plan. Reaching up, I started to unbutton my jacket, hoping to take it off and stash it in some nearby bushes but when I looked around I couldn't find any good hiding-places. Not only that, there was no way I could slip the jacket off without being spotted by one of the drills. This is when I knew I was in trouble.

By the time the sun was illuminating the horizon, most of my buddies were laughing under their breath. I was surprised none of the drills heard their snickers. "Amaru, I told you you'd get caught," Hawker griped in low tone. Unlike the others, Hawk was not happy to see me in this bind.

We were marching due-west singing cadence and it was apparent we were not going to turn around anytime soon. I winced knowing I had to get rid of the jacket in the next few minutes if I wished to escape detection; but on the other hand, I had no idea of our present location so even if I could ditch it without being seen, how would I find it? This was the question burning between my ears.

Along with the rising sun came rising temperatures; it had warmed up considerably. Morning had arrived and I was stuck wearing the cumbersomely hot garment. Seeing I had broken a sweat caused the number of privates laughing to more than double. At this point, the only people who had not noticed my field jacket were the drills. The only thing I could do was cling to the hope we might turn around soon.

After the drills ushered us in front of a non-descript building which resembled a factory, they told us to stand at-ease. When a few of our supervisors went inside, I concentrated on keeping trainees between me and the remaining drills' line of vision while I scoped-out possible hiding places. Before I could make a move, Odom and Dunbar started slap-boxing. This caused me to forget my dire set of circumstances as I reverted to my 'on-the-block' mentality. Within seconds, I was laughing right along with

Brown, Jenkins, and Lonnie.

"City Crew drop! Where the hell do you think you are?"

When Sgt. Maldonado and Sgt. Sandoval sauntered over from their normal 1st and 3rd platoons to check out the excitement, like the rest of the CC, I was encouraging the two combatants. I only let my guard down for a second but that was all it took. With their attention focused on the brawling buddies, the drills failed to notice my jacket—at first.

Once we started cranking out push-ups, the mirage shattered.

"Whoa, whoa, what the fuck is going on here?" asked Sgt. Sandoval. "Are my eyes deceiving me, or is that maggot wearing a field-jacket?" Pausing here, he glanced at his partner. "Sergeant Maldonado, do you see what I see?"

"Jesus H. Christ! I can't believe it but I do," the other drill replied.

"Everyone except the slimeball wearing the field-jacket…recover, get back in line, and shut up!" Sgt. Sandoval yelled.

That task completed, both drills hurried back to deal with the young man who was bold enough to be different from everyone else. Including them. Sgt. Maldonado, a tough-looking Mexican who could do flutter kicks all day, initiated the dual-pronged attack.

"So what do we have here?" the drill asked while I continued doing push-ups. "Looks to me like a total fucking disregard for authority!" Then he looked at a huge, mud puddle about ten feet to my right. "Roll right!" he commanded.

In response to his command, I rolled to my right and continued to do so until I reached the edge of the icy liquid.

There I stopped.

"What the hell did you stop for?" screamed Sgt. Sandoval. "Roll in!"

For a split second, I considered standing up and saying, "Hell no!" because I was certain there were regulations prohibiting this kind of treatment in the so-called 'modern Army.' However common sense dictated if I did not follow this order, these two would find some way to get me kicked out. After all, it wasn't like they had singled me out of the crowd for no reason.

"What the fuck you waiting for?" yelled Sgt. Maldonado, cutting into my moment of indecision.

So I rolled-in.

To my surprise, the water was not so cold. That is, until they ordered me to low-crawl back-and-forth through it several times. A couple minutes later, I was freezing. If that was not enough, Sgt. Maldonado then commanded me to lie still in the puddle. "Put your face in the water!" he added. This was the only thing I did not comply with. For a few seconds, we were at a stand-off. When Sgt. Sandoval walked toward me, I thought he was going to push my face down, so I jumped to my feet.

"What the fuck are you doing?" the Filipino drill vented.

Although he was angry, I could tell by his demeanor he was not planning to assault me. So before he could grab me, I got back down in the front-leaning-rest position.

"In cadence, exercise!" he boomed, commencing another PT session.

"One drill sergeant, two drill sergeant, three drill sergeant…" I yelled at the top of my lungs.

As I reached muscle-failure for a second time, Sgt.

Sandoval crouched down close to my ear. "Lemme guess, you flea-bitten swamp rat," the enraged drill taunted, "you woke up this morning and felt cold, so you were like, 'Fuck what the day's uniform is, I'm gonna do what the hell I please!' Is that about right, asshole?"

By this time, I had had enough. Furthermore, I was sure these two were breaking the rules. Since Billy was always looking to instigate trouble, he stepped to the drill's challenge before I could respond. "Yeah..." he replied, using a smart-alec tone. "Everything except the part about feeling cold." Whenever Billy spoke, my voice sounded different. His words were evocative; they were more biting and insulting than mine ever could be. I couldn't believe he made me snap at the drills but I have to admit I was pleased to see their shocked expressions. Due to the Beast relishing the opportunity to cause pain—*even in the form of fatigue and humiliation to me*—I imagined it had sided with Billy. This was the only way I could explain my outburst. My feeling of satisfaction barely lasted a second. This is because from this point these drills did their best to make my life miserable. And once again the odds were two-to-one against me.

"What the? Hold up, what did that degenerate just say? I know he wasn't talking to you, was he?" Sgt. Maldonado asked his partner, resuming their two-man, *Manzai* performance.

"I don't know who the asshole *thinks* he's talking to," responded Sgt. Sandoval, "but he sounds mighty disrespectful, don't you think?" Then he looked at me and screamed. "Flutter kicks...move!"

Following several reps of flutter kicks, my abs reached the muscle-failure point. As I struggled to keep my feet from resting on the ground, Sgt. Sandoval ordered me to assume a karate *kata* in the middle of the puddle. Standing with my legs shoulder-width apart, I felt the frigid water saturating my socks. Then things went from bad to worse when Sgt. Maldonado tossed a forty-pound sandbag at me.

"Hey fuck-face, catch!"

Missing it badly, the sandbag slammed into my shoulder and fell into the water, splashing a bucketful of icy liquid onto my face. Had any part of my body still been dry, it was now drenched like the rest of me. These sandbags, which can be found everywhere on Army posts, have multiple uses ranging from building safety-bunkers to well…more creative uses in the training environment.

"Pick it up ya goofy bastard!" Sgt. Maldonado yelled.

I can take this for five more minutes. This is the mantra I was repeating over and over in my head. As terrible as the PT and the mud was, let there be no mistake, the most unpleasant part of my ordeal was having to endure the drill's jokes, taunts, and insults.

"Okay, let's see if the retarded muthafucka can follow simple directions," Sgt. Sandoval said pointing at me. "Hold it with both hands in front of you like this," he commanded, demonstrating with another sand bag.

Once I was holding the waterlogged, burlap bag with both elbows extended at eye-level, something odd happened. Instead of getting angrier, I became amused by the ornery pair. Having been raised under the lash of my larger-than-life, cock-diesel father, just the very idea of this dwarfish duo intimidating anyone made me smile.

"What the hell you grinning at?" blared Sgt. Sandoval.

"You mocking us Private?" added Sgt. Maldonado.

In the heat of the moment, Billy converted my private thoughts into public remarks.

48

"You know who you two remind me of? Those two, polite gophers on the *Loony Tunes* cartoons. What're their names again?" I asked before answering my own question. "Oh yeah, *Mac and Tosh.* You know who I'm talking about, right?" In case they didn't, I imitated the animated, *Looney Tunes* rodents. "After you... No after you, I insist!" Then, I busted-out laughing at my own joke.

Seeing this, the two drills turned around to confer with one another.

Seconds later, Sgt. Maldonado began walking in the direction of the company, which was standing in formation about fifty yards away. I took this as a sign of weakness. "Hold up, where you going li'l man?" I razzed the departing drill. "I thought you said we're just getting started?"

"At ease scum-bucket!" Sgt. Sandoval yelled, dropping to one knee next to me. "You're lucky we even allowed a punk like you try-out for this man's Army! You know what happens to big-mouth sissies like you in jail? Which is where you're probably headed after you get kicked outta here!"

"You speaking from experience, shorty?" I countered between clenched teeth. "By the way, ain't there a minimum height-requirement for this man's Army?"

Once our collision of wills extended beyond thirty minutes, the company started marching away. I felt a chill go down my spine as the familiar sounds of cadence faded into the distance, leaving me alone with this feisty drill sergeant. In silence, we eyed each other warily for an extended second. Me in the front-leaning rest and him standing ten feet in front of me with his arms folded. This is when I got the idea he appreciated that despite my woeful situation I was prepared to meet every one of his barbed insults with two of my own.

49

"In cadence…" After another excruciating round of flutter kicks, low-crawls, and push-ups, my task-master again ordered me to hold the sandbag. *Smile!* Sgt. Sandoval taunted as a result of my continual habit of grinning at him. Truth be told, this was probably the only thing I did that really got on his nerves. "Raise the sandbag up to eye-level and keep it there! What's the matter tough-guy from Philly? It ain't funny no more? I know you ain't tired. Keep smiling!"

That day I committed every ounce of my energy to not breaking. Simply put, I would have rather died than allow Sgt. Sandoval to get that satisfaction. Somehow the drill seemed to know this; but more importantly he also appeared to be waiting for something not visible to the uninitiated eye.

"Private Amarooo!" This is how Sgt. Sandoval always called me. "You look like you got a little chink in you. Am I right?"

Had he not unmistakably been of Asian descent himself, this would have easily qualified as an ethnic slur. Once I detected the drill was coloring outside the lines of military propriety, this really fired me up.

"Yeah," I countered and hissed at the same time. "I hail from a proud Samurai lineage. One of the clans that tap danced all over that bullshit island you're from!"

"Is that right, Shogun?" he replied with a grin. Far from insulted, the Filipino drill was having a ball. It was almost as if his own platoon lacked privates with enough spunk to amuse him.

"That's right Sergeant," I responded in an angry tone. Even though in my heart, I had nothing but respect for Filipinos—I mean Ant was Filipino—I was just attacking him any way I could think of.

Due to Sgt. Sandoval being the type of drill who

welcomed the challenge of melding soldiers out of rebels, he let my over-exuberance slide. It took nearly an hour for my personal session to conclude. Once it did, the short drill marched me to the barracks and left me standing outside at attention. Before he walked away, he added one final remark.

"Private, if you think this is over, you're wrong. See ya sooner than later."

"Clear Drill Sergeant!" I blared glaring right back at him. Like I said, there was no way he was going to get the last word because I was one pissed-off private, covered in mud.

Once he left, I calmed down. Waiting there by myself, I could hear the others inside cleaning up this morning's gigs. As I stood outside by my lonesome for about thirty minutes until our next formation, I had a lot of time to reassess my situation.

When I say drills are masters at dealing with rebellious spirits, I am speaking from experience. In the same breath, allow me to also mention that Sgt. Sandoval was the very emblem of professional and I will never forget that. Had he attended to his *own* platoon, like he was supposed to, I would have been sent home an even more confused mental case than when I left. I saw this happen to a high-school classmate who got kicked out of Marine boot-camp.

At the end of our senior year, Ben and I had joked back-and-forth about which branch of the military, the Army or the Marines, was superior. He told me he was leaving for Parris Island in July, so you can imagine my surprise when I happened to run into him at a neighborhood barber shop in mid-August. Even before we bumped fists, I was already disturbed because the Ben I knew was a gregarious, up-beat kind of guy but the dude I exchanged a pound with was quiet and timid. With his confidence shot, Ben had an invisible tag of failure dangling around his neck like a scarlet letter. A week later, I heard Ben got arrested for selling crack to an undercover cop. What made this especially odd was Ben had never done any drugs or even been associated with them while we were in high school.

Sgt. Sandoval, being an ex-LA gang member, seemed in-tune with these types of grim tales from the hood. Although he did not divulge any of his personal information in the beginning, it was easy to tell he was from 'around the way.' It was in our final days together when the Filipino drill revealed details about his background. Once, that is, we became cool. I cannot say we were ever tight, because that would imply he had been less-than-professional in his conduct. So yeah, we were cool. However at first, our enmity was official. Following the mud incident, more than anything, I wanted to get back at him—even if that got me kicked out.

"You, the dirt ball, drop!"

For the remainder of that day, the drills took turns dropping me for having a dirty uniform while everyone else rested on break. By doing this, the drills demonstrated their teamwork method for dealing with extreme personalities like mine. Together they smothered me.

Over the next several days, the fiery-eyed drill stopped by any time we were given a few minutes to take a break. More times than not these visits resulted in me, along with whomever I was goofing off with, assuming the front-leaning rest position. Usually it was Odom. Try as I might, I was unable to get back at Sgt. Sandoval. Once he sensed I was not giving up, he really stepped-up the pressure. Any rivalry I concocted in my head was resolved midway through the second week. This occurred on an extremely cold night.

At 0100 hours, we were rudely awakened and ordered to hold formation outside 'as is.' This meant practically naked. After ruling out the possibility of being in the wrong uniform again, I dejectedly descended the stairs to shuffle outside with my fellow, condemned mates. The sergeant in-charge of quarters that night was, you guessed it: him. As we stood at attention, it was impossible not to notice how snugly Sgt. Sandoval was dressed for the occasion. He even had the nerve to wear an Army-issued scarf.

"What a low-down, dirty muthafucka!" a nearby private vented under his breath.

"Alpha Company…" Sgt. Sandoval began while we battled the bitterly cold wind.

He proceeded to chastise us for some trivial nonsense before dropping us. Honestly, I can't even remember what it was about. Following some push-ups, and a minute or so of the all-too-common tongue-lashing, we were ordered to stand at attention. This indicated the punishment was drawing to its conclusion. With first-call less than three hours away, everyone was eager to get back to the warmth of their beds.

"Alpha Company!" Sgt. Sandoval yelled again. "I just remembered something I forgot to do today. It was something important. Can anyone guess what it is?" he asked in a gleeful tone. When the drill noticed no one was in the mood to play along with his childish antics, he motivated us. "No one goes inside until you guess what it is."

Naturally he was bombarded with suggestions.

"Umm, you forgot to do your daily routine of a thousand flutter kicks?" said one brown-noser from 1st platoon.

'Brown-nose' is slang for ass kisser. It is said these individuals kiss ass so often they have permanent brown,

53

fecal stains on the tips of their noses.

"Negative!" the drill boomed in response. "Real soldiers never forget to train. It's not an option, it's an obligation. I'm a drill sergeant, I ain't like you sorry-ass privates. Whoever said that, drop!"

While the unlucky private got down to crank out his push-ups, everyone else laughed. Meanwhile, the guessing game resumed. The 2nd platoon squad-leader, McCormick, tried his luck. "You forgot to tell your wife that you loved her?"

"Not married to a woman, I'm married to the Army. But good guess." This meant that although McCormick was wrong, he did not have to do any push-ups.

This scene lasted for the next couple minutes. By the time a third of the privates were doing push-ups on the frigid pavement, Sgt. Sandoval appeared to lose interest.

"Everyone recover!" the drill suddenly blared out.

Once everyone was standing, we eagerly anticipated going inside. And it could not happen too soon because my hands and feet were showing signs of frostbite. But instead of releasing us, the short drill started talking again.

"Yeah Alpha Company, I forgot to do something today…something important. Since you dummies can't guess what it is, I'll tell you. I forgot to drop someone today. Where's that tough-guy from Philly? Private *Amarooo!*"

I couldn't believe my ears.

At the clowning of my name, I heard Brown and some others bust-out laughing. In spite of clearly breaking their military bearing, this normally unpardonable sin was overlooked after Sgt. Sandoval revealed the answer to his trivial pursuit. In hindsight, I don't believe he called this formation for the sole purpose of harassing me. Waking us up in the middle of the night was probably part of our training but Sgt. Sandoval was an opportunist. Therefore he took advantage of this wee-hour affair to humiliate the company's favorite, rebellious field-hand.

After positioning me in front of the barracks' entrance, Sgt. Sandoval dropped me into the front-leaning rest position. Then he walked back to the head of the formation and quieted the company down by asking a simple question.

"Who wants to join Amaru?"

Once he was satisfied everyone was quiet, he concluded the evening's festivities. "Alpha Company, you have five minutes to be in bed. And I swear, if a single private—other than Amaru over there—is out of bed one second after that, we'll all come back outside for PT! Is that clear?"

"Clear Drill Sergeant!" everyone but me screamed.

"*Fall out!*" came Sgt. Sandoval's order. And with it, hundreds of stampeding feet came directly at me.

Obviously everyone wanted to escape the cold. Nevertheless it was equally reasonable many privates savored the chance to stomp the jerk who had refused to help with the morning duties. While scores of men dashed over my body, I never considered the victims of my selfishness needed to exact some form of punishment for my misdeeds to be pardoned. Or that Sgt. Sandoval was doing me a favor by making this happen.

What I did understand was, my scheme was not working. It was on that frigid night, doing push-ups under a stampede of privates which proved to be the straw that broke the camel's back. Although I had no idea what to do next, I knew something had to change because Sgt. Sandoval made it clear he intended to continue taking shots at me. Beyond admitting he had won, I realized the larger challenge was making it to graduation. And this chess match would prove itself to be more complex than maneuvering by any single drill sergeant, even one as astute as Sgt. Sandoval.

At this point it may be difficult to imagine but basic training was a game I eventually mastered. After graduating however, I was discouraged knowing the next step, called AIT, which stands for Advanced Individual Training, was waiting to make me a *newbie* all over again. Comprehending this, I understood my Army experience was woven into cycles just like the journey called "life." This led me to wonder how many levels a person had to ascend to master it all.

Chapter 5: Operation Speedstick

On Sunday evening, just prior to being released into the messhall, the drills announced the following day we had a scheduled visit to the Post Exchange. Since the Army shared the huge shopping-center with personnel from the adjacent Air Force base, this was also a Base Exchange, or BX too. With members of both branches, plus their families, frequenting this PX / BX, it had three-times the number of customers as any *Wal-Mart*.

Although Uncle Sam provided us with most of our basic necessities, the penny-pinching bastard got stingy when it came to luxury items like deodorant, toothpaste, soap, and letter stationery. These regular trips to the PX translated to a thirty-minute break from the rigors of boot-camp. During this time, we were allowed to pretend we were still part of the real world. Therefore even if a private had no money, these half-hour-respites were a more-than-welcome-alternative to the toils of training.

On previous visits to the PX, I took notice of some things I had taken for granted in the civilian world. The plush aroma of leather coats, wallets, and handbags dazzled my senses beyond belief; but even surpassing this was the fragrance of ladies' perfume. This scent alerted me to how much I missed *all* women. Incredibly, simple things like cotton candy, fast food, and sporting goods stimulated countless memories of hanging-out with my friends.

However, some other observations aroused my attention too.

With several dozens of patrons crowding each aisle, I imagined it was impossible to keep a vigilant watch for shoplifters. Scheming in this way, I cased the joint and concluded the PX was ripe for profits. As I planned the thieving spree, I recalled my stealing sessions at the 7-Eleven with my on-the-block, partner-in-crime, 'A-Rock.'

My boy, *A,* was the only guy I ever met who was a bigger kleptomaniac than me. In fact, he was the person who schooled me on the finer points of 'Five-finger Discounts.' He claimed he did this in order to create a worthy partner— slash rival. A-Rock's real name was Aaron but he insisted on using street monikers so he furnished me with the nickname 'Sev,' as a shortened version of 7-Eleven. This was where I did my best work. Together, A-Rock and I took shoplifting to whole-nutha-level.

Whenever we were lucky enough to enter a convenience store during its peak hours, we knew the cashier would be too busy to pay us much attention. This was our signal to get busy! At times, our competitive spirit lead us to unload our plunder behind the building, only to return inside for another go-around at filling our pockets. In addition, it wasn't about swiping a hundred packs of gum either. Believe it or not, we actually had the nerve to heat our snacks in the microwave oven; not to mention steal items that most thieves thought were too large to hide, like *Big Gulps.*

The truth was, back then, I was always looking for a hustle to exploit. Not only for personal consumption, but rather, I also procured items my peers wanted so I could sell them—for a small fee, of course. Due to my practice of selling *Bubble Yum* and *Jolly Ranchers* in middle school, when I switched to drugs in high school, my classmates never stopped calling me 'Candy Man.'

In boot-camp, the most sought after commodities were flavorless confectioneries like deodorant and shoe polish. Understanding this, my plan was to pilfer these items and sell them to my fellow GIs at half price. Although I only stood to profit about fifteen bucks, if I was lucky, more than the chump change, it was about establishing a 'rep.' As *Guru,* of *Gang Starr,* claims in his song, *'Just to get a Rep,'* it is vitally important for some youth to be acknowledged as cool. And some will go to insane lengths to earn that rep.

Minutes after we entered the mess hall, I went in the latrine to attend a CC meeting. These scheduled congregations, which involved representatives of all three platoons, fell on different days and meals each week. Since the drills had warned us that 'contraband meetings' would not be tolerated, we made sure to change the meeting times and days in order to avoid falling into any pattern that might get us caught. In these forums, we passed information back-and-forth to each other.

Once the eight attendees greeted each other and took a piss, we kicked all the non-members out of the latrine. Once we were satisfied there were no prying ears in the vicinity, a brother named Thomas, from 3rd platoon, kicked-off our meeting of the minds.

"A-ight y'all, let's do this," he said stepping away from the urinals toward the back of the room where most of us had already congregated.

I had to wait because I was not the only private with something to share that day. After Thomas finished speaking, Taz, the guy I met in the recruiter's car, stepped to the podium.

"Check-it-out," he said, "this is one of the benefits of

having KP duty." Saying nothing else, he reached into his cargo-pockets and handed each of us a *Hostess* pie. Cherry, lemon, apple, he had every flavor. Since we were about to eat dinner, everyone put their pies into their pockets for later. "When you're on kitchen patrol, it's easy as shit to vick these," Taz assured us. "So tell everybody in the crew, whoever got KP, grab about five or six. Not too many or they'll notice. We'll just keep passing 'em around…just for us." Then, Taz reached into his shirt pocket and pulled out some more. "Give these to a few of the brothers who ain't here," he said, distributing them as well.

"Five or six? You got way more than that," said a guy named Brunson from 1st platoon in a suspicious tone.

"That's because I had KP two days in a row," Taz responded rolling up his sleeve to show us the bandage wrapped around his sprained wrist. "But my medical-profile ends tomorrow."

Seeing his injury, many of us were reminded of witnessing Taz fall down awkwardly while we were running through an obstacle course a few days ago.

"Word!" I said, happily receiving two more. I already knew who I was going to give them to. Brown and Hawk. Even though Hawk was not in the CC, he was down with me. "Yo, lemme holler next," I said bumping fists with Taz.

"What you got, Sev?" Taz replied, taking a step back to give me the floor.

"I gotta fifty-percent discount-coupon for all CC members. But you gotta sign-up today so tell the others," I declared with a sly grin. Seeing no one understood what I was talking about, I revealed the details of my schematics.

When I was done, two privates attempted to discourage me from my criminal vow. Hearing this, I cracked a series of jokes on them which basically amounted to me labeling them as 'soft.' Soon, other privates joined in, which prompted the two teens to shrug their shoulders and walk toward the exit.

"Exactly!" I yelled at their departing silhouettes. "Get your punk-asses outta here, so the real men can discuss their business."

With my critics exiled, I got back to my plan. I honestly believed my calculations were foolproof. To prove my point, I promised the crew I'd hook those two wimps up with freebies. *Since I had it like that!* This convinced the remaining privates to have faith in me, and they began writing their orders on toilet paper. Once this happened, I romanticized my pettiness into some full-blown, gangster shit. Seconds later, I collected the flimsy order-forms and confirmed that *Speedstick* deodorant was the most requested item in Alpha Company. For this reason, I coined my mission, 'Operation Speedstick.'

Aside from athletes or singers, every rich person I knew of or ever heard of was linked to criminal activity. To me, this was a sure indication the nine-to-five working-man was a sucker. Once Jeff revealed this was also true amongst celebrated, billionaire-families like the Kennedy's, the Vanderbilt's, and the Rockefeller's—world-renowned families known as the 'Illuminati'—you couldn't tell me shit! As an attentive student in a world of drudgery, I learned that crime pays. *Fuck what you heard!* Although my present endeavors were only for nickels and dimes, I figured I had to start somewhere.

The next afternoon while we were standing at attention in front of the PX, I was dyin' to get started. As soon as we entered, I began snatching stuff at a crazy pace.

Efficiently locating the items on my list, within minutes, I had packed so much into my shirt and pants' pockets, I actually considered going outside to unload, like back in the 7-Eleven days.

Before long, nearby trainees began to shun me. Nevertheless, I was so busy scanning the area for MPs and NCOs, I didn't care if they saw me. My entire strategy rested on one premise: there were so many privates roaming the aisles simultaneously; so many similar-looking crew cuts and BDUs, that it would be nearly impossible to pick little 'ol me out of the crowd. To think, I risked everything on this 'strategy.'

Once I double-checked my list and confirmed I had everything—plus a few bonus items—I strolled toward the exit, trying my best to appear bored. Considering many privates did not make a purchase, I calculated my actions should seem normal enough. In spite of my confidence, I sensed something was amiss. *Someone was watching me!* When I heard rapid footsteps approaching from behind, I spun around.

"What do you think you're doing?" Blaine demanded in a stern tone, grabbing my forearm. He sounded like a protective father when he catches his son involved in some mischief.

"Nothing cuz, I'm rollin' out," I said faking a yawn. "I'm done shopping, what about you?" Uttering this casually, I tried to escape his vice-like grip.

"Shop-*ping?*" he repeated sarcastically. "You mean shop-*lifting* don't you?" Saying this in a not-so-low tone, Hawk then continued before I could respond. "Sev, what're you trying to do? Go to jail?"

"Yo chill out!" I muttered in anger, trying to keep my

voice down. Wrenching my arm free, I ducked into the nearest aisle to be less visible.

Blaine followed me.

"Everyone's watching you!" he declared, remaining firm in his stance. Hawker behaved like he did not notice my hushed voice. "Tak, you're gonna get caught!"

Once we were both in the aisle, I vented. "Hawker, shut-the-fuck-up and get outta my business!" Losing any cool I might have maintained to this point, I snarled at him, completely vexed.

With Blaine's good ol' boy reputation preceding him, I knew the 'square from the countryside' would try to stop me if he got wind of my plan. For this reason, I made a point not to mention anything to him beforehand, preferring to drop the science on "gettin' yours" later in the barracks while passing out the goods and collecting my cash. Long story made short, I had no time to be bothered with him now.

Seeing I was beyond being persuaded, Hawker surrendered. "Amaru, no doubt about it, you're the stubbornest fool I've ever met! I hope you know what you're gonna say to Asia after you get arrested." Getting this off his chest, Blaine penetrated my eyes with one last glare before disappearing.

Suddenly, I felt alone.

Gathering my wits, I prepared to follow Blaine out the glass doors that were thirty feet away. Shifting my weight, I took my first step toward whatever fate might lie beyond the exit. Then I stopped. This was due to a fleeting memory of something A-Rock had dubbed "Mission Negative."

"There's no such thing as coincidence." A-Rock used to preach this whenever we discussed our schemes. He claimed whatever occurred before, during, or just after our

risky ventures needed to be carefully analyzed. "We have to study every possibility. The ability to adjust *any* unexpected situation is the tactic which separates the master-thief counting dollars in the bank with the jailbird counting years in the pen," he asserted one night at his house while we munched on our stolen food. A-Rock aspired to be a big-time cat burglar. He wanted to crack rich people's safes and sell their jewelry and paintings on the international black-market. Therefore he insisted on paying attention to details to create what he called, 'good-thieving-habits.' Having been on the frosh basketball squad a year before me, A-Rock liked to quote our former coach. "Like Coach D used to say…whatever you do in practice is what you're gonna do in the game." In spite of A-Rock's vow to become a career-criminal, to my knowledge, he never advanced past the shoplifting level. Food, clothes, or sneakers; but he never sold drugs or did anything beyond committing misdemeanors. A-Rock was involved more because it was fun than for his own personal consumption. Knowing this, I was not surprised like so many others when he discarded his delinquent undertakings after high school. A few years ago, I heard he turned into a stable guy with a wife and three kids, and even works for some high-falutin, financial company on the Upper East side of Manhattan.

Even though I was already counting the dead presidents in my head, my instincts warned the present circumstances fit A-Rock's mission-negative-scenario to a tee. Anyone could have overheard my argument with Blaine. How this had occurred was irrelevant. The fact was, to walk out would be equivalent to dismissing the credo which had saved my hide numerous times in my illegal pursuit of happiness. *Danger Tak!* the walls themselves seemed to be echoing the warning.

Right then and there, before Billy had a chance to chime-in his opinion, I terminated Operation Speedstick. Reaching into my pockets, I started placing the booty on a cart showcasing a men's gloves display. I was livid! Of course I blamed the aborted plan on Blaine. "If he would've just minded his own fuckin' business, everything would've been cool," I complained under my breath. The only thing on my mind was picking a fight with him as I patted my shirt and pants with both hands to ensure everything was gone.

Following a final look at the assorted goods sloppily piled in the men's clothing area, I snatched the item I wanted most: an *Anita Baker* cassette. This was because the song *'Sweet Love'* reminded me of Asia. Plus, just in case Blaine was right and someone had been watching me, I figured buying something was the best way to assert my innocence.

Taking a look around, I located the cash registers and angrily stomped in their direction. Along the way, I checked to see if anyone was paying any unwarranted attention my way. An expert at identifying *narks,* I stopped here and there to inspect various articles of clothing. This allowed me to look in every direction without appearing conspicuous. I detected nothing; no one was following me. By the time I was standing in-line with the other suckers, I wanted to kill Hawker!

As the idea of fighting him obsessed me, I handed the cashier my last, crumpled ten-dollar bill. The fact Blaine had acted in my best interest, as a friend, never entered my mind. After the lady handed back my change, I shoved it into my pocket along with the PX bag. Then I exited the rear-doors of the building.

Being trainees, we were required to leave via the rear

exits of most places we entered. Due to our formations being held in front of these buildings, this made arriving on-time challenging for a private who was running behind schedule. Following any meal, this bothersome detail proved significant as there were always privates who did not have enough time to eat. The last trainees inside the messhall had to keep their attention fixed on the drills to estimate when it was a few minutes before they were finished dining. If a private ended his meal when the drills stood up, he would not have enough time to run around the building because the drills, of course, exited through the front door.

"Fuck that! Blaine's gonna shoot me a fair-one for this." Once outside, with no one near me, I allowed myself to vent out-loud. Having expressed my intentions, I broke into a jog before reaching the first corner and just like a four-hundred-meter sprinter, as I accelerated, I leaned into the turn…and ran smack into the backs of a group of privates who were gathered just around the bend.

"Damn!"

"What the fuck!?" shrieked one of the privates I collided with. Before I could screech to a terrifying halt, three more dudes were jolted forward.

"Sorry!" I apologized to the foursome, "I couldn't see y'all from around the corner," I explained before asking what they were doing. "But yo, why are y'all standing here?"

"You with the big-mouth! Shut-up and stand in-line!" After a pause, the angry guy asked a question. "Where're you running off to anyway?"

Turning in the direction of the vulgar directive, I saw a dark-skinned man with a distinctive, black-and-yellow band around his left bicep. It read 'MP.' The guy yelling seemed to be in charge of the gathering. "Nowhere…Corporal," I said after searching for his insignia and dipping into my memorized list of Army ranks. "Just stretching my legs—"

"Shut up!"

In silence, I looked behind him and saw four privates standing apart from the others. Seeing their hands placed against the side of the building and their feet spread apart, I realized what I had thought was just a bunch of sneaky privates kickin' it was, instead, my worst nightmare. *Oh shit! This is an MP checkpoint for shoplifters.* With this understanding, I broke-out in a cold sweat before remembering I didn't steal anything. In a split second, my emotions went from sizzling anger, to stark fear, to a smug arrogance when I realized I was clean.

"Next line, step forward!" barked the charcoal-complexioned MP. "Empty your pockets—*move!"*

Following his command, I reached into my pocket, pulled out my bag with its stapled receipt...and smiled. My grin quickly dissolved once I noticed one of the guys in front of me getting frisked was Blaine. With his hands against the wall, he was staring at me with his head pressed against the concrete while a MP patted him down. After being released, Hawker hesitated to make sure his eyes expressed his contempt. To escape his scowl, I glanced to my right. This allowed me to discover five privates which had been out of my field of vision until now.

Separated from the others, three of the guys wearing handcuffs were CC members from other platoons. Unbelievably, two of them were the very pair who had tried to dissuade me in the latrine. What got my attention more than the convicts' identities, or even the shiny bracelets adorning their wrists, was the pile of items which had been confiscated from them. Lying on a nearby table, it was easy to see in one glimpse that it was eerily similar to the stockpile desecrating a men's glove display near the exit. And like the other collection, *Speedstick* was in abundance.

When the MPs released me, the condemned privates gasped in disbelief. Grinning back at them, I issued my trademark wink. I had no compassion for those sucker-ducks whatsoever. As far as I was concerned, they got what they deserved for trying to move-in on my racket.

On that afternoon, Blaine demonstrated true friendship to a hard-headed fool who did not deserve it. Considering this was not the only time he went above-and-beyond the call of duty to save me, I'd like to dedicate this moment to showing my appreciation. *Hawk, if you're reading this, thank you! I can never say 'Thank you!' enough times!"*

Basic Training Note: Feeling the Pressure

Drill sergeants taught us a vast number of soldiering skills. Nonetheless, more than teaching how to kill or survive, their main task was to indoctrinate us into our new roles. This means they taught us how to behave. To do this, they resorted to any form of pressure they could think of. One of their favorite techniques was to congratulate the success stories and publicly-humiliate the failures. Not only were the results of every test announced to the formation, they were also posted for all to see. This inspired privates to pass every evaluation and avoid mistakes at all costs.

For those unfortunates who scored too low, remedial training was provided. Since these gatherings of subpar personnel were held during breaks, and within earshot of the larger group, these pep-talks also served as comedy-relief for the 'good' privates to enjoy. The drill's method to inspire improvement was to make fun of the lackeys. While some training did occur in these special-ed assemblies, for all those not up-to-snuff, there was no end to being isolated together. Because the drills in-charge were especially cynical and condescending, it was impossible for a trainee to feel good about himself after attending one of these sessions. This ensured the feeling of humiliation was effective both in a social context and on a personal level.

Introduction to BRM: Redneck & the Comedian

The day following Sgt. Sanford's departure to Georgia, we were waiting outside after lunch. After commanding us to sit down, Drill Sgt. Terrier launched into a corny, stand-up routine. It was the kind of humor which requires a drum hit after each punch-line so the audience understands when to laugh.

For some reason, I felt disrespected by his slap-stick performance. Like many emotionally challenged youth, I had a tendency to take everything personally. As a result, I glared at the drill using the hardest, most challenging face I could muster. After all, he was my enemy, right? I truly believed most privates would likewise feel insulted. Therefore, I was rudely awakened to reality when my comrades fell over shaking with laughter. Amongst the giggling throng, I spotted many CC members too.

Later, Brown tried to console me with some advice. "Amaru, you don't have to laugh but just try to smile a little bit."

I was shocked to hear Brown felt this way. "Cuz, you

69

starting to sound like an Uncle Tom," I snapped back at him.

Hearing my pessimistic response, Brown shook his head and sighed. "Philly, all I'm saying is, ain't no reason to make any unnecessary enemies."

As usual, Brown's advice was right on point.

When Sgt. Terrier's final series of one-liners produced nothing more than my most callous stare, the lanky drill changed tactics. "Second Platoon!" he boomed. "It seems Private Amaru here doesn't think my jokes are funny." Saying this, he pointed at me. "Amaru, ain't that right?"

"That's right Drill Sergeant," Billy responded without the slightest hesitation.

Turning away from me, Sgt. Terrier again addressed the entire group. "Well I wonder," he began. "Since Amaru's such a bold critic, maybe, just maybe, he can come up here and tell some funnier jokes than this old, drill sergeant. How about it second platoon? Who wants to see Amaru's stand-up routine? Let's hear it!" Using an amused but slightly confrontational tone, he seemed pleased when more than a few brown-nosers cheered him on.

Once Sgt. Terrier challenged me, friendly or not, Billy responded in a tone that maintained military bearing but expressed sarcasm and arrogance. "Yes Drill Sergeant, you're absolutely right. *Maybe* I could tell funnier jokes. But *maybe* I came to Fort Leonard Wood to learn how to be a soldier…not a comedian." Prior to completing my brash reply, I could feel the privates in my vicinity shrinking away. This is why what the drill did next took everyone off-guard. Especially me.

He did absolutely nothing. Following an extended moment of staring at me, Sgt. Terrier, appearing calmer than ever, walked to the head of the formation and signaled for everyone to stand up and prepare to enter the tortuously, humid building.

Due to my limited scope of understanding, I judged everyone as either soft or hard. Taking this to be further proof of Sgt. Terrier's softness, it never occurred to me he had compiled enough data on my character to categorize me as a "failure to adapt," hardhead case. So that's why he didn't punish me. In his mind, I was already gone. Once again, there I was trying to force everyone to play chess when the game was obviously checkers.

Chapter 6: Basic Rifle Marksmanship

In the 1980s, the military-industrial complex launched an aggressive, media campaign to resurrect its reputation. Somewhere between the '50s and the '70s, i.e. Korea and Vietnam, their 'good guy' image had been tarnished by thousands of college students on television labeling them as drug addicts and baby killers. This was very threatening to the power structure, so of course they were forced to hijack the movement. If you ever watch footage of those anti-war protests, it's ironic to imagine that the disgruntled teens chanting "Hey, hey, LBJ, how many kids did you kill today?" were the same up-and-coming professionals who took over the murderous reins a couple years later. It seems the most vocal participants at the demonstrations were the very offspring of the monsters who were sponsoring the killing.

The powers-that-be vowed to never again allow the media to drag their image through the mud. They realized whoever dictated the messages on the news and in the movies ultimately controlled the asses of the masses. It took over a decade, but they finally pulled off their polish-up crusade. Once sanctioned by the ruling class, it became official policy for big-time screenwriters and directors to "get the cooperation of the military or forget about making the picture[3]." *Red Dawn, Rambo, Commando*, *Platoon,* and *Top Gun* heads a long list of military motion-pictures that were

---

[3] See *Embed Miltarism*

73

filmed in Hollywood only after being approved by the
Pentagon.

Being bombarded through popular entertainment with
'feel good' soldier-adventures, which included the new, war-
like video games, Odom, Hawker, and I believed shooting a
weapon to be a God-inspired activity. This is why we were so
disappointed after our first visit to the firing range.

"You know what?" Odom asked us.

"What?" Blaine and I chorused together.

"I think guns, especially rifles, were created for
cowards. Think about it: what kind of bitch-ass muthafucka
would even think of inventing something to kill a man from
so far away?"

"A weak chump that can't handle his business up-
close-and-personal," Hawk expressed before I chimed-in my
opinion.

"Like a true warrior!"

In spite of our Bushido-driven visions, we knew
passing BRM was compulsory in order to graduate. On that
note, every drill warned us several times of the dire
consequences which accompanied failing. "If you maggots
can't learn to march or master your rifle, you'll be outta here
in the next ten days!" This is what Sgt. Terrier yelled the first
time we filed into the arms-room to collect our M-16s.

For the next week, we did everything with our rifles
except shoot them. Mainly, we used them as exercise
equipment. I was surprised how heavy my rifle became after
shoulder-pressing it a hundred times over my head. In spite of
the drills reminders to never let our weapons out of our sight,
soon, many rifles were found lying 'unsecure' on the ground.
This normally occurred near the latrine on our breaks.
Whenever a drill found an M16 without its owner holding it,

the entire company was penalized with push-ups and flutter kicks.

Intimately getting to know our 'new girlfriends' meant learning to disassemble and reassemble her in record time, not to mention keeping her parts clean too. Unable to shoot the cumbersome objects, it did not take long for us to become sick and tired of these cold, metallic bitches. In spite of this, at dinner on the eve of our first day of shooting, everyone was excited to see what the lightweight, 5.56 mm, air-cooled, gas-operated, magazine-fed, assault M-16A2, also known as the 'Black Rifle,' could do.

The first morning we arrived at the range, the scent of gunpowder and burnt metal was strong in our nostrils. After introducing themselves, the cadre in-charge told us the do's and don'ts at their facility. Heading this list was to strictly follow the orders coming from the tower because, in their own words, we would be "wielding the power of life and death!"

Once everyone had a chance to shoot one time, the excitement died down and it became business as usual. Between each wave of firing, Sgt. Terrier and Sgt. Lavendar studied each private's paper target. It was necessary to group six shots together in one area. To do this, we were told to aim center-mass. By the location of these strikes in relation to the bullseye, the drills ascertained how much the front and rear-site assemblies needed to be adjusted. This calibration process is known as 'zeroing' the weapon. It is important to note that by zeroing the rifles, the drills specifically tailored each M-16 to match the body dimensions of its owner.

In between firing, we compared our results. At first everyone's targets pretty much looked the same, with either very few holes or holes scattered everywhere. Gradually, some privates began showing progress. They offered advice to those of us who were still struggling.

By day 3, everyone's rifle was zeroed but I was not comfortable shooting mine. Perhaps I was being too hard on myself but it seemed everyone was improving except me. At first, I took it in stride, believing I just needed to get used to my weapon. Like most, during our days of prep work for BRM, I became sick and tired of my M-16. That said, considering how many boring, high school classes I had devoted to reading assassin novels, it never occurred to me I could amount to anything less than a superb marksman. Nonetheless, my skepticism found firmer ground once we began shooting at the pop-up targets because I couldn't hit anything. *I mean, not one target!* Looking downrange, I could see dirt flying-up in the air so I knew my weapon was shooting bullets, but I couldn't hit a target to save my life. After a couple sessions of missing *every* target, I became one of the ten privates requiring remedial training. Since Sgt. Terrier was the drill who zeroed my weapon, I explained to him that something didn't seem right with my M-16.

"Shut up, stop making excuses, and aim center-mass!" Sgt. Terrier severely reprimanded. Aside from that, he ignored me.

Next, I tried speaking to Sgt. Lavendar. After he likewise brushed me off, I proceeded to complain to every drill sergeant in Alpha Company, including my personal drill sergeant. Completely frustrated, I was reminded of the times I had debated with Coach D about putting me in the game. And just like back then, I refused to remain silent and my soldierly complaints about my faulty weapon were loud and frequent.

"Drill Sergeant, the private requests permission to speak."

"Amaru, if this is about that dog-gone rifle again, just go on ahead and get down in the front-leaning rest."

"Drill Sergeant, if you'd just shoot it yourself, I'm sure you'll see what I'm talking about—"

"Drop!"

By the end of the week, I almost lost my temper when it became obvious all the drills had agreed to drop me the instant I hinted at my weapon's inefficiency. With this conspiratorial edict in effect, I ended up doing push-ups following every wave of firing until the afternoon prior to our qualification test. Being one of the six remaining dunces, I had been reminded every day that failure to qualify in BRM was equivalent to an early-exit back to civilian life. In spite of showing no signs of improvement whatsoever, I refused to give up.

Simply put, with no place to live, getting kicked out was not an option.

During my days of dreadful shooting, I had retained a sliver of hope I could somehow figure a way to accurately fire what had become, from my perspective, a useless piece of junk. As I prepared for my final practice before the test, I was desperate; so I decided to try something new. I prayed. Perhaps, I was more spiritual than I thought. "God, if you really do exist, I need you now!" This was the closest I had ever come to petitioning a higher force.

Upon hearing the command "Commence to kill!" reverberate through the loudspeakers, I placed the selector-lever on 'Semi,' focused down-range, and squeezed the trigger. Hearing the retort of exploding rifles all around me, followed by scores of metal casings hitting the dirt, whatever optimism I had about miraculously passing the next day's test quickly disintegrated.

For over a week, I had tried aiming too high, too far to the left—anything I could think of—to compensate for a non-calibrated weapon. Despite my gravest efforts, I watched each pop-up target go up-and-down completely untouched. Seeing this, I felt a dark cloud of despair hovering over me. When I got down to my last, two rounds, I had a brief notion to turn around and shoot at the drill sergeants. In fact, the only reason I decided against it was I knew I'd miss!

Once my last bullet whizzed harmlessly downrange, I felt like a total and complete failure. "No matter what the drills say, these muthafuckin sights ain't zeroed!" I complained to myself through tears of bitter frustration. In my mind, the only thing worse would be if the CC saw me crying; so I remained in the prone-position well after the formation had gathered thirty yards to my rear. Caught up in my moment of misery, I failed to sense the approach of my personal drill. This guy was always right on time.

"All ready for the big day tomorrow?" the short drill opened up in a way-too-cheerful voice.

Following that cold night of doing push-ups at the barracks' entrance, which I referred to as my 'revelation night,' I had striven to become a soldier. Nonetheless, being at my wits end and feeling like I was kicked-out anyway, for the first time since that incident, I expressed disrespect by simply ignoring him.

"Private, do you hear me talking to you?" Sgt. Sandoval inquired in an authoritative tone. As soon as he ordered me to respond, all at once, the emotional implosion I was experiencing inwardly erupted outward.

"What!?" I opened up without a hint of deference. From there, it briskly plummeted downhill. "Fuck you, and fuck all you fake, monkey-ass, drill sergeants! I told you this

fuckin' gun wasn't zeroed. Get the fuck away from me you bitch-ass muthafucka!"

As you have probably noted, in my frustration, I could not say 'fuck' or any variation of it enough times. My pride was hurt this badly. However Sgt. Sandoval, always the professional, immediately took action by joining-in my screaming tirade. Although I'm certain he heard every vulgar detail I uttered, everyone else probably only heard two people yelling at each other. *Only God knows how that situation did not escalate into a fist fight.*

The next thing I remember, I was doing push-ups with him squatting next to me. But I was still cursing up a storm. So was he.

"Shut the fuck up! Shut the fuck up!" he repeated in a muffled voice like it was a secret.

After I had pumped-out about thirty reps, I quieted down enough for him to question me.

"Amaru, who zeroed your M16?"

"Drill Sergeant Terrier did, Drill Sergeant," I angrily replied.

"Did you report the problem with your weapon to either of your drill sergeants?"

To me, this was a stupid question. "Muthafucka, I told you this same shit three days ago!" Following my venomous response, this was the only time I ever peeped the *Kool* drill show any raw emotion.

Crouching closer to my ear, Sgt. Sandoval spoke in a tone of controlled fury. "Amaru, if you call me 'muthafucka,' or out of my name one more time, I swear to Almighty God I will put my boot so far up your ass you'll be tasting *Kiwi* shoe-polish your entire ride back to Philly. Now regain your military composure and answer the goddamned question!"

His burst of emotion actually calmed me down. The truth was, I found it amusing. Despite this, I never came close to smiling. "Yes Drill Sergeant, I have reported the problem to both of my drill sergeants repeatedly, Drill Sergeant." I replied demonstrating the finest military bearing.

"Much better!" he vented before returning to his usual, wise-ass demeanor. "Ya know what *Amaroo*? In spite of what everyone says about you, I still believe we *can* make a damn soldier out of you yet."

Although he had regained his sense of humor, I remained tense for the remainder of his interrogation.

"After reporting the situation," Sgt. Sandoval resumed, "did anyone re-adjust your sights?"

This question set me off again. "As I said ten times before—"

Before my rant could gain momentum, the drill cut me off. "Just answer the question!" he screamed into my left eardrum. "I won't warn you again. Am I clear?"

"Yes Drill Sergeant!" I said returning to my senses. No longer wanting to fight with him, I cleared my throat, humbled my tone, and responded. "Negative Drill Sergeant, no one has re-adjusted my sights. I have been completely ignored."

At this point, the questioning stopped and he began yelling again. For some reason, even though he called me every nasty thing he could think of, I wasn't offended by his insults. While I was making heads or tails of his suspect verbal assault, the unmistakable sound of a magazine being inserted into my weapon got my full attention.

With the 'cease fire' order having been given several minutes ago, when Sgt. Sandoval fired three shots downrange, without a shadow of a doubt, the other hundred or so privates, drills, and cadre had to be stunned at this clear violation *by a drill sergeant!*

For his part, Sgt. Sandoval joked around like we were the only two people at the range that day. "Well I'll be damned Amaroo! For once, you were actually right, your weapon does need a slight adjustment…" Too far away for his snickering to be overheard, he continued babbling while he adjusted my rifle's sightings. "Okay, that should do it." Saying this, he fired once more to confirm his handiwork. Then, he removed the magazine and returned my weapon to its stand. "Amaru recover," he commanded.

Once I was standing at attention, Sgt. Sandoval again rebuked me using his loud, fake voice before ending in a volume that only I could hear. "Tomorrow, just relax and aim center-mass and you'll do fine. Good luck Private."

Overcome with joy someone had finally heard my pleas, all I wanted was *one* chance to practice before the test. "Drill Sergeant—" I began.

At ease big-mouth…shut-up!" Sgt. Sandoval warned in a muffled tone before booming in a much louder voice. "All firing is done for today! I just needed to get rid of those last, four rounds from a weapon that jammed."

When I noticed he had again reverted to his dramatically loud voice, I began to catch his drift.

"No more questions, understand?"

"Yes Drill Sergeant!" I replied with the utmost respect. Although I did not understand everything, what I did comprehend was this fiery-eyed drill was blessing me with the chance I had prayed for. Most importantly, I felt my confidence returning.

What most people living in so-called 'developed countries' fail to realize is, even if the odds are a million-to-

one against us, the only thing the disenfranchised crave in life is a chance.

Qualify or Go Home

The next morning, the skies were cloudy and grey when we were marched to breakfast. However, by the time we arrived at the range, the weather was crisp, clear, and sunny. An absolute perfect day for shooting, I was slated to fire in the last wave. Standing amongst my fellow privates, everyone was visibly nervous while the senior drill-sergeant greeted us.

"Alpha company, y'all been working over-time at the firing range. I know 'cause I been watching. Hell if today ain't the easiest part. Just relax, aim center-mass, and have some fun out there. When you pull that trigger, imagine you're killing a no-good *commie,* son-of-a-bitch!"

"Hooah! Hooah!" my comrades energetically responded.

While my peers had polished their skills for over a week, I was keenly aware that I was about to shoot my M-16 for the first time. To say I was skeptical whether Sgt. Sandoval could compensate for the difference in our height, is putting it lightly. Sitting there, I was contemplating if I should aim a little above or below each target to offset any slight, calibration errors. Confused and on-edge, I returned my attention to the senior drill once he resumed with a description of the task we faced.

"As you already know, this final exam consists of forty, pop-up targets from fifty to three-hundred-yards. Although twenty-three is the number you gotta hit if you plan on still being a member of Alpha Company at lunch time, the company commander, the first-sergeant, and myself, are looking forward to personally congratulating all those sharp enough to qualify as experts. Men, for that honor, you gotta hit thirty-seven targets."

After being lined-up chronologically by wave, I watched the privates before me fire their rifles. For some reason, by sitting still and smelling the gunpowder, my nerves were calmed. Soon I was in a daze. By the time my wave received the command to step forward, I was still split on my course of action. Then, in my mind, I heard the last words uttered by Sgt. Sandoval the previous day. "Just relax and aim center-mass, and you'll do fine." Silently nodding to myself, I deduced this was my only chance to pass.

Once I got set in the foxhole, I had all but forgotten my shooting woes to this point; even the fact I had not been permitted one practice session to prepare for this monumental test of skill. Following two deep breaths, I heard a baritone voice from the towers deliver the phrase we were all waiting for.

"Gentlemen, commence to kill!"

Closing one eye, I waited for the first target. When a twenty-five-yarder popped-up, I aimed downrange, squeezed the trigger...and knocked it down.

"Oh shit, Amaru hit it!" screamed an unknown voice from somewhere behind me.

"Shut-up!"

After a drill reprimanded the private, I heard nothing and felt even less. Target after target popped-up only to be blasted back down. Seeing this, I was ecstatic but remained locked-in; my concentration never wavered. Even when I missed a three-hundred-yarder, I managed to remain calm.

83

This is because I remembered Sgt. Terrier teaching us to aim an inch-or-so higher for these, due to their great distance.

I proceeded to hit four more targets, from from fifty to two-hundred-yards, before I missed a two-hundred-fifty yarder and another one at three-hundred-yards. After that, I tweaked my technique just right and dropped the next, long-range target. Having made the correct adjustment, I became absorbed in the killing zone. From that point, I did not miss again.

"Cease fire!" blared the faceless voice from the towers.

On his command, I grabbed my weapon and stood up. I felt exhausted standing there waiting for the senior-drill to order us to join the company. Once he did, I struggled to shuffle forward. Still in a mild stupor, it appeared everyone's eyes were riveted on me as I drew near the formation. In spite of this, no one spoke to me when I reached our platoon. In silence, I walked by two groups of trainees who were shaking hands and slapping each other on the back. Then I stopped because I saw Sgt. Sandoval walking toward me. I will never forget the first person to congratulate me was not even from my platoon.

"Not bad Philly, for an amateur. But like I've always said, expert should end at thirty-eight…not thirty-seven." Although he tried to suppress his emotion, Sgt. Sandoval was obviously moved by my effort.

His cocky remarks snapped me out of my dream-like state. "What was that Drill Sergeant? How many did I hit?" Still delirious, I whipped my head around.

"Amaroo," the fiery-eyed drill replied with a chuckle, "I figured your dumb-ass couldn't read words, but damn, you don't understand numbers either?" This is how my personal drill informed me of what was already old news to everyone else.

While I digested his words, a warm sensation caused me to perspire. It was unbelievable to think that, beyond merely passing, I had qualified as one of the seven experts in Alpha Company.

"Congratulations soldier!" Beaming with pride, Sgt. Sandoval then honored me by shaking my hand before returning to his own platoon.

It took a couple seconds before anyone else said anything to me. When I reached the second squad, Brown and Hawk were there waiting for me.

"You know what, Amaru?" came Brown's scratchy voice as he hugged me. "I ain't even gonna ask how you pulled that off. Nothing you do amazes me anymore."

"You just got lucky!" Hawk screamed from behind him.

Then the CC, along with several others, rushed toward me. Soon, I was being mobbed with hugs, handshakes, and pats on the back. While I was laughing at their gibes, everyone was startled by a booming command.

"Alpha Company, attention!"

After we ran to our places and locked-up with military precision, only then did the company commander and first-sergeant make their regal appearance. Once the proper salutes were rendered, Captain Yates assumed command of his company.

"All expert shooters, front and center. *Move!*"

On his command I, along with six others, swiftly took a step to the rear before sprinting to my newly designated position in front of the formation. Having arrived there, we were ordered to stand in a single line, shoulder-to-shoulder, facing the company.

Approaching us individually, the captain, the first-sergeant, and the senior drill, took turns shaking our hands. For several minutes, while the rest of the company remained standing at attention, the seven of us stood at ease as we answered questions about our families and hometowns. By the time Cpt. Yates executed an about-face to address the larger group, the significance of the moment was setting in.

"Alpha Company!" he yelled at the throng, "I want each and every one of you to take a good, long-look at perfection." Following a short pause, he continued. "While it's true none of us can measure up to the perfection of God, the privates lined-up in front of you are as close as you can get in this man's Army!" He then pointed at all three platoons. "Every last one of you should be aspiring to qualify as experts with your M-16s." With that, the CO gestured back toward us and bellowed in a deep voice. "Here before you, I present the elite members of Alpha Company, 3rd Brigade, 4th Battalion." Beaming like a proud father, he pointed one last time. "Men, we're damned proud of you!" Then, Cpt. Yates faced the company and concluded the ceremony. "Well?" he said. "What the hell are you waiting for? Show them your respect and appreciation!" With that emphatic declaration, our company commander began clapping to initiate the curtain-call round of applause.

In less than twenty-four hours, I went from being one of the six remedial dunces (by the way, my five special-ed classmates were sent home a week later), to entering Captain Yate's 'Elite 7' of Alpha Company. Staring at the cheering horde, I picked out my friends before spotting Gimenez wearing a sour expression and Sgt. Terrier's glaring countenance. To keep my shining moment in perspective, I contrasted their frowns with Sgt. Sandoval's hearty smile. That day, I respectfully smiled back; no condescending grins.

The next morning, the CC in 3rd platoon reported Sgt. Sandoval and Sgt. Terrier had a boisterous argument on their floor after lights-out. In fact, they said the two drills nearly came to blows!

Following the CO's speech, the first-sergeant added a couple more minutes of compliments. By this time, I was really showing off my pearly whites. When I looked at Sgt. Terrier again, his face was flushed with embarrassment; it was flaming red. Seeing this, I came to understand why folks called guys like him 'rednecks.'

Now I was in the mood to tell some jokes.

Chapter 7: From Dunce to Elite

"After fourteen years in this man's Army, not many things surprise me anymore…" This is how a smug, but earnest Drill Sgt. Sanford opened after approaching where I sat cleaning my M16 with several other privates. "But Amaru, when I got back this morning and noticed your ass was still here, I have to admit…" Stopping here, the tall drill rubbed his chin and squinted suspiciously before completing his sentence. *"I was surprised."*

It had taken Sgt. Sanford two weeks to mourn the loss of his father before returning to Missouri on an evening flight. Having gotten used to being supervised by two drills, everyone was surprised to see his imposing silhouette at the morning formation.

"And guess what Drill Sergeant?" piped up a nearby private. "Amaru has really cleaned up his act. Not only did he shoot expert at BRM, he maxed-out our last PT test too. Why, he's even volunteered to work-out with Pvt. Lonnie every evening to help him raise his PT score!"

"You, drop!" Sgt. Sanford barked, appearing genuinely disgusted. "And get off his dick!" Following a brief glare at the parrot-like private who had popped out of nowhere with his unsolicited comment, the drill asked me a rhetorical question in a deadly serious tone. "Amaru, how much you payin' this clown for promo?"

The truth was, I had no idea who that guy even was.

After BRM, I became cool as hell with Captain Yates. Our CO made it a habit to personally greet me and a few other 'elite' privates whenever he stopped by to supervise our training. This status promotion had the effect of dispelling any denigrating character assessments circulating throughout the company about me. In short, it was the difference between night and day. Sharing much in common with my first days of riding to school with Ant and his crew, now that I was participating in the morning chores, the entire atmosphere lightened up. As a result, I was able to make friends with privates outside of the CC and they started telling me about their families, wives, and girlfriends. Due to my early wake-ups, I was amongst the first to begin cleaning, dusting, and mopping the common areas each morning. No longer the cranky son-of-a-bitch everyone had come to know, although most of my comrades were pleased with the 'new me,' not everyone was convinced it wasn't just a ploy with an ulterior motive. Honestly, it was an act of desperation.

Realizing the drills were playing for keeps, I learned to sit back and quietly arrange my schemes in accordance with, not against, the rules. While the added patience changed the complexion of my game, the goal remained the same: to get over like a fat rat. Perhaps, the best example of my new school of thought was my decision to attend church. I remember when I first decided to go.

On the Saturday afternoon ending our third week, Dunbar, Odom, Brown, Lonnie, and I were enjoying a two-hour pass together. At that time, we were experiencing difficulty just relaxing. Sadly, something as simple as walking-and-talking freely, meaning not marching and singing in-cadence, had become a foreign activity. As much as we hated to admit it, we were lost without the constant supervision of the drills bearing down on us. This new trait of helplessness became evident when we were crossing the street in front of the PX. We had difficulty judging the oncoming, twenty-five mph traffic. If one person decided to go, some others hesitated. Or, it was the other way around. Finally, Brown, Lonnie, and Odom went ahead, leaving me and Dunbar on the curb. After a car honked at the bumbling trio, Dunbar summed up the glaring truth.

"Man, we don't even know how to cross the street anymore!"

With everyone more relaxed in my presence, that evening at dinner, I overheard enough of another private's conversation to understand we were permitted to attend church the following morning. Having little reverence for the divine nature of things, this in itself was no big deal. That is, until it was revealed the privates sojourning to their Sunday morning sabbaticals were doing so by themselves. That means without a drill sergeant. *Alone!*

Being left unsupervised with my own thoughts was such a rare occurrence, the significance of this privilege cannot be overstated. I just wanted to walk around out of cadence. Play a video game. Eat a doughnut. You know...live a little. Not to mention, I urgently needed to use the pay phones on the other side of the post. Outside of the training area, there were no long-lines of waiting privates. I was stressed-out by my lack of mail from Asia, so I needed to find a consistent way to contact her.

The next morning after breakfast, I stayed away from my usual CC counterparts. Relishing the thought of pulling this off, I did not risk telling anyone about my plan, fearing it might leak like the PX incident had. Unlike my friends, I hadn't attended church as a child. Therefore, I did not understand what these services were all about. *Nor did I give a damn!* Since my goal had nothing to do with prayers, priests, or bibles, I feared someone might take exception to me involving their god in my scam.

At nine-forty-five, when Billy Bad-Ass stepped on the scene, the eighteen privates gathered at the main entrance appeared surprised, if not altogether intimidated. When Drill Sgt. Lavendar arrived, he also did not conceal his astonishment. After doing a double-take in my direction, while many brown-nosers chuckled, the drill began reading a list of the available types of deity worship. Catholic, Protestant, Baptist, Episcopalian, and others. There were probably facilities for Islamic or Jewish practitioners as well; I really can't remember. Immediately following the drills' announcement, three of the sanctified privates cautiously approached.

"Good morning, Pvt. Amaru. Will you be joining us for the Catholic service?" inquired a rotund, Caucasian with red cheeks as he gestured toward his two, devout buddies standing next to him.

"Good morning, umm Cox...Pvt. Cox", I responded after straining my eyes to read his nametag. "No, I'm not Catholic," I responded trying to hide my confusion.

Once he departed, gradually other privates began approaching to ask if I was going to their church. Not knowing what to say, I just repeated the same answer to each group. This turned out to be a blessing-in-disguise because by the time Sgt. Lavendar inquired about my church affiliation for the record, I had compiled enough information to make a decision. Knowing the only religion that could serve my spiritual needs was one which would set me free for a couple hours, I blurted-out the only denomination listed no one had asked me about.

"Lutheran, Drill Sergeant".

"Lutheran huh?" echoed Sgt. Lavendar, again surprised but this time trying not to show it.

Initially, I feared he would not believe me. To this day, considering I have never met anyone who told me they were Lutheran, it's hard to conceive he never checked to see if I actually attended the services or not.

The Road to Graduation

After BRM, Drill Sgt. Terrier never spoke to me again. From this point, boot-camp almost rolled along smoothly. Although not quite fitting the description of a reformed soul, I was much more able to blend-in and socialize with my mates. Having earned their respect, I started to shed my 'bad boy' reputation. To be accepted felt damn good, and being acknowledged for my achievement was even better. Nevertheless, neither of those rosy sentiments could stop me from jettisoning myself from our second-story window after I read a disturbing letter from Asia one night.

It had been weeks since I last received any mail from her. When I tried calling the previous Sunday while 'at church,' the line had been busy. Even when I did manage to get through, our conversations lasted for less than ten minutes, and were always within earshot of her mother. In her letter, Asia wrote the fighting had increased. As a result, Ms. Kalif was threatening to send Asia to live with her older sister, Ursula, in Mississippi. I remember Isis saying she had an aunt who lived 'down south' that didn't take no shit.

Sitting on my bunk, I was stressed realizing if she left now, she wouldn't know where I got sent for AIT. Nor would I know her new address. How would we contact each other? In total silence, I was drowning in sorrow while my roommates polished their boots and talked about their wives, children, and girlfriends. It seemed they didn't have a care in the world. At any rate, this was the sentiment which prompted my irrational decision. *Fuck waiting until Sunday, I need to talk to Asia tonight!*

In hindsight, this dramatization is laughable because Asia never came close to moving away from her family. It seems, this story was a fabrication concocted by Ms. Kalif to scare her. Or, more likely, it was a lie that Asia created to scam me. Years later, I bumped into Asia and her husband at a friend's party. I was startled when she pulled me off the dance floor claiming she needed to tell me something important. After we walked outside on the porch, Asia said she felt I had abandoned her when I left for basic training. She claimed her feelings of loneliness were so severe, she got drunk a couple times in her bedroom. During her tearful declaration, she apologized several times; but she never admitted cheating on me.

After I donned my field-jacket and cap, I started walking toward the same window I had hurled Jones' linen out of six weeks before. All at once, my roommates stopped their conversations to stare at me with dumbfounded expressions. "Shhh," I said. "Keep it low and I'll be right back. This is an emergency." With my index-finger stuck to my lips, I opened the window and stuck my head outside. Once I confirmed nobody was there, I crept out and jumped. Just before my body disappeared from my roommate's view, I looked at their bug-eyed expressions and grinned.

In mid-descent, I heard Brown yelling. "Amaru, you're the craziest bastard I ever met… and I know a lot of sick muthafuckas!"

Landing on the grass, my body rolled with the momentum before I sprung to my feet in one motion. Already running full-speed, I knew there was a good chance a drill would show up in my room any minute. I was also aware that with my extensive reputation, getting caught outside would undoubtedly result in being kicked out. *I figured I had twenty minutes, tops!*

Following dinner each evening, the phone booths designated for trainees were always jam-packed with AIT privates. Since Advanced Individual Training was the next step beyond boot camp, these lucky individuals were allowed to go outside for a few hours after chow-time. With several companies sharing the same payphones, anyone planning to hear his sweetheart's voice knew he might have to devote his entire evening to just waiting in-line.

Knowing I could not afford this luxury, I chilled-out at the rear of the gathering to formulate a plan. Maintaining a low profile, I lollygagged close enough to view all seven booths. Once the opportunity I was waiting for presented itself, I boldly stepped passed scores of waiting privates. The guy who was eagerly waiting to enter the booth being vacated never saw me coming.

Snatching him by his collar, I rudely yanked the freckle-faced teen out of the way while simultaneously stepping through the entrance. When the lanky private who was leaving the booth tried to protest, I used my other elbow to 'assist' him out the door. As soon as I slammed the door shut, everyone demanded to know what was going on.

"Hey! What the hell does he think he's doing?" yelled

one guy.

"That jerk just cut in front of me!" complained the freckle-faced trainee.

"No, he cut in front of all of us!" declared an infuriated voice from the back of the line. "Let's kill that muthafucka!" With that, a scene reminiscent of a public lynching unfolded as dozens of GIs expressed their violent intent with vulgarities.

These young men who had been patiently waiting did not take kindly to this violation. Intent on spilling my blood, they started kicking the door in an attempt to open it. Within seconds, the assault was raining on my tiny cubicle from all sides, proving beyond a doubt the booth was indeed made out of shatter-proof plastic.

Holding the door shut with all my might, I cringed realizing I had underestimated the consequences of my actions. At this point, the only thing I could do was wait. Since the booths were next to one another, the racket was interfering with my neighbors' conversations. Soon, these privates began voicing their complaints about the noise. This is really what saved me. However, before the atmosphere had a chance to settle down completely, two members of the lynch mob ran up holding steel pipes.

Where the hell did they find steel pipes laying around?

Before either of them could take their first hack, many just witnessing the spectacle stepped-in to prevent the attack. Believe me, I was shittin' bricks by this point but I knew I had to play my hand to the end, come what may. Once the vengeful group agreed they would not damage the phones, for a split second, I was relieved. That is, until they also conspired to jump me when I exited the booth.

"Hey Slick, you don't really think we're gonna let you

get away with this, do you? We'll be right here waiting for your wise-ass when you come out!" Although only one private spoke, there were many murmurs of agreement amongst the milling throng.

"Ay man, do what you gotta do," I replied to the spokesman twelve inches in front of me, on the other side of the plexiglass door. "All I know is, the longer you keep up the noise, the longer you'll have to wait." Following my bold reply, I spoke in a more sincere tone. "I do apologize but this is an emergency. After I finish my call, I'll step outta here and fight like a man. I won't run anywhere. I promise." Having completed my statement, I tilted my head downward and closed my eyes to disengage from the conversation.

It seemed my chivalrous response took the belligerent horde off-guard. Although my words accurately reflected my feelings, the gallantry in them may be credited to the *Conan* novels I had read at Charlie's house.

Five minutes later, the amount of threats and kicks began to subside. Once I determined the noise level had been reduced to a bearable level, without looking outside, I picked up the receiver, inserted my coins, and dialed. I was relieved to hear Asia's voice after only one ring; it was almost as if she had been waiting for my call.

"Hello."

"Ssup," is all I said.

"Oh my god, it's *you!*" she said in exasperation. Then she went on a ten-minute rant explaining how everything had gone wrong in her life since my departure. Before pausing to breathe, she had already asked when I was coming home three times. "I need to see you and you don't even care!" she stammered.

"Asia, you know basic training lasts over two

months," I tried to console her. "We're in the second half, but it's still gonna be some time before I can take leave." Feeling in love all over again, I tried to sound calm.

"If I get sent to Mississippi, we'll never see each other again," Asia responded like she hadn't heard anything I said. After reiterating my worst nightmare, she resumed talking about her disagreements with her sister, mother, and assorted friends.

As Asia grieved about her unfavorable circumstances, I felt my heart being stabbed by red-hot pokers. In those twenty minutes, Asia stressed me out so much, by the time I placed the receiver back on its hook, the Beast couldn't wait to face the bloodthirsty mob.

Without so much as a glance outside, I opened the door and stepped out. Having readied myself to be pounced on, I was surprised to find no such threatening situation. It seems as the other booths opened up, the would-be avengers lost their blood-lust. This is reasonable if you consider their trip to the phones that evening had been about love, not hate.

Accordingly, the only private remaining from the original outraged cast was the little guy with freckles I had yanked out the way. Scanning the faces surrounding him, none of them seemed to recognize me, or know anything about the daring move I made almost a half-hour ago. Without a second thought at my good fortune, I sprinted away, hoping the drills had not yet detected my absence.

Running down the street, I passed various groups of trainees enjoying their final minutes prior to curfew. Seconds later, I stopped to sort out my surroundings; I was having difficulty remembering the way back. *Shit, I'm lost!* Realizing this, I almost asked someone for directions before realizing how foolish I would look asking an AIT trainee the way to my basic-training barracks. "What the fuck am I going to do?" I murmured as I started running again. Without any conviction, I turned right at the next corner. This is when someone yelled in my direction.

"Hey asshole!" the unfamiliar voice screamed. "Slow the fuck down!" This was followed by laughter from other members of the slowly sauntering group.

In basic, we got cursed-out so often that privates inadvertently started talking down to one another like they were the drills. It was a kind of monkey-see-monkey-do type of situation, if you know what I mean.

I was irritated by the strangers' catcalls but in my desperation I had no time to pay him any mind. Thus, when he repeated his vulgarities, I never slowed my pace. I had to concentrate on figuring out where the Alpha Company barracks were. However, when his third wave of insults coincided with the sounds of rocks hitting the pavement all around me, the Beast promptly manned its post. Having been cheated at the phone booths just minutes ago, it did not take much to re-summon the violent entity.

Without interrupting my stride, I circled around and accelerated toward the soldiers hurling the stones. When I arrived within twelve feet, I stopped and pointed an accusing finger. "Which one of you bastards is throwing rocks at me?" I demanded through my labored breathing.

I was facing about ten privates. They were walking toward me in three, distinct groups clutching bags from the PX in their hands. When the four guys in the first row stopped in their tracks and pointed back over their shoulders, I knew they were frightened by my hostile appearance. Stepping toward them, the Beast shoved one of the middle guys in the chest. As he crashed into someone in the second row, this prompted both privates to squeal on someone behind them.

"It was Bush!" they chorused in unison.

After pushing my way through the heart of their group, I sized-up the three dudes in the last row. It was apparent by their demeanor and positioning they were the cool guys in the crew. "I'm looking for Bush, or any bitches that got a problem with me running," I said in a challenging tone.

Pivoting my body allowed me to keep everyone in view. Figuring I had a thirty-three-percent chance of crashing Private Bush in his jaw before the ten-to-one odds worked against me, I swore I was ready for anything but I was wrong. When I stepped forward with my hands up, the three cool dudes took off running. Then, the rest of them followed suit. Unbelievably, the entire group—all ten of them—just punked-out!

I was aghast but still determined to provoke a fight. Nevertheless, when I chased after them yelling every four-lettered word I could think of, they just kept running. After I stopped, the cowardly crew dared to slow down to a walk. Seeing this, I figured an 'eye for an eye' and picked up some stones. Since they were of the opinion that rock-throwing was such an amusing pastime, I pegged several of them in the back before they could start running again. Watching them escape, I contemplated *why wouldn't anyone fight the Beast?*

Chucking the remainder of my stones in one great heave, I returned to my mission. Retracing my steps, I ran back the way I had come. *I gotta get back!* Turning left at the next corner, I made a right after jogging passed two buildings which looked somewhat familiar, and was relieved when I somehow stumbled upon our building. Before I could relax, I realized I now faced my greatest challenge of the evening;

and one I had not considered until this very moment: how am I going to enter the barracks?

No time to get shy now, I thought as I approached a row of lit-up windows, hoping to locate a CC member in 1st platoon. Seeing inside proved to be impossible due to the thick layer of steam coating the four windows I peered into. No matter how hard I squinted, all I could see was the the outlines of people's bodies; I was unable to recognize any faces. With nothing to lose, I chose the one closest to the stairwell and knocked. Everyone in the room froze.

Initially startled, eventually the privates discovered the source of the tapping sound. Within seconds, a Caucasian figure approached and opened the window. "Amaru, what the hell are you doing out there?" whispered the unknown, private after he scrutinized my face.

"Never mind that, gimme your hand so I can pull myself up." Saying this, I prepared to climb in.

"Hell no! Are you crazy? Sergeant Maldonado just left our room not thirty seconds before you knocked—"

After shoving him out of the way, I jumped up and sloppily flipped my body through the window before anyone else could try to stop me. Just then, Sgt. Maldonado's voice was heard coming from just outside their door. This prevented any other privates from venting their complaints. With the wall-lockers and beds near or against the walls, there was nowhere to hide. In a near-panic, I dashed toward the door while the drill joked with a private in the hallway, just a few feet from the room's entrance. A fraction of a second before the Mexican drill appeared in the doorway, I leapt to the left of it. *We were less than three feet apart!*

"Tomorrow's uniform includes field jackets," the brown-round wearing NCO boomed his announcement from the hallway. When no one immediately responded the drill showed his impatience, "Hey dummies, is anyone home?"

Finally, the room leader, PFC O'Brien, responded. "Clear Drill Sergeant!" is all he said.

From the privates' vantage point, they could see both the drill and me simultaneously. However, so long as Sgt. Maldonado did not enter, I would remain hidden from him. Standing there, looking at these 1st platoon trainees' faces, for the life of me I could not understand why they were so scared. After all, I was the only one breaking the rules. Being caught between a rock and a hard place, I knew I had to force the action.

The instant the drill pivoted toward the next room, I darted into the hallway behind him and turned in the opposite direction. As I tip-toed away, I was relieved the drill did not command me to stop. Reaching the staircase, I exited through the door and carefully shut it, making sure it made no sound. Then I climbed the steps and blindly entered the second floor. Luckily no drills were in sight!

All the privates exiting the showers stopped to gawk at me because I was wearing my field jacket and cap. It was obvious I was returning from outside; this was a clear violation. I also noticed one of the guys staring was Gimenez. When he pointed at me and started to say something, I ran down the hall to my room. By the time I reached my locker, I had thrown my cap and jacket on the bunk and was already unbuttoning my shirt. Before I could completely disrobe, I felt a tap on my shoulder. Turning around, I was thankful it was only Brown. With a huge grin etched on his chocolate features, he was still wet from the shower. Holding a towel wrapped around his waist with one hand, he was shaking his head in disbelief.

"My man Amaru," he said with a chuckle. "Your nerve, my brain, you just wait, we're gonna make some dough yet."

PFC Brown was true to his word too. The next day, he approached me with a 'chump change' venture which lasted for the remainder of basic. However, it was in AIT where we really made our mark. Although I shudder thinking about how we used to con people for a fast buck, at that time, I was convinced this was the way to the American Dream.

"Amaru was outside using the payphones last night! I saw him come upstairs wearing his field jacket. It was past eight!"

This is what a heated and jealous Gimenez reported to the platoon-guide and squad-leaders the following morning. Hearing his allegation, I played the incident down by simply ignoring him. Without responding, I yawned and turned around to walk outside with everyone else.

Later that day, McCormick approached me.

"Amaru," my squad-leader began. "You've really managed to turn things around here for yourself lately. And I have to admit, I'm actually impressed because I was one of the people who thought you were a lost cause just a few weeks ago. My point is: after everything you've been through, with only nine days until graduation, don't you think it would be a damn shame to fuck it all up now?" McCormick inquired without ever directly accusing me of any wrongdoing.

"Gotcha McCormick," I responded with a serious expression.

From that point, the remainder of our training was devoted to three grueling activities: a field-training exercise, the final PT test, and the End-of-Cycle Test.

For the five-day bivouac, Sgt. Sanford ordered McCormick and I to erect our shelter-halves next to one another. Being forced to work together, after a couple days, both of us had to take off the 'tough guy' veneers we used to mask our insecurities. In my opinion, some of the conversations we had on guard-duty were profound enough to serve as a study on race-relations. The one I remember most is when McCormick admitted that before he met me, he actually believed all blacks were ignorant and lazy by nature. "But you ruined it, Amaru," he said. "When I first met you in the reception center, believe me, you fit the ignorant part," McCormick said stifling a chuckle.

"So you still think I'm ignorant?" I asked, looking for a reason to get angry.

"Well if I did, I'd have a difficult time explaining how you could score higher than me on every test we've had so far," he said with a bashful grin.

After we returned from the woods, with one of the three remaining obstacles out of the way, everyone started feeling confident. We were developing into soldiers. On the evening prior to the PT test, McCormick approached me while I was chilling in Odom's room with the CC. This was a first. Once everyone stopped talking to stare at McCormick, he stated that only Pvt. Jacoby was ahead of me on accumulated points. "I saw the tally sheets in the drill sergeant's office with my own eyes," he said when no one seemed to believe him. "Incredible as it might sound," he resumed pointing at me, "in the final week of training, you're one of the top privates in our company."

"Do your thang, Tak!" bellowed Dunbar. Stating this proudly, he slapped the CC's only candidate for Soldier of the Cycle on the back.

The Soldier of the Cycle award was given each training cycle to the private who accumulated the highest score on all the required tasks. In addition to receiving a medal and an accelerated promotion to the next pay-grade, the number-one trainee was required to sit in the stands during the graduation ceremony with the post commander and other brass dignitaries. *Let's be real, even after maxing-out the two remaining tests, I was about as close to being Soldier of the Cycle material as the man on the moon.*

Despite this, after Jacoby faltered badly on the PT test and the grapevine declared me the winner, I conveniently forgot my ominous beginnings when they gave the award to Jacoby anyway. Following the announcement, I was walking toward Sgt. Terrier to complain. This is when you-know-who stepped into my path.

And, as always, he was right on time.

"What the hell's wrong with your face?" Sgt. Sandoval asked, recognizing my brooding countenance. "Please tell me you're not over here actin' angry about not getting some tired-ass, soldier-of-the-cycle award!" he chided me. "Man, you're lucky to even be here, drop!"

As I pumped-out my push-ups, I had to smile at the simple truth contained in his words. When Sgt. Sandoval squatted down to say something, I imagined this scene to symbolize my entire time spent at Ft. Leonard Wood.

"Amaru," my private drill expressed in a muffled tone, "the hell with them damn points, use your common sense. You didn't honestly believe we'd send your crazy ass up there to chat with the post commander instead of that whiteboy, did you?"

Put like that, I guess he had a point.

Chapter 8: Squad Leader

"Good Luck in your New Career!"
This was the last line of a lengthy message from Sgt. Sandoval. He wrote it in the photo album I received at our graduation ceremony. Afterwards, while many privates spent time with their wives, families, or girlfriends, my private drill blessed me with numerous words of wisdom. However, he now addressed me as an indoctrinated brother; not a basic trainee.

"Come on, let's go." This is what he said when he handed me my album and surmised I had no family or friends at the ceremony. The Filipino drill was wearing a sly expression I had never seen before. "Let's go consult *Mayari.*"

"Are you serious, Sergeant?" I asked in disbelief.

Mayari was the drill's nickname for his self-customized, *VW Bug.* Everyone knew his car was the only love in Sgt. Sandoval's life besides the Army. Any weekend he was not on-duty, we saw him working on his beloved automobile in the barrack's parking lot.

"I painted her white because she's a symbol of the moon," he said as we approached the *Volkswagen.* "She's beautiful, ain't she? And you better agree with me or you'll spend the day doing push-ups," he added with a mocking grin.

During our forty-five-minute tour of Ft. Leonard

Wood, Sgt. Sandoval touched on many topics. Beginning with an account of a childhood spent in a fisherman's village on a southern island in the Philippine archipelago, he then explained how at age six, his world was turned upside-down when his family moved smack-in-the-middle of South-Central, Los Angeles. Despite the efforts of his loving, hard-working parents, they were unable to keep the curious boy out of the streets.

"When I was fourteen, I was the only Filipino in the *Cribs,* so you know bruthas were testing my fighting skills."

"You mean 'Crips,' right?" I said, thinking he had mispronounced the name of the well-known street-gang.

"Nah homeboy, I got it right," he replied in a joking manner. "Most folks don't know the Crips started out as the right-hand of the Black Panthers. Back then, as the Cribs, we used to wear black-leather jackets, one earring in our left earlobe, and carry canes. It wasn't until we left the revolution and started *crippin'*—that means robbing and stealing—when the news reporters screwed-up our names because of our canes. And just like that, the media gave birth to the Crips."

"Word?" I asked surprised.

"I wouldn't lie to you on your graduation day," he replied, braking at a traffic light. "So you see Amaru, a couple weeks ago had I granted your wish, the wish you *thought* you wanted, which was to fight me, I would've kicked your ass." Following his statement, he glanced my way to ensure his grin did not dilute his message.

The more I listened to Sgt. Sandoval's childhood stories, the more I understood that kids all over the country were learning the same bullshit I got schooled on at the courts. When we finally parked *Mayari* back in the lot, I was cracking-up listening to what it had been like for him and his sisters to study English from a Chicano teacher.

"I think we ended up teaching him English," the drill said with a chuckle, "and he taught us *Calo.* That's the lingo the *vatos* speak in the *barrio."* After extinguishing the engine, he talked about the unique obstacles confronting men of color in the military before closing his sermon with some advice for my new career. He emphasized caution when dealing with higher-ranking soldiers, especially officers and direct-line supervisors. His final recommendation left a lasting impression.

"Philly if you don't remember shit else I say, remember this: more than spit-polished boots, being competent in your job, or even brown-nosing, using your common-fucking-sense is the key to success in this man's Army!"

A man's man in the truest sense, Sgt. Sandoval commanded respect. The sincerity, concern, and big-brotherly love contained in his words were heartfelt and appreciated. Believe it or not, for a fleeting instant, I considered following in my private drill's career footsteps. That is, until I realized it was necessary to re-enlist before requesting admittance into the coveted Drill Sergeant School.

Like many teenagers, I joined the military as a temporary fix. Seeing my three-year enlistment as a means to pay future tuition fees, I despised this so-called way of life even more than I missed Asia. In spite of being elevated into Captain Yates's Elite 7 or any encouragement by Sgt. Sandoval, I never considered the Army as a career option. Accordingly, my delinquent behavior, while having toned down on the surface, flourished unabated underneath.

Leaving Ft. Leonard Wood meant saying good-bye to Dunbar, Odom, McCormick, and the majority of the Alpha

Company graduates. However, a handful of my boot-camp brothers, including Brown and Hawker, made the long bus-ride to Ft. Lee, Virginia with me. Since we were being trained for various jobs, we were split-up into different companies. Jefferson and I were in the same class but everyone else around me was new. Being surrounded by strangers was beneficial in many ways. Most notably, it was an opportunity to make a positive, first impression.

"Newbie!"

Even though the word 'new' is embedded in this grunt jargon, I had no idea what the insane privates were yelling when our bus approached the Mike Company barracks. After being awakened at a previous stop, Hawk and I bid a temporary farewell to Brown. Then I said good-bye to Hawker at the next stop. Seeing the locations of their companies, I promised to check them out when I received a pass.

Although AIT is technically the second half of basic training, Ft. Lee was a damn vacation compared to the rigors of boot-camp. Attending classes in the Quartermaster School, I learned to be a supply clerk. Talk about boring. It took me about a week to establish myself as a top student by converting my high school, 'get over' tactics to the military classroom. Taking advantage of my new environment, I remained incognito this time around. By laying low, I was able to dodge undesirable activities like weekend GI Parties and afternoon, PT sessions.

In two, short days, I detected enough loopholes in our

daily routine to adopt a comfortable schedule. Each day, after class, while my peers exercised in-cadence, I escaped to the gym, the library, or just lounged at the PX cafeteria with a beer. A few weeks later, I made friends with a civilian who lived in Petersburg. Luckily, he worked nearby, so it was easy for him to pick me up on his way home from work. Following two months of living the good life, my schemes were panning-out so well that Drill Sgt. Barrett promoted *me* to squad leader. According to the drill, the two PFC's in my squad both fumbled the ball.

"Since the E-3's in this shitty squad can't cut the mustard, I have no choice but to turn to the E-2s." This what the drill barked out before pointing at me. "Private Amaru, you're first up-to-bat."

My natural inclination was to turn the assignment down, similar to the guide-on incident. Then I recalled how much Peterson and McCormick had controlled my everyday—not to mention nighttime—activities. So I accepted the assignment and became the leader of the 3rd squad in 1st platoon. This marked the preliminary stage of a transition from a petty crook with an avaricious mindset to a young man with aspirations of attaining a level of self-respect. I must emphasize this change did *not* occur overnight.

However before any of this occurred, I was living-it-up off-post with my civilian friends. Once again, it took another scared-straight episode to petrify me onto the path of lawful living. Despite being less dramatic than the incident with Jeff, for a hot second, it was just as terrifying.

Monday morning was depressing for everybody; especially in the winter months. Following every weekend, there were always a few trainees that would miss formation. It turned-out the majority of these privates were not deserters. For whatever reason, they
just could not make it back to Ft. Lee on-time.

On one such morning, a harsh, frosty wind was chilling me to the bone as I drowsily lined-up in the dark with my platoon. Suffering from a vicious hangover, it was a challenge just to just to keep my balance; so I had to concentrate. In spite of this, I noticed something was strange. In a normal situation, my curiosity would have piqued but with my head pounding like it was, I was more concerned with sneaking back into the barracks than piecing together the fragments of this mystery. If I could just get another thirty minutes of sleep before class, I was confident I could fight-off the nausea in the pit of my stomach without vomiting.

As soon as we were released from formation, instead of walking toward the mess hall with everyone else, I kneeled-down, feigning like I was tying my laces. Once the majority of trainees walked passed, I stood up to complete my disappearing act. Before I could make my escape, however, someone approached me.

"Hey Amaru, did you hear what happened last night?" It seemed Pvt. Dixon wanted to share the latest gossip. "They piss-tested the entire second and fourth platoons at three in the morning!"

"What're you talking about?" I grumpily replied, thinking he was spouting nonsense.

"Yup, all four squads," Dixon resumed, unfazed by my gloomy response. "They think some of us are gettin' stoned, can you believe that?" he asked rhetorically. "At first, I thought hell no, but guess what? Kendricks and Mitchell came straight-out and confessed!" Before I could interject, he continued. "That's crazy right? I mean, with all the shit we gotta do around here, when did those guys have time to go off-post *and* find some pot?"

Now wide-awake, I resisted the urge to say 'On the weekends' while feigning agreement the safest way I knew how. "Go figure," I replied shrugging both shoulders.

Private James Robert Dixon sat in front of me in class. It was no secret he was in-danger of failing the course. Even though my neighbor, PFC Wilkins, who graduated with the second highest GPA, allowed me to copy his answers, I can't imagine those tests were all that difficult to pass the conventional way. Dixon, a rodeo cowboy from Amarillo, Texas, did not share my opinion. Since he associated me with being a good student, *Jim-Bob* never guessed I had been with Kendricks and Mitchell the previous day. In fact, I was the one who had taken them into Petersburg. We hung out all day with my boy, Che.

Originally from West Philly, Che Cordoba was a hard-working brother who had migrated south with his mother five years ago. I never met anyone who was prouder to call himself a 'Black Man' than he was. Che was a big guy. About six-foot-four, he was a couple shades lighter than me and a bit plump around the mid-section. I knew he hated being reminded of his high-yellow complexion, so whenever I wanted to irritate him I called him 'Old Yella,' referring to the yellow-labrador in the Disney film.

Che and I met under inauspicious circumstances at a

Petersburg nightclub. "I saw you when you bolted out the emergency exit," he uttered looking impressed. What I recall about that crazy escape was, I actually had to kick an off-duty cop in the chest to free myself from his grasp before flipping over a fence to safety. Che said when he was driving out of the parking lot, I hurdled over the front of his car.

"Muthafucka looked like Edwin Moses...I almost hit your insane ass!" he had emphasized. "Cuz, after that, I followed you down Sycamore Street but you were running so fast I lost you."

After sprinting a couple blocks, I ducked behind a parked vehicle, barely in time to avoid a pair of MP cars screeching around the corner en-route to the club. Within seconds, I heard an unfamiliar voice beckoning to me. *Thank god it was Che!*

"Yo Philly, it's safe...let's get outta here!" a stranger yelled over.

Although I lied about it later, at that moment, I had no idea who he was. Being desperate, when I heard the word 'Philly,' I came out of my cold, hiding place and approached his car. The only thing I identified was a means of escape. Twenty minutes later, we arrived at a liquor store far from the scene of the crime, and Ft. Lee. To show my gratitude, I bought my savior a quart of *Private Stock.* While we poured libations and puffed on his last joint, Che explained he had been one of the guys in the restroom smoking cheeba when the dealer asked me where I was from.

So lying about being from Philly saved my ass big-time!

Nothing however, could save my bud-smoking buddies in the 2nd and 4th platoons. A week later, both Kendricks and Mitchell were chaptered-out out of the Army for substance-abuse violations. For whatever reason, I just happened to be in one of the platoons that missed the random, drug screening. Nevertheless, with marijuana being detectable for a month, I was shittin' bricks for the next three weeks!

Once I decided smoking cheeba was too dangerous, I became more creative whenever I hung out with Che. Sometimes I asked him questions about whatever he was studying at the time. Che's interests varied from history to the ancient sciences like Numerology and Astrology. Of course he still puffed, but instead of doing it in front of his grandmother's television watching *Video Music Box* like before, I got him to give me tours of his neighborhood. Like most residential enclaves along the East Coast, Petersburg was segregated into the upper-class, the middle-class, and the melanin-rich folks. It was no surprise that Che and his grandmom had been relegated to the latter district.

On the way to his girlfriend's house one evening, Che recounted the legacy of his two, older brothers who fell victim to the streets of North Philly. According to Che, after his oldest brother, Stanley, began pimping girls and selling crack from his apartment, he became a ghetto superstar almost overnight.

"Cuz, Stan went from washing dishes for some racist, Korean people to practically owning the bar next to Seoul Food." As he reminisced about his childhood hero—his version of Ant—he got excited. "When he started rockin' fly-ass gear and sticking tens and twenties in my pocket, no one could've convinced me my brother wasn't the man. Word is bond, everybody on my block was ready to drop out of school, or quit their full-of-shit jobs, to clock dollars with Stan. Sheeit, I was only twelve and I was like, 'Fuck school!' My moms though..." Che became somber at the mention of his late-mother. "She was smart. Instead of arguing with me, she went directly to Stan and made *him* talk me out of it." Saying this, he re-lit his half-smoked stogie after braking at a traffic signal. "But my second-oldest brother, Jeremy, was seventeen. There was no stopping him from cashing-in on what seemed like a sure thing."

At this point, I knew where the story was headed. Nonetheless, out of respect, I did not interrupt.

"So that fall, I entered *Turner Middle School* on 60th & Baltimore. A couple weeks later, word hit the street that one of Stan's bitches had set him up. But you know my brother wasn't going out like no sucker!" Once again livening up, Che represented the warrior spirit of his clan. "When the pigs showed up in riot-gear at Stan's apartment, both of my brothers pulled-out their *jammies* and they shot it out. In the gunfight, Jeremy got hit twice: once in the shoulder and once in the chest and the doctors still expected him to live!"

At this point, I gave Che some *dap* for his fallen brother.

"But check-this-out, even though the doctor said Jeremy would live, the next day he mysteriously died…right after the cop he shot flat-lined in the ICU."

"Damn, that's fucked up!" I said. "And they smoked your oldest brother too?" Hearing how Jeremy had went down like a trooper, I wanted to know how many cops 'Stan the Man' had taken out before they got to him.

"Nah," Che stated as matter-of-factly. "Stan's on his fourth year of doing two life-bids at Trenton State Prison."

Somewhat confused, I wanted to know how it was possible to not shoot anyone, get arrested, *and* not go out like a sucker. In spite of my curiosity, common sense prompted me to bite my tongue. So instead, I stuck my head out the

116

window to spit. By doing so, I hoped to give Che enough time to wipe away his tears without losing face.

"Is that why y'all moved down here?" I asked in an attempt to steer the conversation in a brighter direction.

"Yeah," he said. "When some pigs followed me home in their squad cars, threatening to 'Pull-the-plug on the youngest *moolie* too,' my moms was like, 'we outta here!'" Two days later, we hit I-95 South and came to Petersburg to live with her brother. He was an Army-guy at Ft. Lee like you."

"Nah, not really," I tried to explain. "I'm not stationed here, I'm just training at the Quartermaster School."

"Aw muthafucka, don't get all military on me! He was just like you: deaf, dumb, blind, and fighting for the whiteman!" Because Che detested everything about the military, he got upset whenever I talked about the Army.

"Well, Che *Guevara,*" I joked in response to his militant critique, "lemme know when one of your revolutionary comrades puts together a combat outfit…that'll also pay me twenty-five-grand for college, and I'll sign right up. See brother, what you fail to recognize is, I don't take any of this bullshit seriously. After I finish my enlistment, it's all about keg parties, tackles, and touchdowns. Ya see, I'm just paying my dues on my way to UNC, Penn State, or Rutgers!"

In hindsight, it's amazing Che and I became friends. According to him, it was because I really did not belong in the Army. Che claimed he could see into the past and the future. One night, after a moment of staring off into space, he claimed I was a prisoner-of-war who had been brainwashed into serving the enemy.

"In a previous life," he had stated that evening, "your whole family was slaughtered by a tribe of barbarians called

Tamahu. Tamahus are the ancestor of this present-day cracka," Che continued. "The horrors of the African Holocaust and Indian massacres have left the survivors— *us*—with a severe case of amnesia. Most brothers and sisters have no idea that *we* were the one's runnin' the world back in the day, and *they* were the slaves! They've gotten us to forget all about our glorious past. To make sure we never wake-up and realize what time it is, this cracka's destroying the evidence. All over the world, our temples and sacred places are being vandalized, torn-down, submerged underwater, or straight-up pillaged—that is, after they copy all the knowledge written in glyphs." Having made this accusation, Che then provided some evidence. Reaching into the drawer of a corner-table in his living room, he pulled-out a scrapbook. Flipping through half the pages, he stopped when he came upon some photos of a gigantic, monolithic temple. "This is *Angkor Wat,*" he declared proudly as if he had built the temple himself. "It's in Cambodia. This is the type of masterpieces we were creating back-in-the-day!" After he held the book up so I could get a look at the Asiatic figures gracing the walls, he turned a couple more pages and handed it to me.

Looking at the photo, I spotted a group of Caucasians amongst the ancient ruins. Dressed like archeologists, they were chiseling into the walls of the great pagoda. "This is some fucked-up shit!" I complained. Then he pointed at the opposite page and I saw three US soldiers, probably during the Vietnam War, shooting anti-aircraft weapons at a portion of the ancient structure.

"Last week, in my political-science class," Che resumed, now making reference to the evening lectures he attended twice a week at a community college. "The professor talked about a government policy called 'expansionism.' During his Q & A, I raised my hand. When he called on me, I asked him why we went through so much trouble to avoid calling expansionism what it really is: invading, killing, and conquering. The rise of an empire is nothing new, I told him. Even though my professor's a white man, he had no problem agreeing with me."

"Word?" I said, surprised to hear this.

"Yeah, Professor Cunningham is pretty cool…for a cracka." After we both paused for a snicker, Che continued. "I didn't say this in class but the unique thing about the Caucasian invasion is that it's still going on right now, and along with territory and economic expansion, they're systematically snuffing out our legacy and committing genocide at the same time. You know what? I actually think crackas are tryin' to replace us as the native people of this planet. They tell us colonization is all about controlling the countries rich in natural resources. Yeah right, there's much more going on," Che said with a sneer. "In between stealing gold, diamonds, and oil, not only are they're slayin' the bruthas and sistas living in those areas, they're brain-washing the survivors with Cracka Theology."

At first, I didn't believe the extraordinary claims Che made; especially about white folks being the original slaves. So I made a trip to the library. After I found evidence of hordes of European slaves in the Americas, both before and during the plantation era, I researched the history of Rome and found startling quotes by Julius Caesar and Cicero about their English (Briton) slaves. Caesar called them "The most ignorant people I have ever conquered." And Cicero claimed, "They cannot be taught to read, and are the ugliest and most stupid race I ever saw."

119

From this point, I started taking Che's words more seriously. Although Che was my first 'conscious' friend, Private Colon was the person who revealed a historical perspective not shrouded in Cracka Theology. The ironic thing is, these two guys could pass for brothers; maybe even twins despite having different ethnic backgrounds. *Was this just a coincidence?* Che called himself a 'Moor.' When I heard this, I imagined he was talking about the old white guy on the oatmeal box until I recalled they were Quakers. Then I remembered Rina used this term to describe herself too. Che put a spin on history and politics which made them interesting. However, I still wonder if he could really see the Akashic Records, like he always insisted whenever we were gettin' nice.

Arriving at Che's girlfriend's house, we were startled when two rats and a scantily dressed crackhead popped-out from behind some garbage cans. As they darted in front of Che's blue *Celica,* they could have almost been mistaken for a threesome. After Che screeched to a stop, he glared at the homeless man limping toward his window to beg for spare change.

"And to think," Che disgustedly murmured under his breath, "we came down here to escape the ghetto."

Monie & Weesie

Monica and Louise were 'around the way' girls complete with extensions in their hair, big-ass earrings, name-brand accessories, and some serious attitudes! As 'ghetto' as they appeared, they were the furthest thing from hoes. According to Che, both girls had dissed so many guys before he and *Weesie* got together that everyone suspected the two friends of being lesbian lovers.

Like me, Che graduated high school the previous June. A skilled carpenter, a talent he told me he'd crafted while being locked-up in a juvenile-detention center, Che was one of the few brothers who had a career waiting for him when he left high school. Having proven his merit as an apprentice in his junior and senior year, by mid-July, Che was already a full-time employee, benefits and all.

Che planned to have a home set-up by the time his princess received her diploma. Until then, Louise lived with her mother, Mrs. Calhoun, who was a registered nurse. Because Mrs. Calhoun worked the graveyard shift in a neighboring town, she was usually at work when I arrived for my weekend visits. The first time I met her, she struck me as a very liberal woman. She treated us like adults, insisting we call her 'Yvonne' instead of Mrs. Calhoun but I usually forgot to. Louise and her mother shared the same beige-complexion and slender face, but Yvonne was shorter than her daughter. It seemed Che had earned her respect and trust; and since her husband, Louise's father, had been a casualty of the Vietnam War, Che was in effect the man of two houses.

Che was focused. He reminded me of my buddy, Dan back at home. Like Dan, Che got high and drank beer but only at home in the evenings or on the weekends. And both of them rarely went out. Even on the night we met, Che was only at the club to buy weed. This, of course, turned out to be a good thing for me because it was on his way home when we ran into each other. Che wanted to marry Weesie the following year but had not yet officially proposed. Listening to his marriage plans, I admired his drive and focus. Although Louise was two years older than Asia, I thought there were similarities between our relationships. Che *completely* disagreed.

"Tak, don't get me wrong. I love me some Weesie, and it sounds like you love Asia too. But I'm dealing with a mature, young lady. Please don't confuse our mutually respectful relationship with your sucker-duck scenario." After laughing at my shocked expression, Che then called me a fool for staying faithful to some girl in Jersey who was no doubt, getting *dicked-down* by another dude by now.

"Ay, don't y'all sing a running cadence about some guy named 'Jodie'?" Che abruptly seemed to switch topics.

"Yeah so what?" I said, not understanding how his question was relevant.

"In the song, Jodie's supposedly the low-down guy that steals your girlfriend while you're off somewhere fighting the whiteman's war, right?"

As it became more and more obvious, Asia and I were not marriage-material, I had grown sensitive about the issue. And Che knew it. When I did not respond right away, he resumed like I had.

"Well Tak, that muthafucka Jodie is really me!" he stated emphatically. "So tomorrow morning, when you're out there jogging with the rest of those fools singing that wack-ass song, picture me and your homeboys *running a train—*"

"A-ight ock I got your point!" I interrupted. "You think Asia's cheating on me."

Chuckling loudly, he responded, "Think? Nah kid, you said it yourself—"

"Che!" I snapped, glaring at my friend. Our conversation was at the brink of spilling into an altercation. "I understand your message, so hear mine: if you're my homie, chill-out with the Jodie jokes."

Like Hawk, Che had my best interests at heart. He was a kid from the streets who was simple in his mannerisms, so he expressed himself the only way he knew how. Hanging out with Che every weekend allowed me to get to know Louise and Monica very well. Since Weesie and Che spent every weekend together, by default, *Monie* and I became paired-off whenever Che and Louise wanted to be alone. During my five-month stay at Ft. Lee, it was "Monie-Love," as I affectionately called her, who provided the much needed feminine balance lacking in my life.

Although Monie's smiling claims of virginity were suspect, when three of Che's friends warned me she was 'tight with her shit,' she automatically earned my respect. Monie was almost the same height as me. Not having to tilt my head down to see her made it easier to get lost admiring her beauty. On a few different occasions, during our hour-plus conversations, I became aware I didn't have the faintest idea of what she was talking about. This was because, for several minutes, I had been staring at her without listening. Almost in a trance.

Her eyes were wide-set and even more slanted than mine. But their most intriguing feature was how they seemed to constantly sparkle. Contrasted against her ebon-flavored skin, they glimmered like two crescent moons on a clear night. Monica was so dark Che used to joke saying she was 'blue-black,' which Monie did not appreciate at all. I actually think purplish-black was more accurate because her skin was shiny, like a black-olive. Her complexion was perfect. It was so smooth and flawless, I can't imagine Monie ever having a pimple in her life. From this account, it should be apparent she was attractive. Nevertheless, any physical description of Monie-Love would be incomplete without mentioning her lower-half.

Now I knew plenty of women with a nice booty, but hands down, Monie had the biggest, the roundest—the most perfect ass I had ever seen! The thickness of her hips and thighs brought to mind the ancient statuettes of the goddess, Venus. While her relatively small breasts and thin waist seemed, upon first glance, to be an unfit match, they were actually the perfect complements to her *steatopygia* figure. Much like Rina and Asia, the term 'natural beauty' applied to Monie too. This is why I was astonished to discover she was not considered a dime-piece by many guys due to the shade of her skin.

"Monie's dark-skinned *but* she looks good." This is how Che's friends usually referred to her. Hearing this, I was not surprised the 'black is evil' stereotype had negatively affected Monie's own self esteem. This was revealed one night when she asked me if I had ever thought about growing locs.

"Believe me sista, when I get outta the Army, the first thing I'm gonna do is grow my hair. What about you?" I reversed the question. "You ever think about going natural?"

"Please," Monie exclaimed sucking her teeth, "my hair doesn't grow like yours does."

"Whaddya mean?" Looking at her sleek ponytail and long side-bangs, I did not understand.

"You know this ain't my real hair, right?" Saying this, she grabbed a few locs of her extension. "My hair isn't soft like yours."

"Oh, I see," I said rolling my eyes with disdain. "This is some of that 'bad hair vs. good hair' bullshit, right?" Then I continued without allowing her time to respond. "If your hair doesn't grow, it's probably because of all those poisonous chemicals you put in it whenever you get a perm. If you leave it alone, it'll grow."

"Takuan, your mother's Japanese, right?" Monie replied, blowing me off with a wave of her hand. "You don't understand." Without another word, she walked out of the room.

Although at times I was blinded by Monie's aesthetic qualities, this does not mean our conversations were not interesting. We used to talk about everything from sports and entertainment to politics and history. Che would usually chair the discussion if it was on either of the last, two topics. Our favorite pastime, however, was watching science-fiction movies. *Star Trek*, *Back to the Future*, *Poltergeist*, etc., we watched every flick made in the '80s featuring an alien, a time-machine, or any evidence hinting at ghoulish, paranormal activity. Due to our habit of falling asleep on the sofa together, everyone believed we had something going on. The truth is, we were just good friends. In many ways, kicking it with Monie reminded me of my relationship with Rina—before we had sex.

Don't get me wrong, I have pleasant memories concerning my first sexual encounter. But let's face it, Rina and I were never the same afterwards. Realizing all things, both good and bad, must come to an end, it's easy to selectively remember only the positive moments I spent with Rina, Asia, or even Monie for that matter.

Speaking of Asia, when we broke up, Monie was there to lend an ear to my love woes. Nevertheless don't get it twisted, this does not imply that she succeeded where Che had failed. Nor, does it infer any ladylike sympathy on her part. For as beautiful, witty, and intelligent as Monie was, remember one thing: homegirl was from around the way.

"Boy, snap out of it! What's wrong with you?" Monie scolded, laughing loudly. "Don't make me come ova there and slap you *black* into reality!" Walking closer to me, she then balled-up her fist. After feinting like she was about to sneak me, she exhaled in disgust. "Alright lemme spell it out for you, as if my girl didn't already: she don't want yo' ass no mo'!"

Although Monie's words stung to the core, it still took a phone call to Jersey to convince me. One evening, I dialed Asia's number determined to get the truth. After Ms. Kalif politely told me Asia was studying, thereby declining my request to speak to her daughter, I called Herb.

"Yo, what's up boyee?" my homie yelled into the phone.

I was relieved to hear a friendly voice. Somehow, Herb's updates on the latest music and fashion trends in Philly were soothing, almost therapeutic. Minutes later, sensing a break in the conversation, I took the plunge by asking if he thought Asia was cheating on me. Herb, being one of my young boys, seemed more embarrassed about the situation than I was.

"Yo man, it really ain't none of my business," Herb started slowly before gaining momentum. "But since you asked, lemme put it this way. If I were you, I'd get that *crush* State Champs jacket back from her. You know, the one with your name on it." Following a slight pause to collect his thoughts, the polite barriers came crashing down. "Fuck that, get everything back and kick her funky ass to the curb with-the-quickness!"

In December, I took leave and went to New Jersey because I still had to settle my debt with Belkis for the weed I lost. Always the big sister, Belkis did not even accept the chump change. Instead she made me a delicious, Cajun dinner to show her gratitude. She appeared touched I had not forgotten the IOU.

At that time I was disappointed Rina was not there. I knew she was going to St. John's University, but I expected her to be between semesters, on winter vacation. When I asked Belkis, she explained that Rina's parents got separated; so with her father out of the house, Rina did not have to live with her anymore.

I did not see anyone in my family but I visited Charlie and Herb before making my last stop at Asia's house. By this time, our secret was out so I knocked on the door. I was surprised to find her there alone and she was shocked I wasn't angry. Even though she still looked good, I sensed the magic disappeared since I had been gone—right along with her virginity.

Upon returning to Ft. Lee in January, Monie-Love and I kissed once. Awkward to say the least, it felt like I was kissing my sister. She seemed to agree with me. Plus, we both knew neither of us wanted to become entangled in a web of emotions with my graduation almost a month away.

"Wake up everybody! We gotta formation in the hallway right now!"

Many privates were not pleased with the rude awakening at twelve-thirty in the morning. So accordingly, some expressed their displeasure.

"Fuck you Amaru!"

"Kiss my ass!"

"Who the hell do you think you are?"

In spite of their voiced frustrations, with some even threatening to report me, no one dared defied a command from their squad-leader to leave their cozy beds and stand in the cold hallway. *I thought that was cool!*

Since Drill Sgt. Barrett named me squad-leader two weeks prior, many privates had voiced their complaints; and they had good reason to be dissatisfied because I didn't give a shit! Following my fourth day-on-the-job, my assistant squad-leader and I were inspecting our wing of the barracks after lights-out. With no one else around, he brought their grievances to my attention. He was shocked when I busted-out laughing.

"They don't respect my promotion, huh?" I said, thinking the irony was comical. "Like I give a damn. Sheeit, I don't respect it either!"

To me, being squad leader meant *I* got to write other people's names on a duty roster. So long as that privilege remained intact, I couldn't have cared less whether they respected my promotion or not. After a few more chuckles at Attinson's rumor reports, I pointed out that despite their moans and groans, our floor was always spotless when the drills performed their barracks inspections.

"That's all I care about Danny-boy," I explained after we entered the empty day-room so we could speak in privacy. "See, those fools still haven't figured out the system. It ain't our job to punish them. As squad leader and assistant-squad leader, we only communicate what the drills' directives are. Oh, and we also report knuckle-heads who don't adapt to the prescribed measures." *I was actually starting to like being in-charge.* "So Dan, let 'em pop their shit," I resumed arrogantly. "If they act up, for whatever reason, they gotta face Sgt. Barrett's wrath, not ours."

Nonetheless this did nothing to appease Attinson.

Pvt. Daniel Attinson, the son of four generations of steel workers in Pittsburgh, accused me of being cold and indifferent on numerous occasions because I didn't take him seriously. He was right. But even after a week of witnessing my listless approach, for some reason, Dan still revered me as a leader.

Eyeing him in exasperation, I wanted to explain my true priorities: not doing any nasty latrine details and no fireguard. Combine this with missing the afternoon PT sessions and I can really say Ft. Lee was a cool stop. I was especially proud of the PT scam because it was instituted on a whim.

At the Sunday dinner, prior to my first day of training, I struck up a friendly conversation with a trainee scheduled to graduate that Friday. This guy loved talking-down his nose to a newbie. Probing him for information, I learned that each week, as one group graduated, another crew of newbies arrived to take their place. With such a high-turnover rate, I realized the only guys that would really get to know me were the six privates in my class.

The next afternoon, when some unknown sergeant called us to attention and barked commands to start stretching, I smiled. There were no drills in sight; so the NCOs sprinkled amongst each class led the workouts. Once I confirmed PT was being conducted without attendance being taken, I enjoyed that two-mile jog knowing it was the last time I would participate in such an unorganized fiasco. Only at our brigade run, when even the drills participated, did I bother to show up.

It was past midnight when I snuck passed the CQ desk. Upon entering the barracks, it was not immediately apparent anything was amiss. Tip-toeing through the day room, where the weekend, television excitement takes place, I chuckled at how one University of Miami fan had chosen to celebrate his team's victory over their in-state rival. After adorning a life-sized cut-out of *Elvira* with a *Seminoles* jersey, he had hung the normally propped-up beer advertisement from the ceiling. There, it remained lynched with a rope lassoed around its neck. However, aside from this easy-to-clean-up violation, everything appeared spic-and-span. Then, I quietly opened the door separating the day room from the area designated for 3rd squad; i.e. my squad.

Even before stepping through the doorway, I knew the scheduled, GI party had not followed the weekend's games. Despite the hallway lights being extinguished, it was not difficult to spot discarded pizza boxes and empty cans of *Kiwi* shoe-polish lining the corridor. Not to mention the bottles laying around reeking with the stench of stale beer.

As squad-leader, I knew this situation could not be ignored. But first, I had to take a shower to sober up. Desperately wanting to sleep, I got heated in the shower thinking about what had to be done. By the time I toweled off and brushed my teeth, I was gassed-up enough to make the bold move. Again the keyword was respect.

On Friday afternoon, I heard the two recently-removed squad-leaders, and a few others, snickering while Attinson read the names on the weekend duty-roster. Looking over at them, I almost started laughing too. Minutes later, my assistant cornered me in our room to express his concern of a 'hostile takeover' occurring if I was not around this weekend.

"Pull your panties up!" I had snapped. "Dan, they just gonna talk shit, don't pay 'em no mind. Let 'em gossip if that makes them happy. Just as long as my barracks are up-to-snuff come Monday morning," I said mimicking the drills. Not only was I not concerned with the burden I left in Dan's hands each weekend, I was barely listening to him. Instead, I was scheming on how I could get him to leave the room so I could drop my already-packed night-bag out the window. Glancing at my watch, I knew I had to move quickly because Che would be arriving at our rendezvous point on his way home from work in fifteen minutes. A virtual stranger amongst the guys I was supposed to be in charge of, I had no concern whatsoever about my social standing within the barracks. Sound like someone you remember?

Even on the night I stood in the hallway facing a squad of angry privates, it was difficult to keep my poker-face straight. If only Sgt. Sandoval and Sgt. Sanford could see me now, I thought. Oh, and Terrier too!

"Amaru, this is some bullshit, and you know it!"

"At ease!" I yelled back. "Y'all don't have to respect my squad-leader title, that's okay, this ain't even about that." Once the troops deduced I was not about to bore them with another played-out, 'I'm the squad leader so you must do my bidding' speech, everyone calmed down to hear what I had in-mind.

It was only after the hallway grew quiet when I realized I didn't know what I was going to say. "A-hem," I cleared my throat to buy an extra second to think. "Since only a couple of y'all are in my class, y'all muthafuckas don't really know me. So lemme fill you in on something: I never asked to be squad-leader. It was only because a few of you proved to be, hmm…I believe 'incompetent' was the word Sgt. Barrett used, that I even got the job." Considering no one had tried to cut-in, I figured so-far-so-good. "To be honest, I only accepted the position so I could chill." Figuring honesty might be the best policy, I experimented. At first, it didn't work so well.

"Yeah we know!" said a big, Italian private from Linden, NJ, named Fiorino. "Your ass ain't never here!"

"Hey everybody, we got the fuckin' Invisible Man for our squad-leader," PFC Riley chimed-in.

As laughter and other forms of jeering took center stage, I noted that Riley still seemed upset over his recent demotion. Fully aware that taking on the whole squad would be suicidal, I decided to separate the ring-leaders from the rest and let the chips fall where they may. "Riley, first of all," I began my rebuttal by addressing the stocky kid from Idaho. "I may be invisible, but when your punk-ass was in-charge, you were *way too* visible. Always up in everybody's face being a fuckin' pest!" Then, in an exaggerated high-pitched voice, I imitated him. "Private Fiorino, you know your name is on the duty roster, right? What time do you plan to start sweeping the staircase this evening?" Turning toward Fiorino I offered my recommended response in my normal tone. "Fiorino, you should've told him to 'Blow it out his ass and fuck off!'"

Once everyone started laughing at Riley, I pressed my advantage.

"How many times did this fool," I again pointed at the ex-squad leader, "looking like *Richie Cunningham* on steroids, come in the day room and turn down the TV…just to tell us to get ready for the GI Party? Like we had to stretch

132

and run some warm-up laps or something." With the privates chuckling, this gave me time to figure out how I was going to return to the topic of cleaning the barracks. "Folks let's face it: in AIT, squad-leaders ain't nothing more than baby-sitters who report to the drills. And Riley, you couldn't even handle that!" Strangely, I wasn't even angry at Riley. I just needed a scapegoat to divert everybody's attention away from my chronic absences; and Riley, with his big mouth, had volunteered. Honestly, I had not even given him much thought until that moment. Judging it came down to him or me, of course, I went for the jugular. "Let's be real," I continued, "all you gotta do to keep this gig is either brown-nose, or know how to avoid drawing attention to yourself—"

"You forgot something Amaru," Pvt. Gooden cut into my soliloquy. "And not fuckin' puke on a drill sergeant's boots!"

"Especially when you're not even old enough to drink alcohol yet!" added Pvt. Hines, a kid from Vermont.

Once the men were reminded of the Sunday formation, three weeks ago, when Riley vomited on Drill Sgt. Barrett's boots, more than a few doubled-over with laughter.

"Right," I resumed my last sentence. "Avoid drawing attention to yourself by doing something dumb in front of the drills!" When the privates burst into another round of laughter, I knew it was time to drop the ultimatum. "Alright, alright, break it up. This is fun and all, but it's almost one o'clock." Mentioning the time grounded everyone back to the present moment. Once it got quiet, I jumped in with both feet. "Listen, if y'all want me to resign, I will, no problem. But tomorrow morning, if Sergeant Barrett is greeted with trash on the floors, *none of us* will see another weekend pass before graduation." Then I summoned my most serious facial expression and blurted it out: "We need to GI this floor…right now!"

As might be expected, raucous pandemonium erupted.

"Hell no! Riley yelled. "We ain't doing it!"

"Fuck you Amaru, you think you're slick!" PFC Gooden expressed his resentment too. "You're just trying to keep your position, we ain't stupid."

Hearing Gooden's response, it suddenly dawned on me that he was the leader of the 3rd squad right before Riley; this led me to toss him into the sucker-ass pile with Riley.

"Ay Gooden," I began. "I heard you and Riley have been talking a whole-lotta-shit about me behind my back since Sgt. Barrett promoted me to squad-leader. Is that true?" When both he and Riley kept silent, I resumed. "What the hell you mad at me for? You got fired on my first day here. I didn't have nothing to do with it." Having singled-out the two loudmouths in the crowd, I confronted them. "You know what? Fuck both of y'all, and fuck this squad-leader bullshit too!" Bellowing this defiantly, I watched the other privates take a half-step back. "Check this out, I'm walking into the day room right now." Saying this, I pointed at them before gesturing toward the door at the end of the hall. "You two punks feeling froggish, leap down there and collect the ass-whoopin' that'll be in the next room waiting for you." Recognizing I was on a roll, I delivered the coup de grace, "We're cleaning house tonight one way or another." Then I pointed at my entire squad. "And that goes for any of y'all!" Ending on this note, I turned and walked away.

Although I was committed to my words, considering this was more of a Billy Bad-Ass moment than a Beast sighting, I was relieved no one followed me.

Five minutes later, the door swung open. Beyond the

grinning visage of Pvt. Attinson, I could see privates behind him wielding mops next to a bucket of water. Following a quick wink at my assistant, I hurried through the door and grabbed a dust-rag.

"Private Amaru reporting as directed, Drill Sergeant," I stated smartly after knocking.

"Enter," rumbled a baritone voice from inside the office.

Walking in, I caught a glimpse of the drill slouched at his desk, looking rather comfortable. Stopping in front of him, I stood at attention. In my peripheral vision, I could see him reading a newspaper and hear the pages being turned. I remained standing at attention. It took about five minutes; but he finally spoke.

"Stand-at-ease, Private."

Upon receiving this command, I separated my feet ten inches, folded my hands behind my back, and tilted my head down to focus on his almond-brown face. He was smiling.

"So," the drill began, placing the sports page on the desk. "I heard you threw a crazy party last night until the wee hours of the morning. Right here in my barracks and I wasn't even invited." Despite his deliberate pause, since he had not asked a question, I did not attempt to explain anything. Seeing my silent stance, Sgt. Barrett resumed his monologue. "Amaru, since you're a stupid-ass private, lemme enlighten you on a few things contained in the Universal Code of Military Justice."

Watching his smile disappear, I feared the worst.

135

"You maggots are guaranteed certain rights. This includes a specified amount of food, clothing, and hours of sleep!" Now yelling, he pounded his fist on the desk. "That means, if my privates are up at oh-one-hundred—*for any reason*—I could be held liable for a grave injustice. You get my point?"

"Yes Drill Sergeant!" I boomed my reply.

"Oh, do you really?" Leaning back in his chair, the drill returned to his relaxed tone.

"Yes I do, Drill Sergeant."

Having calmed down, Sgt. Barrett was again smiling. With both elbows resting on the arm-rests and his fingers interlaced, he revealed two rows of straight white teeth. Following another lengthy hesitation, he surprised me with his next question. "Private Amaru, do you have anything to report concerning last night?"

"No Drill Sergeant," I responded without the slightest delay.

"Good!" Saying this, he picked up the telephone to place a call. This was my indication the meeting was over. "That'll be all Private, you're dismissed."

Careful to suppress any expressions of relief or happiness, I professionally snapped to attention and executed an about-face. Three steps later, as I reached for the doorknob, Sgt. Barrett made one final comment.

"By the way Private," he said sounding nonchalant.

Glancing back, I watched him place his hand over the mouthpiece.

"The hallways, stairwells, and latrines were sparkling this morning…way to keep your boot up their asses! Looks like I finally found someone with enough *balls* for the job."

For the remainder of AIT, I actually turned out to be a

136

fairly dependable, squad-leader. This was mainly because, from this point, Sgt. Barrett demanded my attention. At any rate, my opportunities to meander off-post dwindled to only Saturday and half of Sunday—for the most part.

The Reunion

"What! They made your crazy ass a squad-leader?"

This is what Hawker screamed in disbelief as Brown cackled like an old man with a bad smoking habit. Since Brown was a college-grad, few were surprised to hear he was the platoon-guide of Foxtrot Company. However, everyone reeled at the news of my promotion.

By the time I reunited with my Alpha Company brothers, everyone was in the second-half of their AIT courses. Following a bunch of handshakes, hugs, and astonished looks, the thirteen of us stepped into the *Sword and Key.* After paying the entrance fee and being frisked, we entered the building. This lower-enlisted nightclub was more commonly known for its nickname, the 'Stab and Jab.' Reflecting on this, I looked around and noticed Hawker was missing.

"Where's Blaine?" I asked to no one in particular.

"He went to the latrine," Jefferson responded, unable to shake the military jargon for restroom.

"A-ight, y'all go in and get the first-round ready, I gotta take a piss too."

Suddenly feeling the six-pack Jefferson and I had shared on our walk to the club, my bladder felt ready to explode. Upon entering the restroom, even before the distinct toilet-odor assaulted my senses, I was alerted to the threat of violence. It sounded like two guys were arguing while some onlookers instigated.

Although gangs were not popular in the mid-80s, most dudes had a 'posse mentality.' Thus while at the club, just like on the street, being alone made a person stand out as a target. Hawker had breached this social standard by strolling into the restroom by himself.

"I said sorry," Blaine said in a defensive tone as he tried to walk toward the exit. It sounded like he was repeating himself.

"But you didn't say it fast enough!" said a drunk GI while his buddies laughed along and encouraged him. When the drunkard noticed Blaine looked pissed-off instead of frightened, he became irritated. "Boy, where do you think you're going? Did I say you were dismissed?" When he said this, one of his cronies stepped into Hawker's path while two others crept into Blaine's blind spots.

In all the excitement, my entrance went unnoticed. Seeing my friend surrounded, I knew our only advantage was the element of surprise.

Running forward, I kicked the guy confronting Hawk in his rear end. Hawker, being the only person who had noticed me, sidestepped the human projectile before moving in my direction. By the time the bully sprawled head-first into his loud-mouthed lush of a leader, Blaine had already turned around. Now, with Hawk standing next to me shoulder-to-shoulder and the exit to our rear, Billy-Bad-Ass was in full-effect.

"Oh hold up! I know you muthafuckas wasn't trying to move-on my boy?" I rebuked the group with an extended finger.

In that instant, two things happened that surprised me.

For some strange reason the 'bathroom crew' looked frightened. Before I could figure out why, a loud voice was yelling "Shut the fuck up!" in my ear. Nothing would have been abnormal had this rude command emanated from our enemies but it didn't. It came from my right-side—from Blaine. Turning my head to look at him allowed me to unravel the first riddle. Out the corner of my eye, I glimpsed enough of the silhouettes entering the restroom to know our Alpha Company brothers were standing behind us in battle formation.

"Sev, I didn't need your help!"

"Blaine what the hell is wrong with you? This ain't the good ol' boy, Ohio-countryside, ya know. They were about to drop the hammer on your ass!" No longer a humorous situation, I was getting peeved at what I interpreted as a lack of appreciation.

"They weren't gonna do shit. They were just a bunch of drunk porch monkies—"

"Hawk!" I snapped to shut-him-up. "I did what I did 'cause you were in danger. Whether you thank me or not, I know what I saw." Without another word, I walked away from him. As I did so, my body language expressed my holier-than-thou attitude. This pissed Blaine off.

By the aggressive way Hawk chased me down, for a split second, I thought he was going to throw a punch. But instead, he stopped right in front of me and put his finger in my face. "Sev, okay maybe kicking that guy in the ass was necessary, but I'm really talking about everything that happened after that. We could've left outta there peacefully!"

"What're you pointing at me for?" I complained. "Brown's the one who crashed the big-mouth with the country accent in the jaw. I didn't do shit 'cause you had me in a bear hug."

"You instigated the whole thing!"

Upon hearing Blaine's series of outbursts, two bouncers approached us. Seeing them coming, Brown stepped between me and Hawker before addressing the sentries in a friendly tone.

"Good evening, gentlemen. Just a friendly debate between friends," he assured the guards.

"Is that right?" one of the muscle-bound pair looked at me.

"Yeah, we're debating, not arguing," I replied with a hearty smile. "There's nothing but love over here."

Seeming convinced, the bouncers walked away. Before they got far, Jefferson added his opinion.

"Hawker, I dunno…Amaru might have a point. Those clowns fit the description of a cast of characters that robbed a guy in my company last weekend."

"See!" I exclaimed. "We should've stomped those cowards into the ground and robbed *them!*" As I stated this with emphasis, some Alpha brothers cheered my sentiments.

"Why Sev?" Blaine addressed me directly, ignoring Jefferson. "We just got paid yesterday. You got money in your pocket, right? If you don't, lemme know and I'll *give* you some. But it's not even about the money, is it? *Is it?"* he repeated. "What're you always trying to prove?" Saying this, Blaine then walked to other side of the bar where a group of females were sitting.

Outside, before we entered, Hawk told me he started

kicking-it with a cutie he met at the gym last week. He also assured me he was going to hook me up with one of her blazin' friends because she would be here tonight with several of them. Like all of my buddies, I noticed the fine sistas when we walked in but I had no idea they were the girls he was talking about.

Glancing over at Hawk's harem, I recognized a flygirl with hazel eyes I saw in the PX last week. I surmised she was in the same company as Hawk's girl. Although I wanted to meet her, with Blaine being angry at me, I was not about to press my luck by asking for an introduction; so I walked in the other direction and posted up in an area amidst the shadows. I needed time to ponder things over.

It was only ten-thirty so the club was almost empty. Most of the partygoers were still outside watching the 'GI car-show,' which occurred in the club's parking lot every weekend. Guys with nice automobiles would stand next to them, or sit inside blasting their music, so dudes who either walked to the club or took a taxi had little chance of wooing a female because these ladies were attracted to the guys with cars. All of us being trainees who were temporarily stationed at Ft. Lee, of course we were not equipped with this luxury, which automatically assigned us to the bottom of the food chain.

Hours later, I was still holding the wall up with my back; albeit in a different corner. With the club now packed, I was grittin' on the guys who were lucky enough to bask in the attention of a female; especially the dude talking to the brown-eyed beauty I was supposed to be with. By the time I finally convinced a girl to dance with me, I was dead-tired and my feet hurt. At any rate, my herky-jerky moves on the dance-floor did little to enhance my chances of using the condoms Jefferson issued to us earlier.

"Strap up!" the ex-squad-leader barked while handing us prophylactics in the club's parking lot. Although boot-camp was long over, everyone still respected Jefferson as a cool 'smooth-skinned' leader in many respects.

Once the girl I was dancing with excused herself to the restroom, I never saw her again. This is when it dawned on me that I lacked 'a rap' when it came to introducing myself to ladies. Blessed to have attended a high school ripe with dime-pieces, after my frustrating freshman year, the 'just being myself' approach had yielded gains. In other words, my experience at Garfield High left me ill-equipped to attract a girl in this standing-room-only, GI club. These types of places were filled to the brim with hard-dick privates, so if you failed to make a sista laugh in your opening line, you were lucky if she acknowledged you at all. Holding a ten-to-one advantage, believe me when I say, these *hotties* knew who was calling the shots.

After taking several laps around the club and not finding any more ladies to dance with, I strolled up to the bar trying my best not to look kicked-to-the-curb. As I approached I heard Brown's distinct, grandfather laugh before he called my name. "Yo Amaru commere, lemme pull your coat-tail."

This was Brown's retro-way of saying he wanted to school me on something. It went well with his old-man image.

"Sit down Sev," he said gesturing at the empty stool next to him.

Hawker and Brown were the only guys outside my neighborhood who used my shoplifters' pseudonym. Hawk called me this all the time but Brown only did it in private when he wanted to discuss a scam. For this reason I was all-ears. Prior to talking business, Brown turned toward the three people behind the bar.

"Ay, can my buddy get a Heineken?"

In spite of the ten or so GIs standing in-line, I received my beer within seconds. It seemed Brown had made friends with the bartenders.

"Salud!" Clinking our bottles together, Brown then wasted no time bridging the topic of his latest scheme.

"So them fools in Mike Company made your irresponsible ass a squad-leader, huh? They must be desperate for leadership." Chuckling, he took a sip. "Man, this is going to be even easier than I thought."

Brown was obviously trying to pique my interest. It worked.

"Aight ock, what you waiting for? A damn drum-roll? Spill it!"

"Okay," Brown said before stifling another round of chuckles with a swig of lager. "As platoon-guide and squad-leader, correct me if I'm wrong, but part of our job is to confiscate any personal belongings left unsecure, right?"

"Yeah, so what?" I responded, despite having an inkling of what he was proposing.

"Whenever you find any radios, *Walkmans, t*apes, or whatever else is left behind in the dayroom, check if you're being watched. If you are, turn those joints in to your drill sergeant like you're supposed to."

"And if I'm not?" I asked.

"If you're sure no one saw you..." Taking another swig, Brown casually looked around before responding. "Give them to me."

"Okay I gettit, then you give me the shit you collected

from your company…" Excited, I almost began shouting. "And we sell everything back to the same suckers we vicked!"

"Shh, shh!" Brown cautioned me to quiet down. "Don't announce it to the whole club," he said with a chuckle.

"So when do we start, playa?

"Don't insult me like that, I thought you already knew how I rolled, Sev." After ordering us another round, Brown glanced around before finishing his statement. "I got a load waiting at the barracks right now, so when we roll-out, get in the taxi with me."

"Bet!"

As I said this two other Alpha brothers who had struck out walked over to us. Like Brown and I, it appeared Struthers and Beverly would have to wait for another night to use their Jefferson-issued rubbers.

Brown and I made a decent chunk of change from this racket. What's more, just like the old-head predicted, I soon got a reputation for being 'cool as hell' because everyone loves a bargain; especially someone who has just been robbed. Think about it: I was the nice guy providing these victims with whatever items had been stolen from them. I even gave them a special discount to show how much I cared.

All the action—both the stealing and the selling— took place in the day room. I preyed mainly on that week's arriving class of newbies. My goal was to vick 'em on their first weekend before they became oriented to their new environment. Brown and I met on Monday or Tuesday evening to make the exchange; that gave us ample time to sell the shipment by Friday—just in time to greet the next group of arriving newbies. With trainees shipped in and out so often, it was easy to keep this scam underground and profitable too.

Even though we never got caught, there were consequences for devoting so much time to scamming and chilling. For one thing, much of my newly-attained discipline had evaporated into thin air. This almost spelled disaster at the Army's decorated Airborne School, which was my next stop. So the skies above Georgia, known as the 'Peach State,' is where I would learn to put my 'knees in the breeze.'

Chapter 9: Airborne School

"Welcome to Ft. Benning, USA!" After roaring his salutation to the assembled horde, Captain Smith paused to clear his throat. "As the commanding officer of Delta Company, 1st Battalion, 507th Parachute Infantry Regiment, allow me to congratulate you on being accepted into one of the first-class courses of instruction within the borders of these United States of America. Evidence of this can be seen all around you, in the form of the best and brightest men and women from every branch of military service…"

And it was true.

Far from the normal, shuckin' and jivin' teens from the suburbs, trailer-parks, or project tenements, almost half of Delta Company was comprised of an entirely different caste. Since arriving at the famed Airborne School three days prior, beyond the NCO rank insignias peppering the formation, it was the officers' bars and oak leaves which really got my attention. Training side-by-side with non-commissioned officers was thrilling enough; but seeing the commissioned variety reduced to the status of trainee was easily the best surprise. Most of these future-commanders were cadets, straight from college or West Point.

The Airborne Instructors, who everyone called 'Black Hats,' often referred to the cadets as "cadidiots." Unlike everyone else attending Jump School, the cadidiots were still new to the rigors of military life. And believe me it showed.

147

Since these youngsters were being groomed for leadership positions over the very men and women they were training alongside, fraternization amongst the groups was strictly forbidden. Serving as our platoon-guide, squad-leaders, as well as guide-on, these clumsy buffoons were put on stage every day for the amusement of the entire group. They were the life of the party.

After the company commander finished his prolonged but otherwise effective greeting, the first-sergeant addressed us. Choosing his words carefully, he intensely penetrated our psyche by adding his own personal challenge.

"Gentlemen and ladies, here at the Airborne school, we are dedicated to transforming your chicken-shit, confused, earthbound, frightened masses of flesh-and-bones into highly courageous, confident, flat-bellied, steady-eyed Assassins from the Sky. In other words, bona-fide, US Paratroopers! Oooh-Ahh?"

"Ooh-Ah!" The response from the formation was so loud, for several seconds, the echo reverberated off the barracks' walls.

Using this quick time-out to spit, the grizzled war-veteran then resumed energizing the testosterone-driven throng. "Right now, I want each of you to turn to your right and greet the disciplined soldier or marine standing there. Then, turn to your left and shake hands with the superior sailor or airman looking back at you." Seeing we required further prompting, First-Sergeant Crawford wasted no time guiding the masses to his desired goal. "Why the hell are y'all still standing there looking at me for? Dammit turn to your right, do it for real! I wanna hear some 'Hi, my name is John from Bum-fuck, Illinois self-introductions going on. You have thirty seconds—*move!"*

At his order, a cacophonous murmur broke out amongst the formation.

After saying "Ssup" to my boy Wilkins, who was an honor-grad in my class at Ft. Lee, I shook hands with the Navy SEAL occupying the space to my left. Initially reluctant to respond to my warm greeting, the freckled Caucasian with a buzz-cut stared for an extended second before using his nasal-driven, southern accent.

"Just call me Reid." Neither friendly nor spiteful, he then returned his attention to the front of the formation.

In spite of the daily efforts by members of the Marine Force Recon or the Air Force Para-rescue units to get everyone's attention, the SEALs were without question the stars of Jump School. However, prior to their starring roles being unveiled, I pre-maturely jumped to the erroneous conclusion that Reid was just another goofy, run-of-the-mill whiteboy. This assessment could not have been more incorrect.

"I guarantee you *Airborne…*" the first-sergeant picked up his rabble-rousing speech where he had left off. "If the two men or women you just met are both still here come graduation, chances are you won't be. This is not a threat, it's a promise. This course is not for pogues, punks, nor pansies. We aim to shave this group of wanna-be's by one-third before March 25th. Good luck!"

Top wasn't bullshitting either. Whether they failed to make the grade, got injured, or voluntarily quit during the three-week training cycle, our company was reduced by at least the first-sergeant's predicted amount. Every morning, after calling us to attention, the black hats invariably provided an avenue of escape for anyone having second thoughts about jumping from a 'perfectly good airplane.'

"Who wants to quit?" they screamed.

And each day, dozens of trainees, with their eyes cast downward, ran to the front of the formation. Whenever this happened, I was reminded of receiving my expert badge for BRM because, like the Elite 7, these defectors were required to face the company. But for an entirely different reason. This daily ritual was the subject of many hard-core trainees' wagers at night: "How many pogues do you think'll quit tomorrow?" they asked each other right before lights-out. It was our million dollar question.

On the morning of our last jump, I mistakenly concluded no one would quit with the finish line in clear view. Unbelievably, I lost ten bucks betting with Reid. Following our pre-jump routine, we were lined-up in our respective *sticks* while we waited to receive our parachutes. All of a sudden the SEALs started yelling something back-and-forth to one another amongst the various sticks. In a raucous manner becoming of these *pups,* they barked-out details about a graduation party. After hearing the social gathering was scheduled for Saturday night in a Columbus hotel, I was shocked when Reid tapped my shoulder and invited *me* to their celebration bash.

This was a feather in my cap because everyone knew *frogmen* never associated with anyone outside their clan. What I recall most about this cocky group of outcasts was how they made the rigors of training appear no more trying than a Sunday stroll in the park. As many of us moaned and groaned during our PT sessions, the SEAL pups oftentimes complained the training was too easy. Some even used the word 'boring.'

The entire Airborne School grounds was littered with sawdust. The black hats claimed it was softer to practice our parachute-landing-falls in sawdust pits rather than on top of hard Georgia clay. I don't doubt the veracity of this statement however that didn't explain why we had to exercise in it too. Every time I was lathered-up in sweat, tiny pieces of wood somehow made their way deeper and deeper into my clothing. *Talk about itchy!*

After a couple-hundred flutter-kicks, you could see guys wiping sawdust off their faces or scratching their crotch. In fact, everyone looked uncomfortable except the SEALs. These guys rolled around in the sawdust like pigs playing in the mud. Speaking of mud, I remember one time while they were being reprimanded by a black hat, the whole group suddenly jumped up and sprinted to a nearby mud puddle. Upon arriving, they jumped in and continued doing push-ups. Even the Sergeant-Airborne who had been yelling at them was at a loss for words.

Black hats filter-out the majority of the "wanna-be's" from the more distinguished "gonna-be's" in the initial week, known as Ground Week. On day 3, I was laboring in the front-leaning-rest-position. Hung-over from a night of partying with my newest partner-in-crime, Pvt. Orlando McKnight, whenever the instructors turned their backs, I dropped-down into the sawdust to sneak a rest. When a frogman about thirty yards away spotted me hiding, he yelled in my direction using a sarcastic tone.

"Hey Reid, you over there being all you can be?"

Hearing the well-known, Army slogan[4] twisted to express contempt, Reid chuckled before spitting on the ground to emphasize his disgust. "Yeah, what a joke!"

In Ground Week, altercations amongst the various

---

[4] See *Army Slogan*

branches were everyday occurrences. Although these confrontations usually resulted in nothing more than a shoving match or some angry threats, I did see a couple hot-heads knuckle-up in the latrine one evening. However, since a worthy rival for the SEALs was not to be found within Delta's ranks, following a short pause, one of the black hats filled the void by snapping at the still-conversing pups. "You two with the big-mouths, shut-the-fuck-up or leave now!"

"Clear Sergeant-Airborne!" The twins immediately echoed the proper response before putting their conversation on mute. After being reprimanded, Reid glared at me.

Looking back from the prone position—while again resting—I watched him keep in rhythm with the push-up cadence. Just before I looked away, I noticed there was something odd about his motion. Not only were his feet spread further apart than usual, he was rising and descending at a weird angle. Then it struck me in a flash—he was only using one arm!

Oh, this whiteboy thinks he's hard, I thought as Reid directed his disgust in my direction. Little did Reid suspect, at that very moment, I planned to whip him at his own game. Thank God I was sick! Allow me to explain.

The 'plan' I concocted was to plant my index-finger in Reid's chest with a straight-up challenge to see who could knock out the most push-ups. I really believed, properly motivated, I could take him, as-is. Nevertheless having a queasy stomach, I decided to delay my challenge until the following day. I foolishly concluded that my two months of doing extra push-ups with Sgt. Sandoval could compare to Reid's two years of brutal Sea, Air, and Land training. Never mind boot-camp ended five months ago; this was just another example of me being out of touch with reality.

That night, after I declined a free beer from McKnight, he bent-over laughing as I explained the reason for my alcohol fast.

"Cuz, you're joking, right?" After one glance, he knew I was wasn't. "Reid's gonna destroy you! Tak, those guys *like* doing PT…they can do that shit all day!"

Luckily, the next afternoon, before I had an opportunity to make a fool of myself, the same Sergeant-Airborne from the day before beat me to it. Having taken Reid's slanders about the Army personally, the young black hat picked on the frogman for the remainder of the day. At that time, Reid took it in stride and humbly did his penalty exercises. However the next morning, when the bullying resumed, Reid's attitude was far from submissive. Of course he did the push-ups, but he made sure to express his less-than-respectful attitude every chance he got. As we were being dismissed for lunch, the situation bubbled to a climax when Reid got dropped again.

"Clear Sergeant-Sissy!" Reid blared out. "Because I want to be all I can be…just like you!"

Before Reid completed his reply, other SEALs in the ranks began barking to show their support. This caused everyone to express themselves in one way or another, mostly with random barks or laughter. For a moment, it appeared the frogmen were challenging the black hat's authority. "At ease! At ease!" the Sergeant-Airbornes yelled. It took quite an effort from them to restore order in the ranks.

Eventually the black hats prevailed and there was a stony silence. The area did not remain quiet for long, however. About a minute later, Reid started whistling from the front-leaning rest position. Everyone was shocked until we realized he was whistling the jingle for the 'Be all you can be' television commercial. Then everybody fell-out laughing.

Taking advantage of this timely distraction, McKnight and I switched into 'stealth mode' and snuck passed dozens of trainees who were now singing, "Be all you can be!" To show even further support for the upstart SEAL, some chanted Reid's name while others shouted anti-Army sentiments. But regardless of the branch of service or the rank, almost everyone got a charge watching the SEAL-trainee defy the Sergeant-Airborne. The crowd was so busy watching Reid stick his tongue-out at Sgt. Rasmussen from the flutter-kick-position that McKnight and I practically went unnoticed. By the time the formation was released, we were standing at the head of the chow line.

For the duration of Jump School, McKnight and I entered the cafeteria with the esteemed 'first twenty' at every meal while our fellow trainees stood in line up to forty-five minutes on some days.

Minutes after gulping down our food, we spotted our Delta Company comrades finally entering the building. Once the newest version of the City Crew was assembled at our table, McKnight, who everyone called Mick, asked if I still planned to challenge Reid.

"What's that supposed to mean?" I snapped, as the others looked on in surprise. Feeling insulted, my mouth then placed my butt in a situation it wasn't ready to handle. "See, that's the difference between a big-mouth-busta like you and a thorough-ass-muthafucka like me." Looking around the table to make sure my message was being comprehended, I sealed my fate. "When I say I'ma do something, it's a done deal…my word's my bond!"

"A-ight Philly, chill-out cuz!" Mick replied with equal force.

154

In spite of his defensive posture, Mick smiled like he knew a secret. Some of the other guys were also grinning but since they had to gorge down their meals, they did not have time to say anything. So nobody expressed much on the topic. Well, this altogether changed the instant we exited the mess hall and ran to the formation area.

In the training environment, seeing guys doing push-ups was as common an experience as shining our boots. For this reason, I was intrigued so many bystanders would stop and stare as one black hat punished a trainee. Wilkins, instantly recognizing what had escaped the rest of us, pointed out the significance of the moment.

"Get-the-fuck outta here!" he exclaimed. "Is that Reid and Sgt. Rasmussen?"

Certain he was mistaken, I put on my glasses. After doing so, I was unable to hide my astonishment. I gasped when the huge puddle of effort, grime, and sweat under Reid's pulsating body came into focus. More than a half-hour had elapsed since we entered the dining hall, leaving these two combatants locked in their personal session. Yet, not only was Reid casually pumping out reps, he was still talking shit!

"Hey y'all," Reid said grinning our way. "Today, I'm gonna prove a Navy SEAL can do more PT at lunchtime...than an Army wuss can do all day!"

When Reid made-fun of the same Army commercial for the third time, the entire formation area busted-out laughing. At this point, Sgt. Rasmussen was unable to ignore the jeering catcalls from the crowd; he had no choice but to concede. *This was the closest thing I witnessed to anarchy in my three-year enlistment.*

As you can probably imagine, from that moment my buddies clowned me to no end. Everyday, while sporting huge grins, they asked me the same question over-and-over. "So, is today the big day to face Reid?" This was, by far, the most popular joke at every meal.

Incapable of extracting the foot I had so expertly jammed into my mouth, I cringed knowing what needed to be done. *I gotta go through with it,* I reflected. *So first, I gotta get in shape!* Realizing our daily PT regimen, which was the same amount of push-ups Reid did everyday, would never bring me any closer to defeating him, I started doing multiple-sets at night while Mick and I were drinking beer.

Due to the list of dignitaries in Delta Company, unlike my previous stops, there were few bullshit-duties assigned after training ended each evening. Nonetheless, with so many trainees sharing the barracks, life was hectic. This situation was exacerbated during showers, laundry time, and especially when you needed a toilet to take a dump. It was crowded! Therefore, to ensure everyone had an equal amount of time to eat or use the limited number of facilities, the four companies, Alpha, Bravo, Charlie, and Delta, rotated the order in which they were released into the cafeteria and barracks' areas.

Prior to being excused from formation, we were always given long-winded, hoo-rah speeches. The one after dinner, in front of the barracks was especially wearisome. It was not uncommon for this rambling, repetitive pep-rally to stretch well beyond a half hour. Well, while everyone screamed and waved their fists to the barbaric banter, Mick and I disappeared into thin air. With almost no personal time available, the only worthwhile scam in Jump School was to steal *time* back, itself.

By day 3 of Ground Week, thanks to our twenty-plus-minute head-starts, the final formation of the evening had been reduced to glimpsed fragments through the barracks windows. This occurred while Mick and I ran back-and-forth down the hallway, from the latrine to our rooms.

After throwing our BDUs in the washing machine, Mick and I always rushed into the shower. By the time the hoo-rah, Viking crowd came inside the building, with our clothes already tumbling in the dryer, we'd be toweling off almost ready for another night out in town.

In Jump School, Mick and I hit the streets every night. All in all, we probably had about triple the amount of free-time provided everyone else. It's ironic to think I spent most of it knocking out push-ups while Mick counted my reps like a drunk, black hat. The reduction of stress this additional rest provided could never be properly explained to anyone unfamiliar with the hardships of military training. As Mick and I honed our ability to exit a C-130 and execute a Parachute Landing Fall, which we called a 'PLF,' we also perfected maximizing our down-time.

On Monday of Week 2, which was called 'Tower Week,' beyond feeling confident we had become cocky. On that morning, when all four companies were lined-up for a special formation and some unknown brass arrived to observe, everyone knew something noteworthy had occurred over the weekend. Considering the number of belligerent personalities jam-packed in the down-trodden barracks, I imagined fisticuffs had broken out. Although I was correct, according to First-Sergeant Crawford's stern warning, my prediction was only the tip of the iceberg.

"Airborne!" he yelled into an olive-drab megaphone. "In my twenty-two years of service defending freedom, justice, and democracy, I've never heard of the level of delinquency which took place in my barracks over the weekend!" Exhaling sharply, Top wiped his forehead with a handkerchief. "I got AWOL suspects, privates fighting with lieutenants, and several reports of sexual misconduct. *Geez,* where the hell were my NCOs—the backbone of this mighty fighting machine—when all this bullshit was happening? Boys and girls, I didn't think I had to say this…" Pausing, he looked around the formation. "But this ain't basic training. There's nothing basic about becoming a fit-to-fight, dynamite paratrooper. Ooo-ah?"

"Ooo-ah." Responding with a downward intonation of the same bark, the swelling masses of warriors submitted to being reprimanded.

"Because we gotta whole day of training to get to, I'll make this short, sweet, and to the point," Top resumed. "All of us, together, represent the first-line of defense of this beautiful nation. Therefore we *will* learn to work together! And that starts by showing respect for all those of a higher rank, especially personnel in a different branch of service." Stopping here, he allowed his words to sink in. "With God as my witness," he continued, "I promise the next lower-enlisted soldier, sailor, airman, or marine who responds to someone of higher rank with anything other than 'Clear Sir, Ma'am, or Sergeant,' will not only be kicked outta here, if I have it my way you'll be tossed out of the military altogether!" Pausing again, he glared around the formation. "And I don't give a damn what hot-shot outfit you belong to either!" Appearing satisfied his point had been delivered, Top took a deep breath before calling out a name and title unfamiliar to my Army senses. "Seaman Stewart—front and center!"

After a young man in a Naval uniform ran to the front of our formation, we listened as Top read some monotonous orders promoting the short seaman to NCO status. Once the new *petty officer* returned to his place amongst the masses, the grizzled paratrooper closed with potent words to rivet our attention on the sublime goal of becoming Airborne.

"So remember," Top boomed, "we have zero tolerance for insubordination. If I hear any bullshit, you sorry-ass *LEGs* will be toast for tomorrow's breakfast! Oh, and that includes fraternization for all you horny toads in the group!"

LEG is an acronym meaning 'Lacking Enough Guts.' It's the slogan black hats use to distinguish paratroopers from those without jump-status, whom they consider unworthy. By the time we donned our maroon berets at graduation, we had been thoroughly conditioned to believe LEGs were inferior beings.

Considering the severity of the Top's reprimand, Mick and I should have taken this as a warning. However, by lunchtime, we had forgotten about both his words of caution and Stewart's *petty* promotion. Once our company was halted in front of the mess hall, like always, we were given the command to 'ground our gear.'

Removing our rucksacks and TA-50 webbing, we positioned everything in a neat pile according to a prescribed outline. Like every assignment, failure to satisfactorily perform this tedious task resulted in a gig. For any trainee unlucky enough to receive three such demerits, he or she was sent packing their duffel bags to become a permanent member of the LEG community.

Each time I placed my kevlar helmet, with its stenciled 403 on top of my gear, I was keenly aware of a liberating sensation. This was because, once free of our burden, there was no way to identify which company or stick a particular trainee belonged to. After the black hats went inside the cafeteria, the NCO and officer trainees were required to step-out of the formation to supervise us lower-enlisted personnel. The next step required patience. Having been assigned to the two middle-squads, this provided Mick and I with a clear view of each company standing between us and the mess hall. Each day, when the last threat in the first two squads exited the ranks, I always smiled before glancing over my shoulder to see Mick's thumbs-up signal. This meant the 3rd and 4th squads were all-clear too. *Then it was off to the races!*

Given the penalty for getting caught was being kicked out of Jump School, plus the severe humiliation that went with it, the meager rewards of a few extra minutes in the mess hall or barracks did not seem worthwhile to our fellow, Delta Company comrades. Most of them thought Mick and I were stupid. What none of them could comprehend was, we had the system figured out. In spite of this, our master plan did overlook one, small detail. Promoted just hours ago, our newest non-commissioned supervisor had spent the duration of Ground Week in formation as an E-4. So it was possible he had watched us creep by from his place within the ranks.

Petty Officer Stew

"Hey you, what company are you in?"

I ignored the short Naval NCO in my peripheral vision, pretending I didn't notice him. With no other option available, I hoped ignoring him might discourage him. After all, he might be talking to Mick. However, once Petty Officer Stewart poked my left bicep, I knew my optimism was in vain.

"You! Step out of the chow line—now!"

Oh shit! Although I never uttered a word, this thought

clamored loudly between my ears. Feeling the pressure of the moment, I forgot this guy was in the Navy. "Clear Sergeant!" I realized my mistake the instant the words left my mouth.

"What did you call me, you dumb-fuck? That's Petty Officer!" Stewart sharply reprimanded.

Watching this dwarfish sailor lose his cool nearly brought a smile to my face.

Once he positioned me ten feet away from the line to stand by myself, it did not take long for the other NCOs and officers to pick me up on their radars. Sensitive to any deviation from standard procedure, by the time the PO launched into his fiery indictment, they had begun gathering around us.

"Yeah," began the irate petty officer, "I watched you and your partner sneak by all these hard-working trainees every day last week." Stopping here, he looked around for Mick, but was unable to recognize him standing next to where I had been just seconds ago. "He's probably here too," the PO said after taking a final sweep of the area. "To be honest, I'm not sure because I don't remember what he looks like. But I *do* remember you!"

As the enraged sailor pointed his finger inches from my face, I saw a Caucasian man wearing Army BDUs approaching out of the corner of my eye.

"And you wanna know why I remember you *A-maru?*"

Seeing and hearing PO Stewart make the effort to read my shirt as if to commit my name to memory, my heart sank to my feet.

"It was because of that stupid, wise-guy grin that I can see you're trying to hold back." Stepping closer, he inspected my face closely. "Private, do you think this is some kind of joke?"

"No…P-Petty…Officer."

Although he had just stated his title, it was still foreign jargon to my Army-mind. Later, Mick said it sounded like I'd labeled Stewart 'an officer who was petty.' *Hmm…you be the judge.* What I do know is, when the troops in line began laughing, 'Stew' became livid.

"Okay I gettit, we gotta fuckin' comedian here. Private Amaru, what's your roster number?" he demanded in an authoritative tone.

Career decision: should I lie or tell the truth? Once the details of Top's warning from this morning flashed in my mind, my decision was far from complicated. "Roster number six-oh-three, Petty Officer," I stated just as the older white-guy stepped toward the PO.

"Bullshit! You're a fuckin' liar and a disgrace to the uniform you're wearing!" Spitting more than yelling, the PO's face was blood-red from the flash-flood pumping through the swollen veins in his neck.

Seeing his burst of anger, I was optimistic my *guess-timate* had hit its mark. It was pure luck that I guessed Mick and I were amongst the trainees in the six-hundred-series. I didn't even know of which company so I'm glad he didn't ask me.

"Petty Officer, may I have a word with you in private?"

Sergeant First-Class Ripkin, who had been standing there observing for several seconds, never looked in my direction before leading the PO a discreet distance away to discuss the matter. Nevertheless with the area bathed in silence everyone heard the tongue-lashing dished out by the E-7 on 'being a professional NCO.'

As Top reminded us, Airborne School was a far cry from boot camp. With a mature group of trainees in attendance, outside of serious violations, we were left alone during our down-time. In a nutshell, any unnecessary readings of the riot act was frowned upon, especially while on-break.

Before being out-ranked and otherwise shutdown, PO Stewart did try to argue his point. "Sergeant, with all due respect, I'm sure he's not lined up with his stick because there's no way I never noticed him before today—"

"At ease, Petty Officer Stewart!" Sgt. Ripkin was now yelling. Then the E-7's brow creased as he reflected on the last words uttered by the frustrated PO. "Wait a minute," he snapped in an incredulous tone. "Are you telling me you don't even know this private?" Once Stewart looked unsure of himself, Sgt. Ripkin shook in his head in disgust and ended any further debate. "Petty officer, it is now lunchtime. This is your decision but I will say this: if you proceed any further— *you better be right.*" Then turning his head and shoulders, he pointed in my direction. "But my recommendation is, for you to walk back over there and release that soldier so he can get some chow and be ready when training resumes at thirteen-hundred." Finished chewing out the newest kid in the NCO club, SFC Ripkin was already walking back toward where, minutes ago, he had been having a pleasant conversation with a Marine E 7. Before leaving the scene, he added one more inspirational anecdote. "Petty officer, I'll be watching you."

When PO Stewart returned to where I remained standing at attention, I was aware that his former overbearing, herculean aura had been reduced to that of a sulking child. In silence, the petty officer stared at me for several seconds before murmuring something in a low tone.

163

"Amaru, get back in line."

"Clear Petty Officer—Airborne!" I stated smartly.

As I returned to my place, Mick whispered something. "Fuck that li'l *Mighty Mouse* muthafucka!"

Now I was struggling to suppress my wise-guy grin.

"Yeah laugh-it-up Amaru!" PO Stewart hissed. "It might be a big joke right now but we'll see how funny this shit is after lunch—when you're *not* wearing a kevlar with six-oh-three stenciled on it." Visibly angry, the PO tried to appear calm while he served up his final threats. "See smart-ass, it's what you don't know that'll get your ass burnt every time. In this case, what you happen to be ignorant of is, I'm roster number six-two-oh. That's right genius, do the math! So, according to you, I'm in the stick right after yours." Now wearing a devilish grin of his own, he fired his best shot of the day. "We'll see who's doing the laughing tomorrow morning when Top's kicking your ass outta here! You understand me, Private?"

With his feathers ruffled like they were, I could not resist teasing him one last time. "Clear…p-p-petty, umm, officer!" I responded in a military tone before using a softer voice to correct my obvious blunder. "Oh, I mean the petty officer named Stewart."

When a new chorus of laughter leaked out behind me, the PO's smile melted into a frown. "At ease! At ease!" he screamed at the crowd before stepping toward me and yelling one last time. "We'll see who gets the last laugh on this A-ma-ru. Consider this incident far from being over!"

Once the little agitated man left the area, Mick gave me a friendly elbow to my ribcage. Although I returned his grin, my thoughts were racing ahead to after lunch. Exactly how did I plan to evade this five-foot assassin?

Undercover Brother

"Hahahahahaha! Man, what the fuck is wrong with you?" Alternating between laughing and scolding me, everyone in the CC agreed I was about to get kicked-out of Jump School.

"Damn Amaru, we were all supposed to make it to graduation together. Now that oath's fucked up!" Wilkins loudly lamented.

"Like he said, it ain't over."

Although I tried to sound confident, no one was buying it. Nonetheless, everyone chuckled as they recounted watching the petty officer not only get played, but to add icing to an already humorous cake, this was followed by a public dress-down by an *Army* E-7. Yet, since *PO Bonaparte* had expressly warned the gig was up after lunch, everyone wanted to hear my plan.

"What're you gonna do?" Wilkins inquired on behalf of the entire clique.

"Patience plus a little slickster in your nature, these are the only virtues necessary to pull off Operation Time Extension." This is what I had bragged to Wilkins two days earlier when he insisted it was only a matter of time before we got caught.

"How the fuck should I know?" I snapped. Beginning to squirm under the pressure, I dug into my breast pocket and removed my Army-issued glasses. "But for starters, everyone please sit down and relax!" After I put on my glasses and everybody was seated, I took a bite out of my chicken sandwich. "Stop making a scene," I pleaded. "If he locates me in here, I'm done." Slouching down in my seat, I tried to buy time to think.

"Hey y'all, when Amaru puts on his birth-control glasses, he looks like Bruce Lee in the *Chinese Connection.*"

Busting-out laughing, Mick agreed with Wilkins. "Yeah he does, when Bruce went undercover as a telephone repairman!"

Barely noticing their wisecracks, I was concentrating on bringing-forth every tip from my spy novels on remaining incognito. For the next ten minutes, while they continued having fun at my expense, I inhaled my food. My buddies were still laughing when I stood up without saying a word and walked over to set my tray on the rack for dirty dishes. Then I left the mess hall by myself.

On my way to the formation area, every time I spotted a navy or marine uniform—their BDUs and cap looked the same—I dipped into the shadows. Since it was of paramount importance to keep a low profile, I went into the latrine nearest to Delta Company. Once inside, I took off my cap and stared into a mirror.

For several minutes, I stretched and contorted my cheeks and mouth. Then I put my cap on and pulled it down to my ears. This allowed the brim to shade my eyes. *Not bad,* I thought but I needed something more so I enlarged my nostrils just a hair and extended my chin forward. Doing this made me look like a different guy up-close, I thought. To alter my appearance from a distance, I practiced walking and running with a limp. I did this until the last, possible minute before formation.

It was seconds before we were called to attention when I hobbled-up to the formation. With my glasses on and cap pulled down, at first, even Mick failed to recognize me. In spite of arriving in the nick of time, I actually brushed shoulders with PO Stewart as he combed the crowd in his desperate search.

The PO never looked twice at the shy boy hiding behind his thick glasses and a gimpy gait. Instead, he grabbed the arm of another melanin-rich male about my size and weight.

"Get the fuck off me!" snarled Private Lloyd, the CC representative for Chicago. Then realizing who it was, he soon relaxed. "Oh, you're that little Navy-guy looking for Amaru, right?"

"Who're you talking to like that Private?" Initially taken aback by Lloyd's aggressive response, the newly promoted NCO was unable to assert his authority before Lloyd apologized in an exaggerated fashion.

"Oh excuse me Petty Officer Stewart, I don't what came over me!" Then he looked in the opposite direction from where I was and pointed. "There's Amaru right there!"

When the PO spun around to see who he was pointing at, he found a bunch of Caucasian trainees.

"Oh my bad, the guy in the middle looked like Amaru a second ago," Lloyd added with a huge grin as the first-sergeant called us to attention.

For the remainder of the day, Wilkins, Mick, and I collectively held our breath at every break while more than a few trainees chuckled as they watched the petty NCO scour the area. What made this extremely funny was that everyone knew where I was but nobody told him. It became Delta Company's source of entertainment.

That evening before dinner, which incidentally was the only time Mick and I played it safe by not sneaking ahead, PO Stewart again pushed me out of the way to rough up another guy near me.

After Wilkins saw the PO release my arm and grab someone else's—while never taking a good look at either one of us—he called Stew a "Stupid-ass whiteboy!"

"Who said that?" demanded the infuriated petty officer. When no one responded, and instead ripples of laughter began to infect the crowd, *po-po* promptly moved his search-and-destroy mission over to Charlie Company.

The irony was, despite being lost in the sauce, my 'private petty officer' intuitively knew where to search. As a result, after nearly being caught when I stayed in place, Mick and I decided it was better to slip by him rather than to risk being snuck-up-on from our blindside. Furthermore once we determined Stewart could not see beyond my glasses—*he never once glanced toward my chest*—after only one meal on the disabled list, Mick and I were back to the races.

In spite of his apparent color-blindness, since the petty officer knew my name, that evening I took the precaution of borrowing one of McKnight's BDU shirts for the remainder of training. "Yeah I'll lend you one if you want but you don't need it," Mick chuckled, tossing me the shirt. "Stew's looking at every brother except you…as long as you got those glasses on."

By Friday of Tower Week, every brother near my size had yelled 'Get off me!' at least twice. This little man appeared to be everywhere. "I know one thing for sure," Wilkins commented while we grounded our equipment before lunch. "Homeboy's hot under-the-collar he can't find you." As several trainees in my stick expressed their agreement with a round of laughter, Mick and I prepared to sneak away before the super-sleuth disguised as a Naval NCO showed up.

When Jump Week kicked off, a light illuminated within every soldier, sailor, marine, and airman as we began to shape-shift into rookie paratroopers. Ready to demonstrate what we had learned over the past two-plus weeks, we were dying to put our wobbly knees in the breeze. Unlike firing our rifles for the first time, since our parachutes saved us from experiencing a terrifying death, jumping from airplanes qualified as God-inspired. Once we notched a couple jumps under our belts, the black hats verbally promoted us from lowly, wanna-be status to the more respected title of 'gonna-be's'.

From this point, we thought we were the shit!

Boarding the airplane on Wednesday evening, everyone was eager to get over the hump of our night-jump requirement. Even though this was our third exit from a C-130 in as many days, jumping into the unseen blackness was indeed an eerie experience. Following Thursday afternoon's jump from a C-141, the black hats announced our graduation ceremony was scheduled immediately after our fifth PLF— right on the drop zone.

After we deposited our spent chutes in one pile, and the reserve parachutes at a separate turn-in point, the big question before being marched to dinner was: who planned to have 'blood wings' pinned-on tomorrow? It was during this high-tide of emotion that, like everyone else, I began to relax and enjoy myself.

I was standing in the chow-line, next to Mick, when I recognized *Inch-High Private Eye* approaching. *Damn!* I knew it was too late because my glasses suddenly felt heavy…as they snugly rested in my breast pocket.

"Son-of-a-gun, lookee who finally showed up!" Gloating unabashedly, Petty Officer Stewart was beside himself with joy. I, on the other hand, was browbeating myself in silence for forgetting to wear my glasses. "You know Amaru, for the life of me, I don't know how the hell you avoided me for this long. *But I got your ass now!* Step out of the line, Private Wiseguy!"

Having devoted a healthy portion of his time and energy working to achieve this very moment, it was no surprise Stew wished to celebrate for an extra minute. Or two. Once the PO separated me from the others, he jumped in my face.

"That's right, I caught your wise-ass!" he reiterated, striking a fist into the palm of his other hand. "Guess what Amaru? Tomorrow morning, when you're cleaning out your locker, I'm gonna make it my personal business to pay you a visit, you low-life scum!" Then, switching to a huge smile, he turned toward the onlookers standing in-line. "Where're all your cackling buddies now? Huh Amaru?" he thundered in a loud voice. "I told you I'd get the last laugh on this! Remember I said this, he who laughs last—"

Far beyond a desire to see justice served, Stew's mission had become personal in nature. Standing there, I had no choice but to watch as he repeated over-and-over how bad my punishment was going to be. Looking at him, I was reminded of Batman's archrival, the Riddler. For those unfamiliar with this pompous villain, he caught the Dark Knight on numerous occasions. But instead of dropping the hatchet to kill his enemy outright, he always wasted time verbally masturbating over every detail of his deadly intentions. In each of these episodes, while he was steadily babbling, some incredibly unlikely loophole would present itself—just in the nick of time—to save the ill-fated, Caped Crusader from what seconds ago had seemed to be a hopeless predicament.

"What the hell is going on over here?" SFC Ripkin,

screaming his way onstage for his second cameo appearance, rudely cut into Stew's thirty seconds of fame. "Petty officer, you'd better have a damn-good reason for all this noise!"

"Ahh, Sergeant-First-Class Ripkin, it's so nice to see you again," the PO snobbily greeted the silver-streaked soldier. "And yes, I'd say we have sufficient cause for some 'noise' as you put it." Confident he had hooked the biggest fish on the boat, the pint-sized petty officer arrogantly grinned before rolling his eyes in my direction. "Not to mention some disciplinary measures to be enacted, whaddya say Amaru?"

"Excuse me?" The E-7's fury snapped Stew out of his delusions of grandeur.

"Sergeant, what I meant was, I caught Private Amaru committing a serious violation. Top needs to be notified immediately," the petty officer replied, quickly regaining his military composure.

"Oh really? That serious, huh?" Sgt. Ripkin replied in a condescending tone. He was obviously irritated. "What happened?"

Stew then explained our prior encounter in graphic detail, even taking the time to mention my wise-guy grin. A couple minutes later, SFC Ripkin appeared to have heard enough.

"Okay, I get the point," he snapped before pushing PO Stewart out of the way to take his place in front of me. Standing there, scrutinizing me, this was the first time he had acknowledged my existence in either of our meetings. "Private, humor me by telling me none of this is true." Although the mildly greying soldier used a casual choice of words, his grave, facial expression communicated the seriousness of the situation.

"Sergeant," I replied using my most soldier-like voice. "The private requests permission to speak freely."

While Stew was squealing, I recalled the words of the master-shoplifter, A-Rock. He preached if the cops ever questioned me about something they couldn't prove, the best defense was to deny the crime and say nothing more. In his own words: "Cuz, you have no idea how many stupid-ass muthafuckas talk themselves right into the pen trying to over-explain shit. Sometimes a simple "I don't know" works better than any of those high-priced, lyin' lawyers!"

"Relax," Sgt. Ripkin said in a commanding tone. Now in front of me, he was standing flat-footed with his arms folded. It was clear the Army NCO was losing patience. "Now speak up and make it snappy."

"Sergeant, I don't know," I simply stated.

"What!" With his eyebrows arched to the top of his broad forehead, Sgt. Ripkin was flabbergasted. "Private, you'd better have something better than that—"

"Sergeant!" I deliberately cut him off for added effect. "The petty officer is making some serious charges against a private named 'Amaru'." Saying this, I was aware in a matter of seconds I'd either be kicked out, or I'd be the big fish that got away. Now taking advantage of the permission granted by the E-7 to relax, I pointed at my breast pocket. "But you can clearly see by looking at my shirt that my name is *McKnight.*"

The next few seconds seemed to take an hour. As I watched both NCOs tilt their heads to take in the offered data, I remembered the ID tags dangling around my neck. If either of them requested to see my dog-tags, I would be 'toast for tomorrow morning's breakfast.' Fortunately before Sgt. Ripkin had a chance to consider this, Stew's jaw hit the ground in utter disbelief. Then time sped back up to its normal pace.

"Private McKnight…" Following a deep breath, Sergeant Ripkin rubbed his face brusquely with both hands and exhaled in frustration. "Accept my apology for this rude interruption during your break. Please step back into the chow line and enjoy your lunch." Then, in much sterner tone, he turned to the shortest member of our threesome. "Petty Officer, I'd like to have a word with you in private—*now!*"

People always ask me: 'What's it like to put your knees in the breeze?'

Well, for one thing, please don't confuse paratrooper missions with any free-fall, recreational activity. Far from being fun, combat jumps are tiring, discomfiting, and hurt like hell every time you hit the drop zone. In addition, these nocturnal missions involve a degree of surprise; so clear nights and brightly reflecting moons are generally frowned upon. While captivating to the senses, these scenarios make paratroopers feel like sitting ducks. That said, imagine stepping through a portal…

And almost being thrust from your body as you're violently sucked through a wind-tunnel by the breath of Almighty God! Within seconds, an invisible braking mechanism slows your descent as you merge with the darkness to become one with the night-sky. Upon regaining your bearings, you must ensure your parachute is functioning properly and steer clear of any potential hazards. After checking your velocity and the direction of the wind, there are a few seconds to appreciate the backdrop before the tree-line comes into view. This is the signal to pull the release straps that jettison your rucksack. The final step is bracing for the jarring crash we called a PLF.

Upon completion of our fifth jump, we stood proudly in formation on Eubanks Field. Even though I remember feeling a sense of accomplishment, unlike many of my fellow graduates, I elected to have my silver wings pinned to my uniform, as opposed to the less conventional blood wings, which meant having the wings stuck through the soldier's BDUs directly into his chest. *Ouch!*

Graduation Night

Before linking up with the City Crew at a local bar, I went to check out the SEAL's party. With no mud to roll around in, I was intrigued to see what these raucous roughnecks called a good time. Besides, I still owed Reid for our bet. Far from being upset about parting with the cash, I was proud to be the only non-SEAL socializing at the members-only event.

Correction: the only *male,* non-SEAL.

Being the flamboyant loners they were, the twenty-two of them had arranged a private celebration with about an equal number of sexy women. The fact they managed to decorate three adjoining rooms at the *Howard Johnson Inn* with carloads of girls blew my teenage mind at the time. In retrospect, I am fairly certain those women were hired professionals. In any case, being the odd-man-out at the exclusive venue, I didn't stick around long enough to find out if this was indeed the case, or not.

After selecting a bottle of *Moosehead* from a bathtub full of ice, champagne, and beer, I placed a ten dollar bill into a pointy, Navy cap being circulated around the room for the losers of various wagers. It seems these SEALs had a proclivity for betting on things. Although Reid won his bet with me, I noticed he balked on taking any money when the hat was passed his way. Instead, before putting it on his head, he removed the loot and combined it with some greenbacks taken from his own breast pocket. Following a brief grin in my direction, he then distributed the cash to three unknown characters in the room.

During my introduction, a few in the close-knit fraternity started telling Army jokes to make it clear they were not happy about my presence. Still early, most people were busy meeting and greeting each other in the first room. I remember feeling awkward listening to Reid being interrogated about why out of the 391 graduates in Class #13-87, he had invited *me* to their esoteric gathering. As the conversation neared erupting into an argument, Reid, seeming fed up, pulled hard on his Marlboro Light before standing up and raising his hand in a grandiose gesture to get everyone's attention.

"Brothers!" he shouted, pointing at the two nearest SEALs. "According to Piper and Smitty, there seems to be some misunderstanding about why our Army guest was invited this evening. Allow me to clarify so there'll be no more questions."

Instantly, the gathering came to a stand-still. Many SEALs who had been outside, ran in to hear Reid's announcement.

"See Amaru here, he didn't learn some of the fundamentals of life." Pausing, Reid gestured at me and took

175

a healthy swig of his Budweiser. "Before he met us, he didn't understand the meaning of honor. Especially when it came to being a yellow-bellied coward."

Detecting sarcasm in his voice and hearing my name associated with 'yellow,' I instinctively braced for a Jap joke. Sweeping the area for the nearest exit, I noticed—for the first time—there was only one other melanin-rich face in the room.

Reid seemed to notice my change in demeanor. "Naw man, I ain't talking 'bout you," he stated. "I'm talkin' bout them yellow-bellied quitters who have no respect for themselves. For anything! How the hell could those wimps know anything about honor? Not to mention higher principles like uncompromising integrity?" Now confident he controlled the attention of all three rooms, Reid turned to address his larger audience.

"When I met Amaru he was just like the rest of 'em." Thinking back to that moment, he started laughing. "Actually, he might've been worse!" Hearing this, the crowd chuckled along. "But he surprised me because he changed."

Until his last sentence, I was afraid Reid was going have me lynched. Now I understood he was paying me a compliment.

"Just two and-a-half weeks ago, this guy was struggling to do thirty push-ups." Taking another swig, he slapped his knee in laughter. "In our morning PT sessions, he'd hide in the sawdust whenever the black hats weren't looking. Am I lying Amaru?" Turning toward me wearing a sly grin, Reid then asked another question. "How many can you do now?"

Surprised he asked me a question, I was slow to respond. "Umm, I dunno…more than thirty," I replied not knowing what to say. I was relieved when everyone laughed.

"After I *heard* you were gonna challenge me, I noticed you were getting stronger..." Hesitating here, Reid scratched his chin in a gesture of contemplation. "But tell the truth, you must've been burning some serious midnight-oil to git to where you're at now!"

In case some in attendance were still not convinced, Reid turned up the drama.

"Gentlemen, although we're really common men, just like *them,* unlike them, we have an uncommon desire to achieve success," he eloquently stated. "This is what sets us apart." As the meaning of his words sank in, Reid lit another cigarette. "I don't think, I *know* Amaru-here now understands that desire." Again he turned toward me. "How many push-ups did your friends count-out after you challenged me Wednesday morning? A hundred-fifty...a hundred-sixty?"

Beyond revealing he'd heard about my plan to challenge him, Reid also confessed he and three others had placed wagers on whether the Army guy had the balls to go through with it or not. He lost that bet.

As I squatted on a nearby bar-stool, one tall, obviously prideful SEAL stepped close to where Reid was giving his dissertation. His blue eyes blazed under his high-and-tight crew cut; he looked pissed off. Doing his best to not acknowledge my presence, he hooked his thumb at me and spoke in an irritated tone.

"Reid, I know you didn't let this guy take you out?"

"Sergeant-Airbornes broke it up before we could finish," Reid replied. "So out of respect, I felt obligated to give Amaru another chance—right now if he wants it."

Had I waited until the final day of training, it would have been too easy to rationalize I did not need to go through with my promise. For that reason, I decided to deliver my challenge to the pup on Thursday of Jump Week. The only problem was, I didn't know exactly how to do it. Obviously, poking my finger in Reid's chest was no longer something I was considering. This is what I was pondering as we pumped-out the last of our push-ups at Wednesday morning's PT session. While we waited for a black hat to give us the order to recover from the front-leaning rest, all of a sudden, the answer to my enigma became crystal clear. *What better time than the present?*

Peering over at my adversary, Reid seemed to be reading my mind. Once our eyes locked, both of us remained on all fours after everyone else stood up. Never uttering a word, I glared hard at my adversary just as he had done two weeks before.

"In ca-dence…" When I yelled out the military command to initiate an exercise, everyone in the sawdust pit spun around to see what was going on. "Exercise!" I continued before proceeding to count out loud. One, two, three…"

Wearing an inquisitive grin, Reid cranked-out reps to my cadence. He was silent. When I reached twenty, I stopped counting in order to conserve energy, hoping he would take over. But he didn't take the bait; he just remained quiet and kept smiling. Three silent push-ups later, the crowd picked-up the count at twenty-four. At first, it was only a few voices, but seconds later, dozens of trainees joined-in. From our location, in the middle of the pit, it sounded like they were chanting.

By the time we cranked out fifty reps, even the black hats had gathered around to view the commotion. I felt pride hearing many express their shock that the guy mixing-it-up with the SEAL was not a Ranger or a Para-rescuer, but instead just a 'Be-all-you-can-be,' regular-Army soldier.

"Eighty-one…eighty-two…eighty-three…you got 'em Amaru!"

I could hear Wilkins and the CC counting and yelling encouragement my way. Reid's brotherhood, on the other hand, remained deadly silent. They just stared in quizzical fashion.

"Ninety-nine….one-hundred….one-hundred-one…." When the cadence began to slow down, Reid's grin widened.

"Yeah boyeee, keep on grinning 'cause I got a lotta-mo!" Feeling re-energized, I stared back into the eyes of the PT adept.

And he kept smiling too.

"One-hundred-forty-nine.....one-hundred-fifty.....one-hundred-fifty-one….."

Before muscle exhaustion fully set-in, I closed my eyes to concentrate.

"Okay, the show's over! We got formation in thirty seconds, let's move!" shouted a black hat. Then all the sergeant-airbornes likewise started yelling.

Hearing their voices, I opened my eyes and was shocked to see Reid standing next to me with his right-hand extended. *He was still smiling.* So technically speaking, Reid quit first. Nevertheless, to anyone who had a clear view of the spectacle, it was apparent he had conceded out of respect. To this day it remains unclear why he did this. Perhaps he demonstrated this warrior-like chivalry to give the Army population, which accounted for over half of the trainees, something to finally cheer about. What I do know is: I was damn sure happy to see him standing!

I politely declined Reid's rematch but I did accept two cold beers plus ten dollars for taxi fare—the same ten bucks

I'd donated earlier. After Reid and I stepped outside the party, we shook hands for the second time in three weeks. This time the SEAL returned my smile.

As the taxi sped off, I glanced out the window and took my last glimpse of one thorough-ass whiteboy.

Twenty minutes later, the cab stopped in front of an off-post, bar named 'GI Joe's.' Before paying my fare, I popped the cap off the second bottle using the seatbelt's clasp. During the drive, 'George,' as the friendly driver had introduced himself, explained he was an ex-paratrooper who had graduated from Airborne School back in the '60s. In our short conversation, he also mentioned he had the dubious distinction of experiencing the loss of both his T-10 and reserve parachute on a jump.

In order to keep the trainee's focus fresh, the black hats had told and re-told horror stories about 'crashing and burning' via the infamous *double malfunction.* The nightmare of every trooper, the only difference between George's narrative and the sergeant-airborne's was, the cabbie had survived to tell his hair-raising tale.

According to my man George, when his artillery unit got deployed above Laos in response to the bloody *TET Offensive,* both of his parachutes failed to open. With nothing to brake his fall, the 180 mph PLF into the side of a mountain left him partially paralyzed from the waist down.

"That's why I didn't get out to open your door."

Listening to the details of the grim episode, I concluded that George had recited his terrifying account hundreds of times to recent Jump School graduates just like me. Despite sensing the scam, the fact this able-bodied cab driver was clever enough to stimulate gratuities while avoiding carrying his patron's luggage brought a crooked smile to my face. Taking another sip of my free beer, I reminisced on some of the details which had paved the way to the very spot I found myself in. I had to admit I was pretty fortunate. With this in mind, I dug deeper into my pocket for an additional ten dollar bill. More than tipping George for his story-telling ability, I was paying homage to the game called 'getting over.'

"All the Way!" Beaming an almost toothless grin, the taxi-man saluted me when he received the monetary offering.

"Airborne!" I replied, returning his salute as the cab took off.

There were a lot of people standing in the bar's parking lot. While I crossed the street, I overheard a strange, high-pitched voice. It sounded like the guy was speaking in falsetto.

"Yo, yo, who's that guy who just got out the taxi?" Then a different person, who sounded like Wilkins, asked another question.

"Is that Amaru? Or McKnight?"

"I'm not sure," replied the first person before switching to his normal voice. "All those darkies are starting to look alike…just ask Stew!"

When this was yelled by none-other-than Mick himself, the crowd of Delta Company graduates—both black and white—busted-out laughing.

Hearing my friend's voices, I began walking in the direction of the loud boozers but I still had not located them.

"Look at him," yelled the voice I was sure was

Wilkins'. "Blind as a bat without his birth-control glasses. Yeah that must be Amaru!"

From their voices I knew who was there even though I had not found them yet. Turning my head, I finally spotted Wilkins waving his arms to get my attention as another round of laughter erupted. Having pinpointed their whereabouts, I smiled before breaking into a jog. Upon joining my Delta Company comrades, I gave Mick a pound and was about to dive into a round of dozens with Wilkins. This is when another, more authoritative voice, startled everyone by yelling *my* name.

"Private Amaru! Front and center—*move!*"

Hearing this, I immediately became conscious of the beer in my hand while recalling Top's warning about taking it easy tonight. He had especially emphasized all those underage. With my groove busted, I squinted my eyes in the direction of the unfamiliar voice. Barely able to make out the blurred silhouette of a melanin-rich gentleman standing under a lamp post, I was relieved he was not wearing a uniform. Once the man started walking toward us, I noticed he was a little shorter than me. The remnants of grey hair along the edges of his short afro revealed he was in his fifties. More confused than ever, my thoughts raced, considering every possibility. Yet, it was not until he arrived and extended his hand to greet me when the mystery unraveled. Spying his youthful grin, it somehow jolted a genetic vibration within me.

"You're my Uncle Mattias, aren't you?"

Uncle Mattias

Although I wanted to meet my uncle and had done much to arrange the encounter, I never thought it would happen. After all, considering Kay and I had never met any of our relatives, like children often do, I was convinced something must be wrong with us.

I recalled my father saying one of his brothers had retired from the Army and settled down a few miles outside of Ft. Benning, so on the day I received my orders for Airborne School, I called Kay from Ft. Lee to confirm if this was true or not.

Even after writing down his phone number, I was hesitant about making the call. Just thinking about how to introduce myself was embarrassing enough. What was I going to say? 'Hi, I'm your long-lost nephew from New Jersey. We never met before, but I happened to be in town and thought I'd stop by.' Therefore, to stall for time, I made a promise to call during Jump Week—if I made it that far. I figured by then, I'd know what to say.

On the Thursday evening following our fourth jump, I was on cloud 9. Not only was graduation a day away, I was also celebrating my success with Stew from that afternoon. In addition, I had already earned my stripes by confronting Reid so there was no pressure to do any push-ups that night. In short, my confidence was soaring. With my promise to contact my uncle in mind, I grabbed my phone book on the way out of the barracks.

"Ay, where you going?" Mick asked.

"I gotta call someone, I'll be right back." Replying thus, I entered a phone booth, leaving Mick sitting under a star-filled, Georgia night.

After pulling out my phone book and inserting the coins, I placed the call. Nine rings later, a man's recorded voice revealed I had reached the Amaru residence before politely requesting I leave a message after the beep. Still undecided on what to say, I simply stated my name, the fact I was his brother's son, and that I planned to celebrate my Airborne graduation at GI Joe's on Saturday night. Since I failed to specify a time, I never expected him to show up.

"Wait!" my uncle spoke in a stern tone, "don't sit down yet." This sudden warning symbolizes my lasting impression of my father's younger brother: he was a hard-working man who didn't take no shit.

Waiting outside the passenger side of his silver, '81 Cutlass, I watched my uncle climb into the driver's side and reach for a small towel lying on the passenger's seat. Removing the cloth, he revealed a grey .357 snub-nose revolver.

"To hell with a credit card," my uncle stated while inserting the pistol into the glove box. "I never leave home without one of these."

Unsure of how to respond, I chuckled and said nothing; so I was glad my uncle filled the void by making his point clearer.

"Down here boy, you gonna need some firepower for them racist-ass crackas. You in the deep-south now!"

Before going to my uncle's house, we stopped at my barracks. Because I was scheduled to leave the following morning and I had to wear my Class A uniform on the bus, I packed my duffel bags and took all my stuff with me. During our thirty-five minute drive, we became acquainted rather quickly, and were having a good time until he rocked the boat with another peculiar comment.

"You look just like your daddy when he was your age."

I did not agree. Even though my sire was regarded as good-looking, it was my animosity for the Serpent which made me resent his opinion. From that point, I was quiet for the rest of the ride.

Arriving to his modest three-bedroom home, he introduced me to his wife, Renata, and their daughter, Kendra. Like me, Kendra was shy, but my aunt hugged me like we had known each other for years. Looking at them, it was obvious they were mother and daughter. Kendra was a slightly darker-skinned version of her mother. Both women were average height, heavy-set, and had their perm-straightened hair pulled back into a small bun. After getting a good look at all three of them in the light, I decided people would never guess we were related. Once my aunt released me, I was overtaken by a tantalizing aroma billowing-in from the kitchen. I almost replied 'yes' before my aunt asked me if I was hungry.

Barely hearing her apologies for only having left-overs, the barbecue chicken, potato salad, and collard greens treated my taste buds to heights and delights which truly nourished my soul. While the three of them asked questions about my family, I gorged down my first serving and was working on my second plate. The food was so good, it was difficult to chew and speak at the same time. Of course, I did not want to exhibit bad table manners, so I asked a question, hoping to get a few minutes to munch while someone else talked.

"I never met any relatives before. Can y'all tell me something about our family?"

"Sure," my aunt responded before asking another question. "What do you wanna know?".

"Um, anything. Do you have any pictures?"

"Of course we do," replied my uncle. "The Amaru's, with the exception of your family, are tight. We're like these four fingers." To illustrate his meaning, he raised his hand with his fingers extended. "And your family," saying this he closed the same hand into a fist, flipped out his thumb, and wiggled it. "This is your family." Following a hearty chuckle, he gestured at Kendra. "Bring over them photo albums and a bottle of rum…the good stuff."

While my uncle spoke, I savored the last morsels on my plate. Although I wanted more, I thought it would be rude to ask for a third helping. Sitting there, I wondered how I was able to survive on the bland, mess-hall rations. When my cousin returned to the living room, she put three binded albums down in front of my uncle. Then she surprised me by handing me another plate of food. I thought the dish she was holding was for her.

"By the way you put away that last helping, it seemed you weren't done yet," my cousin said. In spite of her serious expression, I suspected she was being friendly because I could see a hint of a smile glinting from the edges of her eyes. "Gimme the other plate," she said revealing more of a grin.

"Thanks Kendra," I showed my appreciation and returned her sheepish grin. After accepting the dish and a fresh napkin, I gave her the empty plate.

"Boy, you ain't gotta feel bashful around here. Eat as much as you like. You're kinfolk," my uncle assured me.

Together we looked at photo-after-photo. I saw lots of Kendra's baby pictures, which was to be expected since she was an only-child. My uncle described other people in the photos as your cousin so-and-so, or your daddy's friend from Alabama. About five pages later, he came to a face resonating an almost irresistible glow. It was a head-shot of a young airman adorned in his Air Force blues. Since the blues were the Air Force's equivalent of our Class-A uniform, I deduced it was a graduation photo. Although I did not recognize the man, I instinctively felt something in common with him. His aura reminded me of something residing deep within.

"Now tell me you ain't the splittin' image of your daddy when he was your age!"

Astonished into silence, I found it difficult to speak; so I just nodded my head.

Noting my utter disbelief, my uncle laughed before placing the album on the table next to me. With his hands unburdened, he picked up the bottle Kendra brought from the kitchen and cracked the seal. "This here's Jamaica's best rum. It's called Appleton Estate," he declared. "How do you take your drink?"

"Some ice and a little tonic please," I responded with my eyes still glued to the glossy page.

I remained this way until Kendra took my plate without being asked. With the space in front of me empty, I slid the album over and continued staring at the dreamlike reflection of my own identity. I was still wearing a dumbfounded expression.

"I knew you didn't agree with me back in the car so I wanted to show you this picture," my uncle stated as he poured two glasses. "That photo was taken just after your daddy finished basic training, so y'all about the same age."

When my aunt went into the kitchen to help Kendra wash the dishes, my uncle handed me my glass. Then he rose from his chair, clicked the lamp brighter, and compared my face with the one in the black-and-white photo. "What I tell ya," he verbally patted himself on the back. "Y'all got the same mouth, the same smile...and that same proud look in your eyes."

Having grown up the victim of countless, chinky-eyed jokes, the part about our eyes being similar was difficult to swallow. That is, until I re-examined the photo.

"Before we joined the service," Uncle Mattias chuckled, *"Bubba* used that devilish grin of his to flirt with the girls in town. Yeah your daddy was a real ladies' man. He was always dancing and singing until…" Suddenly his face became rigid. "He served two tours in Vietnam. One of 'em to get me outta that hellhole."

"Two tours?" I said confused. "You mean he volunteered to stay there?" I found this hard to believe.

Instead of responding, my uncle raised his glass and made a toast. "Here's to that proud bastard!" he said, sounding emotional. "Because of him, Renata was spared the life of a young-widow and Kendra grew up knowing her father." My uncle went on to explain that since his infantry battalion had a much more perilous mission than my father's Air Force squadron, Bubba approached his commander to request permission to do a double-tour: one for his service to his country, and the other on behalf of his younger brother. "The Department of Defense had regulations which stated two family members were not permitted to fight at the same time. It was called the 'Sole Survivor Policy'," my uncle explained. "But you know rules like that are usually only reserved for *honkies.* To be honest, I still don't know how your daddy pulled that off." After we clinked glasses, my uncle dimmed the lights to their normal setting and returned to his seat. Then he finished his story. "Exactly two days after I flew back state-side, I was informed my platoon had been completely wiped-out in an ambush. Not a single soldier survived."

For a fleeting instant, we were no longer relatives; we were just two soldiers. The significance of my father's actions needed no further explanation.

In the next three hours, we poured libations in honor of my father's bravery over and over again. During this time, Uncle Mattias talked about growing up in the '30s and '40s as the son of an Alabama sharecropper.

"Back then, crackas didn't have to pretend they liked you," he said before draining his glass and just as quickly refilling it. "We didn't have no running water, no modern appliances," saying this he bursts-out laughing. "Instead, we had an out-house and a well in the backyard; but it wasn't all bad. You need a refill?"

"Nah, I'm okay," I replied.

"Even though we were dirt poor," Mattias resumed, "we didn't know it because we had each other. We were a family. We had everything we needed to live right there on our land. We had chickens, cows, goats, vegetables…and three boys to work in the fields with daddy, and two girls to help mama in the kitchen."

After my uncle explained what it was like living on a farm, he segued into what I really wanted to hear. He offered his opinion on the origin of my sire's nature: the genealogy of the Serpent. He blamed it on a lady named Ms. Ida. She was one of their neighbors.

"Ms. Ida was always saying your daddy was the best-looking boy in town. This went to his head, ya see."

According to my uncle, Ms. Ida spoiled Bubba rotten in her role as one of the surrogate mothers to the neighborhood children.

"It got to the point that you couldn't even disagree with him because Ms. Ida always took his side. She didn't bother me none though," my uncle explained, refilling our glasses. "I argued with Bubba anyway. But I knew if he got upset, I had to grab something: a stick, an axe, a knife— anything for protection—cause your daddy was strong as a mule!" After playfully demonstrating by snatching the bottle of rum by its neck, he resumed. "He was built just like our daddy...your granddaddy. Plus, that boy's head was harder than any man's fist, so you had to find something—quick!"

Hearing this, I remembered my trusty Easton bat and nodded. "I know."

Listening to Uncle Mattias' account reminded me of something my father said about his childhood. One of the few family occasions my family observed was Christmas dinner. Since we ate in the early-afternoon before my father went to work, it was closer to being a Yule-tide lunch. At one such meal, my father claimed folks in his day followed the African tradition, 'It takes an entire village to raise one child.' "Any adult in my neighborhood could give any of us kids an ass-whipping if they caught us doing something we wasn't supposed to be doing," he had emphasized. "Then we got another beatin' when we got home!"

"I know you heard Bubba was a helluva football player, right?" my uncle asked.

"Yeah," I replied.

"That boy earned two scholarships. One of 'em was from Grambling. I can't remember where the other one was from, but back in the '50s if a negro got a scholarship it was a big deal. Well, in high school, once your daddy became a star athlete, he was convinced his shit didn't stink no mo'!"

As the evening progressed into the early-morning hours, I was astounded by much of what I'd heard. *Singing and dancing? Ladies' man? Bubba?* Before nodding off to sleep, drunk off my ass, I discovered two things. Besides my newfound respect for 'my daddy,' I recalled hearing one of my uncles had a drinking problem. Now I knew for sure which one.

"Tak, Tak…"

Feeling a hand nudging my shoulder, I opened my eyes and barely made out the image of my uncle cracking the seal on another fifth.

"Young buck, I know you ain't done already," he smacked my arm with a grin. "We just getting started!"

The next morning I woke-up feeling reborn. I dreamt I died during the night but my spirit had relentlessly wandered through the cosmos in search of my paratrooper avatar. Sitting up on the couch, I looked around at my unfamiliar surroundings and was confused as to my whereabouts. As I continued to scan the room, I spotted *two* empty bottles in front of my uncle's slumbering body. This conjured-up images of the previous night's events. *"Damn!"* I whispered with a grin while stretching my arms and yawning as I realized he had downed the other bottle all by himself after I passed out. Then I removed the blanket someone had placed on me and rose to my feet wondering which way the bathroom was. Looking around the room, I happened to glance at a clock hanging over the entrance to the kitchen. Seeing it was twenty-minutes-past-nine, I was suddenly panic-stricken because first formation was at nine o'clock.

"Oh shi—!"

"Relax!" Stirring in his La-Z-Boy recliner, my uncle

again used his authoritative military tone to get my attention. "I called your company two hours ago and told them you'd be missing formation."

"What?" This was my only response thinking I must still be dreaming. There was no way my retired uncle could call my CQ desk to excuse my absence.

"Still don't believe in your old uncle, huh boy? Listen, I was a GI before you were born. You know I retired an E-8, don't you?"

"I know you're an Army veteran." Although I stated this respectfully, I was unable to see how this piece of trivia might serve to keep my ass out of a sling. Not to mention get me on a bus to Ft. Bragg this morning.

Seeing I was struggling to maintain my calm, Uncle Mattias chuckled before putting my worries to rest. "Me and your first-sergeant...Crawford's his name, right?"

"Yeah."

"Me and Crawford were stationed together in Korea. I was his platoon sergeant." Saying this, my uncle started laughing. "Long story made short, he claims I saved his life." As he laughed again, I watched the war veteran peep into the past. "Anyway, I called him after hearing your message. He confirmed you were graduating." Now pointing at me from his brown recliner, he answered my next question before I could spit it out. "Soldier, all you gotta do is make it to your bus, and it leaves at eleven." Glancing at the clock, he closed the discussion. "So we gotta get moving."

Stepping out of the shower, I was assaulted by another

delicious aroma. This time, it was that of a southern-style breakfast. As it wafted into the bedroom where I got dressed, I hurriedly polished my jump-boots with my uncles' shoe-shine kit. Following the thirty-second sham job, I donned my Class A jacket and beret before running downstairs.

"Umm, umm. Lord, if you ain't every bit as handsome as your daddy was in his uniform!"

"Thank you Aunt Renata," I replied while she and my cousin stared like they were seeing a ghost.

"What about me?" my uncle complained. "I have the same uniform!"

"Mattias stop actin' like a chile," his wife playfully admonished like she was his mother.

"Daddy, you know you look handsome in your uniform too!" Kendra came to the aid of her father.

As everyone enjoyed a chuckle, I joined the ladies at the dining table. Unwilling to pass up any opportunity for a delicious home-cooked meal, I rapidly ingested two, lavish servings of eggs, grits, toast, and waffles. When I saw my uncle reaching for his car keys, I knew it was time to go. Wiping my mouth, I stood up and hugged the only relatives I ever met.

After grabbing my duffel bags, I followed my uncle outside and got into his car. While I was waving good-bye from the passenger seat, I felt a nudge on my arm. Looking at my uncle, I watched him open a pint of Bacardi.

"Take a sip of this," he said, "it'll get rid of your hangover."

"No thanks."

I waved one last time before Uncle Mattias finished backing out of the driveway. Minutes later, when we screeched to a stop at a traffic light, I was reminded my uncle was drunk; so I buckled my seatbelt.

"Don't worry," my uncle assured me. "This is my old route to Benning and I always drank on the way to work."

When the light turned green, he put his Cutlass to the test. Although the ride to his home had taken over a half an hour, seventeen minutes later, we waved at the MPs manning the gate before again speeding-off in the direction of the Airborne School.

While I considered how to thank my uncle for his hospitality, I noticed several buses were departing the barracks area. Once we stopped in the parking lot across from the *only remaining* bus, I jumped out of the car and ran around to the driver's side to hug my uncle.

"You gotta hurry!" warned my uncle as he released me.

Snatching my duffel bags from the back seat, I dashed toward the huge vehicle while my uncle yelled and frantically waved his arms to get the driver's attention. When the bus closed its doors and started moving, I was worried until I saw someone step in front of it with his hands raised. Without my glasses on, it looked like the guy was wearing a white, Dixie paper-cup on his head. Then the blurry silhouette walked to the door and spoke with the bus driver.

Seeing this, I decelerated to a jog.

Once the Naval NCO finished talking to the driver, he turned toward me. "Come-on McKnight!" he yelled, "if you don't hurry, you'll have to hitch a ride to Bragg!"

As I arrived near the bus, the door opened and out popped Wilkins. "Gimme your duffel bags," he said after approaching me. Then he whispered something. "Put on your glasses."

"What's up with you?" I asked, thinking he was acting

194

strange.

Wilkins never responded nor did he look at me. After he took my bags he quickly disappeared into the bus before I could repeat my question. With my hands empty, I followed his advice and removed the glasses from my pocket. As I put them on, the NCO-in-charge of our departure stepped into my path.

"Private McKnight, congratulations on a job well-done!" The short sailor boomed with his right-hand extended.

Hearing this familiar voice, I focused on the bright, white hat, along with the rest of the iconic, naval uniform made famous by that spinach-eating sailor, *Popeye*.

"And umm," he continued, "about the other day, no hard feelings, okay?"

"Airborne, Petty Officer Stewart!" I cheerfully replied.

Shaking hands with my nemesis for the past two weeks, I feared this gung-ho guy might try to tackle me once he realized he'd been clowned but there was no way to stop Billy from exacting his revenge. Once I released his hand, I stepped passed him and closed the chapter on Airborne School in style.

"By the way…" Saying this, I turned around to face him. Now standing next to the bus's door, I felt bold. "Why the hell do you keep calling me McKnight?" I inquired in a pompous tone before imitating the incident which occurred on Thursday. "If you look at my name tag," I said pointing at my chest. "You can clearly see my name is *A-ma-ru.*" While his eyes were transmitting this information through his nervous system, I elevated myself onto the bus. "April Fools," I teased, unleashing my wise-guy grin along with a wink.

As Stew's jaw touched the pavement for the second time in three days, numerous voices from inside the bus yelled, "Let's go!" The driver, no doubt an Army veteran, realized he was going to be alone with the occupants of this bus for the next several hours, so he obeyed. Cranking the door shut, he sped off.

"Hey Stewart!" Wilkins screamed after sticking his head out the window. "Don't feel bad. That shit Amaru pulled wasn't even fair. Everyone knows it's still the last week of March…but he gotcha sucka!"

Needless to say, the entire bus erupted into laughter. This was just another reminder that karma had a sick sense of humor indeed.

Chapter 10: Ft. Bragg, North Carolina

"Amaru, the game's about to start," Wilkins yelled down the hallway.

Seeing him with a brown towel wrapped around his torso and a toothbrush sticking out his mouth, he resembled an Aborigine wearing a loincloth. As I laid another slab of wax on the floor, I shouted back. "Man, I might not get there 'til the second half."

"Damn, you're slow as hell!" Then Wilkins began laughing. "See, that's the penalty for all that gettin' over while everyone else was working," he replied. He was still mumbling when he disappeared into the latrine. "You don't even know how to use that buffer."

Well, that was not exactly true.

Two days after arriving at Ft. Bragg's 19th Replacement Center, everyone received their respective unit assignments. Wilkins and I, being the only CC members with orders for the 82nd Airborne Division, were transferred to the 82nd Replacement Center. On our first night there, I was assigned to buff the floor. Once the NCO-in-charge of the details saw me approaching the buffer like I'd never seen one before, he became perplexed.

"Can't see how it's possible for a private, fresh outta AIT, to *not* know how to use a buffer," commented Sgt. Watlington with a quizzical grin. "You must be one of those slick negroes…" With his arms folded, he nodded his head,

197

"Amaru, I'm gonna do you a favor and get you 'caught up to speed' on the finer details of polishing a military floor."

"Clear Sergeant," I replied never making a fuss.

Unlike Stew, it was obvious this melanin-rich E-6 could easily see 'beyond my glasses.' Under Sergeant Watlington's tutelage, I waxed the floors every night I was there. And I didn't mind. The reason for this was, ever since I sprained my wrist playing around with a buffer at Ft. Lee, I wanted to figure out how it worked.

From the first time I saw one, I was amazed at how this heavy-duty, polishing apparatus appeared to float inches above the ground. It seemed to operate along the same principle as *Luke Skywalker's land-speeder.* Somehow able to dodge this science-fiction-like chore in basic, I had assigned the detail every evening as a squad-leader in AIT. Yet, I had never buffed a floor myself.

The trick, *Sgt. Watts* taught me, was how to be in-sync with the rhythm of the spinning disk. Rotating in a clock-wise direction, once I mastered the balancing act, it was easy to maneuver the heavy, circular brush from side-to-side. Soon, the machine was doing all the work, with me merely guiding it from behind.

"Now that you stopped fighting the damn thing, you gettin' good!" Standing behind me with both hands in his pockets, the smile on the NCO's face indicated he was pleased he had startled me. Standing a full inch shorter than me, with his beady eyes and round face, he reminded me of an owl. "Syracuse is spanking that ass!" he said wearing a confident grin. "It's still early but…" Pausing here, Sgt. Watts looked down the hall again. "By the looks of things around here, you ain't gon' see none of the first half. But don't worry, I'll keep you posted." Before leisurely strolling into the latrine, Sgt. Watts made one more comment. "Oh, and by the way, I want my cash tonight!"

During my 'how-to-buff' crash-course with Sgt. Watlington, he and I began enjoying our time together in brotherly fashion. Once I learned he was a die-hard Syracuse fan, I deliberately tread on sacred ground by declaring, "no team coached by a no-body like Jim Boeheim is gonna defeat Bobby Knight, a.k.a. 'the General,' in the NCAA Championship."

"Get off his dick!" he had shot back at me.

And before I knew what happened, I'd agreed to a twenty-dollar wager. Later, Sgt. Watts came to his senses and changed the bet to five dollars. This is the difference between a 'friendly bet' and a possible violation for fraternizing with a private. Despite the reduced stakes, should Indiana come up on the short end, I still did not have enough money to pay him.

Although Sgt. Watts only stood to earn a couple bucks if the *Orangemen* trounced the *Hoosiers,* he had hyped-up the collection of 'his cash' for the past two days. He was so sure Derrick Coleman and Sherman Douglass would man-handle the All-American boy, Steve Alford and his no-name crew, whenever he saw me, he communicated his loyalty to Syracuse in one way or another. His favorite method included performing a musical jingle. Pretending to jog in formation, he'd sing his rendition of a well-known, running cadence

"If you think Indiana's gotta chance Monday, the Orangemen say F-that—No Way!"

Like some of my punch-lines, his brand of humor was *so* pathetic it moved the listener to laughter instead of scorn. Especially when the down-to-earth NCO capped-off his 'corniness' with a generic sound-effect as he pantomimed pulling back a cash-register's lever. *"Ching-ching!"*

Since I knew Sgt. Watts would be inspecting the floors the following morning, I made sure they were sparkling like sapphire diamonds before calling it quits. In spite of my overwhelming desire to see General Bobby outwit another coach with his usual squad of marginally-talented players, since me and Wilkins were supposed to meet Mick on *Smoke Bomb Hill* later, I decided to shower before checking-out what remained of the game.

After putting on a black, Pierre Cardin sweat suit, which represented half of my civilian outfits, I scraped two-dollars-and-thirty-eight-cents from the bottom of my drawer. This was all the money I had. Closing my locker door, I thought about borrowing three bucks from Wilkins in case Indiana lost. That's when it occurred to me why Sgt. Watts had insisted on collecting his money tonight. *Payday's in a couple days...that means Wilkins ain't got no cash either!* I lamented. As I poured the change into my pocket, I realized this was a bet I literally could not afford to lose.

Being broke the final two weeks of each month was the obvious drawback to allotting a hundred dollars to the GI Bill, plus another two-hundred-eighty to my brother. I loaned Ken this money so he could take advantage of his "can't miss" tips on the stock market. He promised to return fifteen percent on top of any money I sent him. My brother claimed this was triple the interest-rate guaranteed by banks. For Ken, his motivation to engage in this business-venture was he got to keep any money remaining after our agreed-upon amount. In order to hold up my end of the bargain, I learned to live like a pauper because after taxes I was left with only about ninety bucks.

Passing through the door separating 'March Madness'

with the run-of-the-military routine, I entered the day-room just in time to see a lucky shot barely roll in the basket by the Orangemen captain, Howard Triche. As a round of applause—led by Sgt. Watts himself—stung my eardrums, I scanned the television screen. Considering how consistently the Syracuse-dominated-room had been cheering all evening, I imagined the Hoosiers were losing.

"What's the score?" I asked to no one in particular. Despite almost shouting my question, I was ignored until the spellbound, sports enthusiasts realized it was the lone Indiana fan who was making the request.

"Ching-ching!" slurred Sgt. Watts in a loud voice. "That's all you need to know."

While not quite drunk, the E-6 was definitely under the influence of the now-empty bottle of lager rolling around under his feet. Seconds later, Triche stepped to the line and sank one of two free throws. This gave Syracuse a narrow, three-point lead. Confident his team was in control, the sergeant started teasing me.

"Uh-oh, look y'all, the president of the Bobby Knight fan club finally finished buffing the floor. Amaru, you got here just in time..."

Yeah, to get paid!

With thirty seconds left, even after Keith Smart cut the lead to one with an exciting fast-break-layup, the high-spirited NCO continued to babble non-stop. However he, along with the entire day-room, became engulfed in silence when Keith again majestically elevated from sixteen-feet along the left base line. After Smart connected on what became known as 'the Shot,' I actually felt bad for Sgt. Watts. The awkwardness of the moment brought to mind an old-school memory at Wayne's house.

201

One day, out of the blue, Wayne asked me if I knew how to play chess. When I responded yes, he ran into his bedroom and returned holding a wooden chess set. "I'm sick of listening to my step-father brag about how good he is," Wayne complained. "Can you teach me how to play?"

"I could but I gotta better idea," I replied. "Let's go." Without any explanation, I took Wayne to the public library to find a book on chess. Luckily, the librarian was an avid chess player herself. She showed us a book which illustrated a nifty, four-move, checkmate strategy called 'Scholar's Mate.' Together, Wayne and I practiced the moves until we could execute them without thinking. Although they could be done in a variation of sequences, the basic idea remained the same: to attack using the queen and bishop.

I assumed Wayne wanted to beat his father himself but I was wrong. Instead, he bet his step-dad ten dollars that *I* could beat him and invited me to come over one Saturday afternoon. Of course, I knew nothing about his plan until I arrived at his house. Once Wayne put me on the spot, there was nothing I could do but play.

At first, I pretended I was contemplating my moves but when Wayne's father started cracking jokes, calling me the 'Fake Genius,' I became determined to slay him. Barely five minutes into the match, while Wayne's two sisters were enthusiastically cheering for their dad, I put Mr. Robinson in checkmate. Similar to the basketball game, since both Wayne and I were dead-broke, that sticky situation was also a must-win scenario. If I remember correctly, we used the winnings to get into a high-school jam, featuring the funky-fresh, SOS deejays on the 'wheels of steel.'

With Wilkins riding shotgun at my side, I took a ceremonious bow in front of the disappointed spectators before walking over to where Sgt. Watlington was sitting. While I was standing in front of him waiting to receive 'my cash,' I listened to Wilkins be his usual, annoying self.

"Oh Sergeant Watts, say it ain't so," he cried out with both palms stuck to his forehead. "Please tell me my homie ain't got you digging in your pockets like that!"

All the Way...Airborne!

"It's easier to squeeze blood from a rock than to get pussy from any of these wenches in *Fayette-nam!*"

This is how my new roommate, PFC Schwartz, responded to my question about the 'female situation' in Fayetteville.

"You ready?" Schwartz said, grabbing one of my duffel bags once I finished laughing.

"Yeah let's go, and thanks for carrying that," I said showing my appreciation.

With the additional bag of TA-50 we received at the reception center, there was no way I could carry all three duffel bags by myself.

"It's nothing," he replied, "we're roommates now."

Once I shouldered the other two, I followed him toward the barracks area. As we passed the 505th Parachute Infantry Regiment headquarters, I gawked at a statue of their mascot, surprised it was a black panther.

"Just a little further," he assured me, pointing at the first of four huge structures we were approaching. "That's our building." Upon entering the barracks, Schwartz greeted the CQ runner without breaking his stride. "What's up Michaels, this is my new roommate, Private Amaru."

"Nice to meet you," I hastily said on my way by, in my attempt to keep up with Schwartz.

After racing by the CQ desk, we bounded up three flights of stairs. "We're in the third squad, we live on the third floor, and we're in room three-oh-three," Schwartz explained sounding slightly winded. "Oh, and our room happens to be the third door on the right, so everything's easy to remember."

When Schwartz stopped walking and talking, I checked the door to confirm the room number. 303. My lower-back was aching, so I set both bags down. Then I noticed Schwartz was searching all his pockets, almost in a panic. He seemed to be having difficulty locating his key.

"What's the matter? You lost your key?" I asked him.

"Yeah, I can't find it," he groaned. "You got yours, right?"

"Yeah," I responded glancing down the hallway of my new home trying not to appear disgruntled. I was far from pleased with the living conditions.

"Can you open the door?" Schwartz asked, breaking through my silent complaints.

"Ahh, yeah no problem," I responded after focusing on what he was saying.

Putting my hand into my pocket, I grabbed the key I received from Schwartz minutes ago but I did not pull it out right away because something seemed fishy. When I spied a devilish grin on Schwartz's face, I really got suspicious. His expression did not match the grumpy sound of his voice in the least.

"Damn, I can't find my key either," I lied, determined to wait him out. And just as I thought, once I did not produce my key right away, his mysteriously turned up.

"We're in luck, I found mine," he proclaimed. "Here you go." Saying this, Schwartz offered me his key chain, wanting me to open the door. Looking over at him, I recognized he was straining to keep a straight-face.

"You gottit," I said gesturing toward the lock and taking a step back. "After you PFC." I didn't know what was going on but there was no way I was going to enter that room first.

Hearing my reply, Schwartz seemed a bit rattled. Thanks to this small hint, I was prepared by the time he slid the key into its slot. When the door swung open, I peered into the dark cavity but I did not move. Even after Schwartz disappeared inside, I remained in the hallway.

"Schwartz," I almost yelled. "Where you at? Turn on the light."

All of a sudden, the grinding clash of a heavy-metal, guitar-solo blared-out from the blackness. For the next five seconds, I stood there wondering what was going on. Then just as abruptly as the noise started it subsided and the lights were switched-on, revealing eleven screaming people.

"Surprise Cherry! Hahahahaha!"

Hearing my name mixed-in amidst the ensuing confusion, I dejectedly crossed out any possibility we entered the wrong room.

"Alright, alright, turn that mess down!" After the grinning, brown-skinned man in his mid-thirties yelled this playfully, he turned toward me and spoke in a serious tone. "Private Amaru, welcome to the third-of-the oh-five. I'm Staff Sergeant Quick, your platoon sergeant."

Hearing both Schwartz and now my platoon-sergeant call our brigade the 'oh-five,' I deduced this is how everyone referred to the 505th. Before I could reply, I had to side-step a tall, Caucasian man who was pushing his way into the crowded room. On his face was a look of urgency.

"Chief, what a pleasant surprise," Sgt. Quick greeted the tall soldier wearing horn-rimmed frames. "Amaru, this is Chief Warrant Officer Richards."

Without ever acknowledging my presence, the studious-looking man with flecks of silver streaking his mane made an announcement which ended my welcome celebration.

"Gentlemen, we've been called out!"

18 hours... anywhere in the world! This is the well-known slogan that advertises the 82nd Airborne's next-day service to transport thousands of Assassins from the Sky anywhere on God's green earth. It was just my luck, on the day of my arrival, the oh-five was in DRF-1, which is the most critical stage of the mission-cycle. This meant our brigade was temporarily set free of all demands except for its ability to mobilize in a moment's notice. Being 'called out' meant an Emergency Deployment Readiness Exercise had been initiated. During EDREs, even our supervisors were not informed if we were jumping into an actual, combat situation or just practicing. If it turned out to be a drill, that usually led to conducting a field-training-exercise. Although many of our FTX's took place right on Ft. Bragg, sometimes we'd find ourselves on a drop-zone in a foreign land. Most people have no idea the United States has well over five-hundred military bases worldwide[5]. Well, paratroopers know this better than anyone.

The next day, minutes before the break of dawn, I was drenched from a terrifying PLF in waist-high seawater. After

---

[5] See *US Military Installations*

gaining my bearings and standing up, I gazed at the shore and immediately realized the paltry number of troopers trudging onto the beach represented only a fraction of the paratroopers who had sat on the runway at Pope AFB the previous evening. While I wondered about the other soldiers' whereabouts, I retrieved my spent parachute before likewise making my way out of the water.

Once I discarded both of my chutes at their respective turn-in points, I looked around for a familiar face. Seconds later, I spotted CWO Richards walking my way after turning-in his reserve parachute so I slowed down to walk with him. Even though this was a practice-drill, we had not been given any official 'All Clear' order. For this reason, to maintain military silence, Chief whispered once he was next to me.

"Bway-nos dee-as. Bene...bene ve-nido al...Porrto Rico," he said in his gringo accent.

Similar to 'Gaijin' in Japan and 'Toubob' in West Africa, 'Gringo' is the pejorative term used by Latinos to describe the melanin-deficient invaders of their homelands.

Initially, I failed to comprehend his gibberish had been in Spanish. "Morning sir," I replied in a soft voice. Together, we walked toward a group of shadowy silhouettes. I abstained from speaking until I heard others talking under their breaths. "Chief," I then whispered, "what happened to the rest of the troopers from last night?" Just as I completed my question the meaning of his opening remarks fully registered. "Hold up," I said a bit louder, "did you say we're in Puerto Rico?" Before Chief Richards could respond, a loud voice sounded off in front of us.

"Company, attention!"

On this command, everyone snapped erect and placed both arms against their sides. As we gazed toward the horizon, a tropical scene befitting a postcard unveiled itself before our awed senses. Watching the morning star boldly ascend its golden stairway to heaven, I'm sure I was not the only one who was mesmerized. The sounds of men's voices snapped me out of my trance just as Sgt. Quick reported our platoon was missing a soldier. Almost simultaneously, a school of dolphins began testing their jumping ability a couple yards offshore. For a few seconds, I watched their playful antics from the corner of my eye. When a human voice was heard over the crescendo of crashing waves, everyone turned their heads to look.

"Get the fuck away from me!" a man screamed at the frolicking, sea mammals. *"Help!"*

Before I had time to get my glasses out, nearly a third of the formation had already dove in the water to rescue their comrade. This is when it occurred to me that whatever social graces these un-colorful characters lacked, they made-up for with an abundance of courage and soldiering skills.

An hour later as everyone sat down to eat our breakfast MREs, out of nowhere, Sgt. Quick tried to pull a fast one on me.

"Amaru, where the hell were you when that paratrooper was in distress? You didn't so much as flinch a muscle to save PFC Ritchey…he could've drowned!"

Detecting a sly grin highlighting Sgt. Quick's angular features, I figured he was joking. Therefore, I responded in kind. Altering my voice to mimic his slightly southern drawl, I pointed back at him. *"Saw-gent,* like you said yesterday after my Cherry Blast orientation..." Seeing a confused look on his face, I cleared my throat. "And I quote: 'Don't do sheeit unless you receive a direct order from me. Nuthin!' Those were *your* orders." When a few chuckles were overheard, I scratched my head in feigned contemplation. "Hmm," I resumed in my normal tone. "Now correct me if I'm wrong, but I don't recall gettin' no orders to save nobody named Ritchey." Turning my head toward the private-first-class in-question, I then sarcastically apologized. "Sorry Ritchey!"

Ritchey, who was viewing my comical parody from a nearby medic tent, where he was receiving treatment for his dolphin bites, busted-out laughing. It seemed everyone—with the exception of Sgt. Q—appreciated my light-hearted humor. Perhaps my supervisor disliked being made the object of the pun. On the other hand, maybe he deemed, after only two days in the oh-five, I was a tad bit too comfortable. Whatever the case, he brushed my comment off without uttering a reply.

Three hours later, Sgt. Quick was still wearing a sour expression when he read from a jump-manifest log and barked-out my name along with his own and two others. After providing details for that evening's pre-jump muster, he released the formation and approached me.

"So Amaru, how do you like the Division so far?"

"I ain't complaining, Sergeant." This was the only phrase that came to mind.

Similar to Reid's SEAL team, the 82nd Airborne adhered to its own rigid code of ethics and conduct. Therefore it was my platoon sergeant's responsibility to initiate me into America's *Guard of Honor*. A big part of this initiation involved senior troopers making the newcomer, i.e. the Cherry, the butt of their jokes. Several times that day, other solders in my platoon tried to play tricks on me. Nothing major, it was more an assortment of meaningless errands and trite one-liners. For example, PFC Ritchey sent me to Sgt. Quick for the keys to someplace called 'Area J.' Considering

209

we had been transported to Muñiz Air Base in the back of a truck after jumping onto this tropical island, something seemed strange about asking for the keys to an 'area.' So when I approached Sgt. Quick, instead of requesting the keys from him like I was supposed to, I asked my NCOIC for permission to go to Area J.

"How the hell are you gonna do that, Private? Area J's on Ft. Bragg—" Then Sgt. Quick realized I tricked him into revealing the secret. "Did someone tell you to get the keys from me?"

"Yeah, Ritchey did. How'd you know?"

Hearing this, the melanin-rich NCO started smiling before explaining that Area J was the name of a training area on Ft.Bragg. "Ritchey should've waited until we got back to the motorpool before using that one," he said slapping his knee in laughter. "You got off easy, Amaru."

Even after this explanation, I still had no idea what he was babbling about. "So how am I supposed to get the keys for it?" I asked in a bewildered tone.

"It's a joke, stupid! It's part of your Cherry Orientation," he said with a snicker.

"Oh," I replied with a look of irritation.

"Don't tell me your angry," Sgt. Quick said, starting to chuckle again.

"Angry? Nah, nah. It ain't that serious," I said shaking my head. "It's just, this shit is corny."

The E-6 made it known he did not appreciate my remarks. "At ease Private!"

By the time dusk settled in, Sgt. Q was sitting next to me at the base of the runway. He still looked upset. During our our monotonous three-hour wait, we were loaded down with two parachutes, a rucksack, and an M-16 strapped to our shoulders. Looking around, I thought we resembled a bale of beached sea-turtles flipped over on their backs. Having no choice but to remain next to Sgt. Q, I decided to strike up a conversation. Since jumping was the Alpha and Omega in Creation for these guys, I used their favorite topic to break the awkward silence. It didn't work.

"Sergeant Q, after only three days in the Deuce, I'm about to have two jumps under my belt already. I heard other airborne-units only jump once every couple of months. Y'all ain't playing around here, huh?"

Rotating his kevlar in my direction, Sgt. Q snapped his cold response. "Shut up Amaru! You're lucky to get your Cherry Blast outta the way so fast. Most troopers gotta wait weeks. Some even longer." Then glaring harder, he recalled my earlier comment. "And anyway, I thought you said you weren't complaining?"

With no one to talk to, I closed my eyes and tried to fall asleep but soon found it was too hot to relax. This caused me to ponder how long I could tolerate the lifestyle of a paratrooper. Although receiving a hundred bucks for jump-pay was a welcome bonus, after experiencing my Cherry Blast, if I had never put my knees in the breeze again, it would have been fine with me.

Far from being gung-ho, the only reason I signed-up for Airborne in the first place had been to cancel my orders to far-off, Ft. Riley, Kansas—*which was way too far from Asia!* Now that I had been permanently stationed at Ft. Bragg, I wondered if terminating my jump-status would result in getting sent to a different post, or just down the street from the oh-five to another brigade?

Sgt. Quick

In fairness, I must admit Sgt. Quick taught me a lot in his brief time as my supervisor. His daily lessons on 'how a young brutha needs to carry himself' became cherished information once I evolved to the point where I desired to shed my delinquent lifestyle. Unfortunately, this change did not occur until several months *after* I left the Division.

Like other NCOs who had been in my chain of command, Sgt. Quick went out of his way to take me under his wing; and his keen military knowledge was easy to recognize. However, our relationship was absent of the respect inherent in my other teacher-student episodes. This was simply because I viewed Sgt. Q as a sell-out.

I recall Sgt. Quick having high standards. In fact, his criterion even eclipsed the prescribed benchmark used by the famed 82nd Airborne. I also remember he demanded this level of dedication from every soldier in his platoon. One unforgettable example illustrating his above-average yardstick was the first time he inspected my weekend latrine detail.

Anyone needing to use the facilities on Sunday knew they were in for an unpleasant experience. Foul odors and overflowing toilets *always* greeted us. Being the lowest-ranking private in my platoon, I was usually assigned the weekend latrine detail. This meant mopping up the vomit, diarrhea, and whatever other putrid gastrointestinal fluids were on the floor and walls. The first time I was assigned to this horrendous chore, I tried to get away with a doing sham job. On Monday morning, when Sgt. Quick arrived to inspect the barracks instead of one of the E-5s in our platoon, I knew

I was in trouble.

After opening the rusty door to the first stall, Sgt. Q started laughing. "Amaru, what the hell is that?" When I failed to respond, he pointed at the toilet. Even amidst the malodor, my NCOIC managed to retain a sliver of a smile. "Please tell me that's not toilet paper sticking out of the drain, is it?" While he asked me this, he took off his BDU shirt and slung it over the door.

Standing behind Sgt. Q, I glanced over his shoulder and spotted the feces-stained paper he was referring to. "Sergeant, I swear I used the plunger and flushed the toilet several times but the water started overflowing—" *What he did next shocked me into silence.*

Without the slightest hesitation, Sgt. Q stepped into the stall, bent down, and stuck his arm into the murky liquid. Standing a few feet behind him, I listened to the NCO hum *'Use ta be My Girl,'* which is a song by the mighty O'Jays. After flushing the toilet twice to confirm the drain was indeed doo-doo free, he produced a rag from his cargo pocket and dried his arm. Then my supervisor grabbed a sponge, a brush, and a bottle of pine-oil before getting down on his hands and knees. He was in such deep concentration he never once looked in my direction until the entire area was damn near spit-shined! By the time Sgt. Q handed me his dripping brush, I noticed he had broken a sweat.

"No excuses...just results," he stated in a grave tone. "Am I making myself clear?"

"Clear Sergeant!" I responded loud enough to create an echo.

Had I not been there to witness this sanitation feat with my own senses, no one could have convinced me it was possible to transform something so vile and disgusting into the sparkling oasis of pine-oil perfection now before me. No bullshit, I could almost hear the sounds of happily chirping birds in that latrine. *Thanks to Sgt. Quick's stellar example, to this very day, I still clean the shit out-of-a toilet!*

In a less brutal society, free from the pressures which naturally accompany a system of biased inequality, I may have benefited much more from this astute man. However in the so-called 'real world,' Sgt. Q was not speaking my language. In spite of his timely African-American, cultural presentations, I did not respect my platoon sergeant. Whenever only the two of us were present, he would give detailed dissertations on every famous negro from Smokey…to Jackie Robinson. It did not take long for me to grow sick-and-tired of these on-the-low, *Soul Train* commemorations. What irked me most about him was how he hid his 'blackness' from everyone except me. This included the three other melanin-rich brothers in our platoon. Why the big secret? I could not understand this, especially because some of his facts were quite impressive. For example, he told me the famous trumpet player, Miles Davis, unknowingly lined his *chakras* up while performing 'rituals with heroin.' According to Sgt. Q, by doing this, Miles was granted access to musical divinations from beyond the cosmos.

When he was saying this to me, I was like: what the fuck is he talking about? Chakras? Rituals? Spiritual entities beyond the cosmos? Yet, ten minutes later, when I walked into the bay to ask him what a 'chakra' was, I found him doubled-over laughing right along with the motorpool's *Hee-Haw* crowd. To me, this easily qualified as intolerable Uncle Tom behavior.

Every company in the awesome war machine known as the Airborne-Infantry was the target of numerous

214

inspections. Living in such a hectic, stressful atmosphere tends to alter people's personalities. For those individuals who failed to humble themselves in accordance with Division Policy, they were summarily kicked out of the Army with a less-than-honorable discharge. After four months of being saturated in a barracks with a cast of characterless hillbillies, I feared that in such a *melanin-deficient* atmosphere, even the coolest brother would eventually be converted into nothing more than a dark-skinned whiteboy.

On a hot, humid day in mid-July, this situation reached its apex following our afternoon formation as I sauntered back to the motorpool with my platoon. Everyone was quiet and had their heads down trying to avoid the sun's glare. For some reason, I looked up and made eye-contact with a private walking in the opposite direction. He was about the same height and complexion as me, which is probably why I noticed him. Whenever I saw any unknown brothers, I always greeted them to see where their heads were at.

Due to the Army's unwritten segregation policy, most melanin-rich soldiers were cordial toward one another. However there was the occasional bourgeois negro who had been turned-out by society. They were easy to distinguish because their level of self-hatred ran so deep they avoided looking at anyone who reminded them they were not Caucasian. Whenever I met one of these soulless creatures, I could hear Brother-Minister Malcolm's voice in my head: *"Who taught you to hate the shape of your nose…your lips? Who taught you to hate the race that you belong to so much you don't want to be around each other?"*

Kelvin Atkins was not one of those folks; in fact he was the complete opposite. Once we made eye contact, he surprised me by running toward me with reckless abandon and snatching me into his arms. After one look, this guy just ran up and hugged me even though we did not know each other. At any other time if a complete stranger would have tried that, he probably would've gotten punched in the face but in this instance I somehow understood Atkins shared my feelings of forlornness.

"Wassup Amaru!" he yelled with a huge grin after he released me and read my shirt. "Cuz, I been on Fort Bragg for two days and you're the first real brother I'n seen since I got here!"

"Word?" I replied a little embarrassed at his enthusiasm. Besides his height and complexion, the next thing I noticed was one of Atkins' front teeth stuck out of his mouth like a beaver. I was happy we were wearing the same unit-flash on our berets because that meant he lived in one the buildings near mine. "What company you in?"

"Charlie," he replied before repeating the same question to me. "You?"

"I'm in HHC." When Atkins looked surprised, I added, "Yeah, I'm not a grunt, I work in the motorpool."

"I just left the motorpool but no one was there," Atkins continued talking to me like no one else was present. "My squad-leader sent me there to get the keys to Area J. Y'all got them over at the motorpool?"

Before I could respond, my whole platoon busted-out laughing.

"Yo Atkins, there ain't no keys for Area J. You're squad-leader's clowning you—"

"Amaru, mind your own business!" yelled Sgt. Q.

"Good afternoon, Sergeant." Only after Sgt. Quick walked over to us did Atkins turn to greet him. "Sergeant, where's Area J?" Atkins asked, looking perplexed.

Instead of answering the question, Sgt. Q continued snickering with the others. Hearing this, I rolled my eyes in their direction without turning my head. "Atkins, I'll tell ya later," I replied on behalf of my NCOIC.

"Bet," he said, understanding my meaning. "But tell me this, my squad-leader's playing me for a fool, right?" Atkins looked angry.

"Don't sweat it, it's just something they like to do around here to newbies. It's part of your orientation." Saying this, I directed my voice toward Sgt. Quick and the others. "Sergeant, is it okay if I show Private Atkins back to his company headquarters? He just got here and I think he's lost."

Even though Sgt. Q looked disgruntled, he did not object. "Okay but hurry up, Amaru. We gotta lot to do this afternoon."

For the next five minutes while we walked, Pvt. Atkins and I got to know one another. After he finished interrogating me about the 'Area J joke,' his entire conversation was about females and going to clubs; which was cool with me. By the time we arrived at the Charlie Company Headquarters, we were friends.

"I gotta jet to the motorpool," I said reluctantly. "What you doing after work? Let's drink some brews later.

"Cool," he responded but we can't do it near here because I'm only nineteen.

"Me too," I replied with a grin. "I'll meet you at your CQ desk if I don't see you in the mess hall at dinner.

"A-ight," Atkins replied.

Then we bumped fists and parted ways. When I got to the motorpool, everyone just stared at me; it appeared they felt threatened by my interaction with Atkins.

"Hey Schwartz, here comes your roommate, the 'real brother'," commented PFC Parker, one of my neighbors in the barracks.

From that moment, day-by-day, the 'black jokes' gradually increased. It took about a week but I eventually got fed up and challenged the same guy, Parker, to a fight one evening. Shocked—not to mention shook—PFC Parker ran downstairs to tell the CQ sergeant.

The following day, CWO Richards and Sgt. Quick interrogated both of us. I was relieved when Parker finally admitted he and a few others had been harassing me. However, my feelings of relief turned into shock when Sgt. Quick accused *me* of being impossible to get along with. Hearing this, I contemplated my chances of getting chaptered-out for failure to adapt were quite good. It might not occur from this incident, I contemplated, but both my uncle and Sgt. Sandoval had warned me that 'failure to adapt' was the excuse the Army used to dismiss undesirables who were not criminals, or outright incompetent. That night, my barracks mates continued to snub me. Seeing this, I knew what had to be done: *I gotta get out of the Division before they kick me out of the Army!*

Convinced of this, the next morning, I requested a meeting with Sgt. Quick.

"A-ight," he complied. "What's up?" When he replied thus wearing an expression of concern, I was surprised. Then I realized with only the two of us present he felt comfortable allowing his 'black side' to show.

"You mean now, Sergeant? You want to talk right now?"

"Yeah. You can drive me on my errands this morning. Tell PFC Ritchey we're taking vehicle H-9."

"That's a hummer right? Who's driving?" I asked excitedly.

"You are of course, Private."

"Bet!" Happy to get a chance to drive one of the Army's new jeeps, I almost forgot the circumstances for our conference.

Minutes later, we were rolling out the motorpool gates.

"Slow down!" Sgt. Quick reprimanded. "We're going to the 782nd for a pick-up. You remember the way?"

"I think so, Sergeant."

Although these hour-plus tours of Ft. Bragg were boring as hell, they almost registered as fun compared to the humdrum monotony of a motorpool.

"So what's up Amaru?" my platoon sergeant finally asked after he filled-out some parts-request forms on the cover of the truck's logbook.

"Sergeant, yesterday I didn't appreciate you accusing me of being 'impossible to get along with'…especially since Parker admitted he was wrong."

"Well if the shoe fits—"

"Sergeant, Parker said he started everything," I reiterated in a louder voice. "He even apologized."

"Amaru, shut-up and listen!" my platoon sergeant yelled. "You still don't get it, do you? That street-life bullshit is over…your 'tough-guy' act won't last in the Army," he said before pointing out the window. "Turn here and enter over there."

Following Sgt. Q's orders, I drove through a beat-up gate with a sign affixed which read '782nd Abn Ord Maint Co.' Although I wanted to resume our conversation, he jumped out at the entrance of the warehouse and told me to come inside after I parked the experiment-on-wheels.

Knowing how fast my platoon sergeant moved, I quickly parked before jogging to the building. Upon entering, I grabbed a wheeled cart at the door and pushed it passed several gated areas until I reached a bin labeled '3/505.' Inside was a mountain-sized pile of vehicle parts. Before getting to work, I scanned the dimly-lit room and spotted Sgt. Quick having a friendly conversation with a warrant officer and two E-7s.

It took two trips to put the thirty-plus vehicle parts into the back of the hummer. My assignment completed, I had a few minutes to close my eyes and relax in the driver's seat before Sgt. Quick walked outside chatting with his colleagues. Listening to him chuckle just a-little-too-loudly, I imagined he was 'shuffling his feet' like he always did whenever he encountered an E-7 or higher—especially if they were Caucasian. By the time he came to the jeep, I was determined to express myself without being interrupted.

"Wake up, Private!" Sgt. Q snapped. When I opened my eyes, I saw him get into the jeep. "Everything loaded up?"

"Clear Sergeant, Airborne."

"Good, let's go," Sgt. Q stated. "I'm starvin' like Marvin and it's almost time for lunch." Declaring this, my NCOIC fastened his seatbelt.

"Clear Sergeant," I responded, starting the engine and putting the jeep into gear. "And I gottit, I know what's been bothering me."

"Oh come on Amaru!" he complained sounding irritated. "I thought that conversation was over with." Then after a brief pause he conceded. "Okay Private, what is it?"

Knowing my opportunity might not last for long, I got directly to the point. "Sergeant Quick, no disrespect, but I don't think it's necessary for us to act like white people anymore. You know…to be accepted."

"Amaru, what the hell are you talking about?" my NCOIC replied before laughing in a nervous manner.

"Sergeant stop playing, you know exactly what I'm talking about." When Sgt. Q continued to feign ignorance, I shrugged my shoulders and explained. "You know," I resumed, "all those extra chuckles back there…your whole performance. Sergeant we're moving toward the nineties," I insisted, "the 'tap dancing days' are over. I think it's okay for us to be ourselves now." Having gotten this off my chest, I sat back and waited for his reply.

"Like I said," Sgt. Q angrily rebutted, "you don't gettit! Amaru, this racial equality bullshit is an idealistic dream that rich college kids—I should say rich, *white* college kids—can afford to hang onto for a couple years. But you, as a poor *black* private damn sure can't."

"I disagree," I cut-in. "Excuse me for interrupting Sergeant but I think you're only talking about the Division, not the entire Army. Here, especially in the infantry brigades, the atmosphere is a bit more, hmm shall we say 'conservative' than it is, for example, on Smoke Bomb Hill."

"You mean those nasty LEGs?"

"Hold up," I replied using a quizzical tone, "everyone outside the Division isn't a LEG. And furthermore, I've been reconsidering this theory about LEGs."

"What're you trying to say?" Sgt. Q asked cynically. "Just spit it out!"

"Okay Sergeant, if you insist." Taking a deep breath, I followed his order. "Perhaps my personality would be less disagreeable to those outside the Division—"

"You mean terminating?"

"If that's what it takes Sergeant," I responded.

Similar to the Salem Witch Trials, if even a rumor hatched that a paratrooper was considering terminating his jump-status, while not enough to accuse him of treason, it definitely got the soldier kicked out of any red beret social circles. So once I mentioned it to Sgt. Quick—particularly because I preceded that taboo declaration with accusing him of being an Uncle Tom—the bottom of our relationship collapsed. However, to his credit, Sgt. Q did not start yelling right away. First, he tried to reason with me.

"Amaru, you don't know shit about me!" he passionately exclaimed. "When I graduated high school in '76, I was a member of the Baltimore Chapter of the Black Panther Party. Out there in the streets soldiering for General Huey P, we got into all kinds of shit!"

Listening to him pause, I imagined he was waiting for me to express my surprise. Honestly, I was wondering how this was relevant to our conversation. For this reason, I remained silent. Once he saw no reply was forthcoming, he rambled on.

"Nowadays, people don't even fuckin' care to understand the level of expertise that existed in *the Party,*" Sgt. Q claimed. Then he started laughing. "We had a lotta guys who thought they were tough, just like you Amaru. And I admit, back then, I thought I was tough too. Especially after I was assigned to guard Elaine Brown when she visited B-more." Winking, he gave me a slight nudge on my shoulder. "Betcha you don't even know who Elaine Brown is, do you?"

Like I said earlier, this need to prove he was 'down' with his impromptu black history quizzes was a big part of what made him so annoying.

"Sergeant, I don't know what this has to do with me

leaving the Division. But since you asked, I know about Huey's flight to Cuba, to avoid the fabricated murder charges by the pigs. And how, during his absence, he appointed Comrade Elaine, who was also rumored to have been his lover, to the exalted position of Chairwoman."

At that moment, I telepathically shot Che a 'thank you' for schooling me on the BPP.

"Not bad on the history," Sgt. Quick nodded with a grin. "My point is, you can't get no blacker or tougher than we were in the Party." Saying this, the NCO stared at me. "But despite our cool leather jackets and raised black fists, once the government got ready, they snuffed us out like a cheap cigar." Shaking his head, he appeared to be recalling unpleasant memories from the past. "Amaru, after watching the FBI, the National Guard, and SWAT do their thing, I decided if I can't beat 'em I might as well join 'em. That's when I went to the recruiter's office and enlisted. By the time I finished basic training, I wanted to represent the best and the brightest the military had to offer."

Hearing him rehash the same paratrooper catchphrase our commander at Airborne School liked so much, I realized it was futile to continue this conversation, so I surprised him by agreeing. "Me too Sergeant."

"You too what? What're you talking about?" Sgt. Quick replied not understanding my meaning.

"I want to be more than just an 'average Joe' too!" I exclaimed, sticking my chest out.

"All right!" Sgt. Q beamed his encouragement. "Now that sounds like the words of bona-fide paratrooper!"

Following an hour of listening to Sgt. Q's bullshit, my mind was made up to terminate my jump-status; so I was using snippets of information I picked up at the SEAL graduation party in order to steer the dialogue back to the topic of me leaving the Division. Just as I was about to get to the point, I glanced at Sgt. Quick and it was difficult to suppress a smile from appearing on my face. This was because I felt like I was experiencing déjà vu. My platoon sergeant's face reminded me of how angry Drill Sergeant Sanford was ten months ago after his arm-twisting discussion failed to convince me to accept the guide-on assignment. *I bet Sgt Q's gonna be even more pissed!*

"The only problem is," I resumed, "nowadays the Division has been reduced to the ranks of a glamorized clean-up crew for the Ranger units." As Sgt. Quick cleared his throat to speak, I sealed the deal with a very obnoxious offer. "Sergeant, if you give me your word you'll send me to Ranger School within the next six months, I'll stay."

"What? Gimme a break!" Sgt. Quick exploded prior to chuckling in a condescending manner. "Private, in the future, do yourself a favor and read a damn, Army regulation-manual before you spout-off about shit you know less-than-shit about. It makes you look ignorant."

When he abruptly stopped in an effort to calm himself, I imagined he remembered at this moment he needed to be my friend.

"Look Amaru it's like this," he said after lowering his voice. "We've only got a few Ranger School slots for the entire brigade, and there are dozens of paratroopers—experienced troopers may I add—who've already put in their request. Sheeit, I'm on that dog-gone waiting-list myself!"

Appearing confident his lure had my attention, he tried to set the hook. "So even if the CO, Top, and myself inked our approvals—which ain't gonna happen anytime soon—this would only put you at the end of a long line of qualified soldiers." Saying this, he paused to glance at his watch.

I prayed he was as tired of talking as I was of listening. Glancing to my left, I spotted the motorpool coming into view. I figured it was now or never. "So that means no?"

"Of course that means no!" Sgt. Quick snapped. "Okay, we're back at the motorpool. I don't want to hear any more of this foolish talk about terminating. You're fucking up my appetite!"

Pulling into our motorpool gates, it was apparent I had to take the bull-headed NCO by the horns. "Agreed," I blurted out, "no need to discuss this any further."

"Now that's what I was waiting to hear——"

"Let's get the ball rolling," I interrupted before he could finish. "I want out ASAP. Can we go to Top's office after lunch?" Saying this matter-of-factly, I extinguished the engine and got out.

"What a fuckin' coward!" Sgt. Q screamed from the passenger seat. After getting out of the jeep and slamming the door, he continued venting his emotions. "Private, I am truly disappointed in you!" Appearing clammy from his lengthy speech, he shook his head in disgust. "Amaru you know what you are?"

By this time, it was safe to say I'd won my bet.

"You're a frickin' waste of talent, that's what you are!" Then Sgt. Quick finished his critique. "You'll never amount to a donkey's ass! Remember I told you that!" Now that any pretense of friendship was out the window, he went straight for the jugular of any paratrooper. "Yeah we'll go see Top alright…" Saying this, Sgt. Q stomped toward me and unexpectedly threw his right hand toward my head.

I easily ducked under his clumsy assault, and was

about to counter with a left hook to his unguarded chin. Then I understood what he was doing. My platoon sergeant was not interested in harming me on the physical level. He wanted to crush my spirit.

"But only after you take off that beret," he continued. "Go get your LEG cap, you dirty, nasty LEG!"

Nasty LEG. During Jump School, I used the term along with everyone else. However now that I was a few months removed from the training environment, this concept seemed a bit outdated. Perhaps my mind-control programming was wearing off.

"Private Amaru reporting as directed, sir," I stated after knocking.

"Enter," replied a cold voice behind the door; Captain Erickson sounded irritated.

Unlike First-Sergeant Isben, who minutes ago had expressed his professional sentiments of disappointment, the CO looked furious. For an ambitious, company commander looking to climb the promotion ladder, having terminees on his record could have detrimental effects on his quest to trade-in his captain's bars for a major's oak-leaf. In any case, Cpt. Erickson seemed to be taking my decision personally; and he was not shy about expressing his feelings.

"Pvt. Amaru…" Saying this, the O-3 stood up behind his desk while I remained standing at attention. With his hands on his hips, it looked like he was reaching for a six-shooter. "I consider you to be a sub-standard human being…" From here the young commander aired a barrage of insults.

226

While he screamed and hollered, I cleared my mind and focused on the career portfolio stitched to his shirt. Checking to ensure his black bars, Airborne and Ranger tabs, and Expert Infantryman Badge were embroidered in their proper locations, soon, his verbal assault was harmlessly flying over and around me. Despite his impressive list of credentials, I was recalling the numerous times I had witnessed temper-tantrum throwing whiteboys, just like him, get stomped into the ground.

Following his repeated threats to send me to guard the DMZ in South Korea, or even worse, to Ft. Polk, Louisiana, which was nicknamed 'swamp duty,' the captain appeared to mistake my timely meditation for the look of someone who was intimidated.

"Don't just stand there like a fuckin' idiot! What do you have to say for yourself, Private?"

Never thinking he might want me to reply, I had caught only small segments of his inflammatory threats. As I considered what to say, Sgt. Q, who had stood by quietly, cleared his throat. His message was clear: don't say anything stupid!

"Well sir," I began, "it has been brought to my attention that opinions can be compared to a person's nose, meaning everyone has their own. Sir, you expressed your less-than-stunning opinion of my personality. And that's perfectly fine because that's only *your* opinion. Nothing more...nothing less. In other words," I continued in spite of Cpt. Erickson's scowling glare, "I too might consider *you* to be a sub-standard human being as well. But the difference is I don't feel the need to spout a bunch of nasty comments just to hurt your feelings. I mean, what's the point?" After a brief pause, I resumed. "Sir, after all, the Knights Creed instructs

227

warriors to protect the common man—never attack him."

Although Captain Errickson appeared astonished a private would dare assert himself, when Sergeant Quick attempted to interrupt midway through my spiel, he raised his hand to silence the NCO. Since the captain had asked me to reply, to avoid losing face, he was obliged to allow me to complete my statement. Once I finished saying my piece, the CO summarily gave his closing remarks.

"This meeting is over. Sergeant, get this *thing* outta my office!"

Although I never overtly snubbed him, according to Sgt. Quick, my reference to a 'common man' was enough for the CO to charge me with insubordination. Especially since there are no references to any common men in the actual oath taken by medieval knights. Instead it obliges knights to "protect the weak and helpless."

Being a graduate from West Point, it's likely Cpt. Erickson was familiar with the quote, as well as my alteration. So why did he allow this act of defiance slip by? Who knows? All I knew, or even cared about, was despite the statue of a black panther adorning our headquarters, the vast majority of the oh-five was comprised of corn-husking, white dudes who came from places I never heard of. And we cannot forget the non-presence of the black mascots who had had their manhood sapped from them. Once I realized they were likewise trying to break me in, I was like: "Nix that, I'm outta here!"

19th Replacement Center

"Barnes, it's one o'clock. Time to wake up." When

the body under the blanket did not stir, I raised my whisper a few decibels. "Barnes get up!" Mistakenly thinking he was still asleep, I reached out to nudge the private. By the time I touched him, I knew I was busted. Not only was Pvt. Barnes wide awake, he was staring at his illuminated Casio wristwatch.

"Fuck-off Amaru! There's still forty-five minutes before my watch starts. What kinda shit you trying to pull?"

Had I apologized and backed-off right then, perhaps a scene could have been avoided. Normally, in a case where I was caught with my hand in the cookie jar, common sense prompted me to admit my wrongdoing. By doing this, I reasoned my forthrightness might induce a not-so-harsh penalty. *But I was drunk as a skunk!*

Earlier that evening, in order to hang-out with Mick and some chickenheads we had met at Fayetteville State University, I'd defied an order which required all those on the night-duty roster to remain at the barracks. Following two six-packs and several shots of vodka, the highlight of our double-date was a stimulating game of strip poker. As a half-naked girl sat on my lap and handed me another Lowenbrau, my guard-duty flashed into my mind. Having been in permanent party for over four months, I had almost forgotten about this ridiculous detail because fireguard was only assigned in the initial training cycles.

"Oh shit!" I exclaimed, "I got fireguard tonight." Before I finished my sentence, the keys to Mick's Honda Civic hit me squarely in the chest. Groggily picking them up, I buttoned my shirt and shuffled toward the door.

"Good luck soldier!" Those were Mick's last words as the door slammed shut.

Twenty five minutes later, I woke up just in time to

see a sign which read, '19th Replacement Center,' speeding by. Stomping hard on the brake, I turned the steering wheel and fish-tailed into the parking lot. After barely avoiding a parked humvee and skidding to a stop, I glanced at my watch and started to panic because I had less than a minute to spare. Jumping out of the car, I started running but after taking three strides, I realized the Civic's headlights were still on. Retracing my steps to extinguish them used an additional ten seconds. When I finally sprinted up the steps of the WW II barracks, I stumbled and scraped my knee—*but I made it on time!*

Stepping through the door, I spotted the fireguard walking toward me with his head down; he seemed to be looking for something he dropped. I imagined he was returning from making his final rounds, which included waking me up. Because he was looking at the floor, he had not yet noticed me so I used this moment to compose myself. This amounted to trying to look sober and not breathe too hard.

"Yo Rodriguez, I'm here," I whispered.

Even though I spoke softly, he was startled.

"Damn Amaru, you scared the shit outta me!" said the Latino soldier in a muffled tone. "Where were you? I've been looking all over for you. I was about to report your ass missing. Hurry up and get dressed."

"Listen Rodriguez, I need a favor," I pleaded. "I ain't feeling so good, can you help me out?"

"What you mean is: you're too drunk to stay awake, right?" Without allowing me to reply, he continued, "Alright, how much you offering?"

"Check-it-out man, I don't have any money right now. But I swear, I got you on pay day—"

"Pay day?" After repeating this in a sarcastic tone, Rodriguez started laughing. "You mean in two-and-a-half weeks? Man, you're leaving here tomorrow morning and neither of us know where the hell we'll be by then. Amaru, if you weren't so fucked up, I'd accuse you of taking me for a fool."

"Nah seriously *papi*, I got you. I promise."

But Rodriguez was already walking away. "Good luck soldier." Like Mick, these were his last words.

Barely able to keep my eyes open, the only thing I was qualified to guard was my bed.

According to Sergeant First-Class McDowell, the NCO who scolded me the next day, it was the 'unprovoked assault on a sleeping soldier' which prompted him to take disciplinary measures. In his own words: "It takes a low-down snake-in-the-grass to hit a man in bed!"

"Pvt. Amaru, let me get this straight," the E-7 had said. "Last night, you attempted to deceive a fellow soldier into doing your fireguard duty. After Barnes caught you red-handed, you felt insulted because he told you to 'Fuck off!' And that's when you hit him?"

After I plead guilty to assault, deceit, under-age drinking, and other assorted counts of mischief, the slim dark-skinned NCO led me and Barnes to an office. Once inside, Sgt. McDowell shut the door and sat on the desk. He was facing both of us.

"Pvt. Amaru," he stated in a grave tone. "We don't need reckless men who have no regard for authority in the Army. Not only have you broken the law, you've broken every code related to being a soldier." Then he turned toward the stout Caucasian private next to me and made him a promise. "Barnes, if the MPs don't lock him up, I'll personally see to it this low-life is chaptered-out of the Army."

Oddly, while this was taking place, I became aware of a subtle energy force in the corner of the room. It was staring at me. Was it the Beast? In fact, it was the presence of this phantom-specter which distracted me enough to calm my nerves. As I watched it out of the corner of my eye, I hoped it was here to guard me from the consequences of my foolishness. For some reason, I sensed it was guiding me through all this. I say this because some of my indiscretions influenced people I didn't even know. Allow me to explain.

The previous day, which was the last one of my week-long stay at the 19th, a group of newbies arrived. Immediately noticing many of them were sporting the well-known, double-A patches on their arms, I chuckled wondering which brigade within the Division they had terminated from. Minutes later, I saw the only melanin-rich member of their group pointing at me. When I nodded to him, the short broad-shouldered E-4 stood up and double-timed in my direction.

Introducing himself as 'Mouse from Detroit,' he then explained how a few nights ago two-thirds of his *commo* platoon, which amounted to twelve soldiers, had convened in his barracks room. The theme of the evening was to discuss if they should terminate or not. After unanimously voting to pull-the-plug on their jump status, they decided to approach their first-sergeant together the next morning to receive their scathing humiliation.

Although we had some things in common, and despite finding his story most enjoyable, I was baffled why Mouse was so eager to share his platoon's adventure with me. Moreover, another mystery about this guy was he seemed to know a lot about me.

"Amaru, I can't front," Mouse stated with a grin. "Standing at attention in front of Top and the CO, I was scared as hell! And not just me, all of us were. For real cuz, I thought by now we'd be stationed somewhere south of hell." When he finished talking, he waved his buddies over.

"Nah kid," I jokingly replied, "you just terminated out of hell."

"See that's what I'm talking about," Mouse now looked serious. "How the fuck did you have the balls to terminate all by yourself?"

Slightly embarrassed, I tried to downplay his praise. "It wasn't really a big deal—"

"Wha-? That's bullshit! Oh, did I forget to mention that we're from the 3rd of the oh-five too?"

Hearing this, I was surprised.

"Yeah Amaru, we were there when Sgt. Quick and them were dissin' you, calling you a dirty, nasty LEG and shit. And cuz, you wasn't having none-of-it either." By this time, Mouse's disciples had sauntered over to pay homage to the private they claimed had inspired them to 'go against the grain.' "I really respected how you stood up to them," Mouse resumed. "Cuz, I had tears in my eyes when you punked those whiteboys from S-2—" Suddenly stopping himself here, he glanced at the *melanin-challenged* group that had just joined the conversation. "Um, no offense."

As Mouse and I busted-out laughing, he used his sleeve to wipe his face. During this brief pause another specialist stepped toward me.

Extending his hand without introducing himself, the blue-eyed E-4 simply expressed his gratitude. "Amaru, we wanted to do it for almost a year now but we were just too chicken to do the right thing."

233

Initially uncomfortable, the more these guys addressed me like I was someone great, the more I began to envision a different side of me. Did I dare to imagine playing the role of hero?

Billy's Back...

'I know you ain't gonna let this bitch-ass newbie disrespect you like that!' the spirit called Smirnoff hissed its insidious scheme in my ear.

"Who the fuck you talking to bitch-ass newbie!" I repeated verbatim. This, in spite of hearing common sense warning me to back off.

"Ouch…hey!" As Barnes yelped, piercing lights attacked my dilated pupils.

When I opened my eyes, Barnes was standing next to his jump-school buddies. In addition to the twenty or so men, the lights also revealed the huge clock I had set ahead by almost an hour. I never considered Barnes might sleep with his wristwatch on, assuming he would just accept my word and the time illustrated on the wall. Sometime before first-call, I had planned to re-set the clock on my way to the latrine. Looking at the grim faces confronting me, I wished my fan club from this afternoon had been assigned to these barracks instead of another nearby decrepit building. *How the fuck am I gonna get outta this?*

"Barnes, what the hell's going on?" One burly guy with long, ape-like arms and a protruding forehead spoke for their entire group. "And who's this?" he said pointing at me. Due to his prehistoric appearance, I had noticed the private-first-class at a formation earlier that afternoon. By his demeanor, I imagined he had been Barnes' squad-leader in AIT.

"This asshole just punched me!" Barnes whined in a high-pitched voice while rubbing his left shoulder.

With the odds stacked against me, far from any foolish delusions of knightly grandeur, my brain was screaming "Retreat!" But it wasn't that easy. Realizing the lit-up exit sign diagonally behind me was approximately forty feet away, I silently calculated if everyone ran toward the door right now, there were at least two privates who had a shot at beating me there. Knowing from experience that once the chase was on, if I stumbled, got held, or had difficulty with the doorknob—any mishap whatsoever—all would bear the same consequence: a stomp party at my expense! As the realization unfolded that I was in a race where a tie did not go to the runner, I tried to stall, in-hopes of inching myself closer to the exit.

"Is that true?" This time the primitive-looking PFC addressed me directly. Without waiting for my reply, he then casually glanced at the clock. "Guess that also makes you the brilliant guy who's responsible for changing the time too, huh?"

Recognizing desperate times call for desperate measures, I went into my Richard Pryor, 'That Nigga's Crazy!' routine.

"That's right muthafucka, I did it…now what?" To emphasize my hostile intentions, I slapped the black metal flashlight I was holding in the palm of my hand like I was po-po. Once I did so, the two privates nearest to me shrank away ever-so-slightly from the 'angry black guy.' "Oh, I gettit. I'm supposed to be scared just 'cause a crew of punk-ass cherries rolled out their beds?" Using their moment of indecisiveness

235

to press my advantage, I stealthily stepped to my rear in an attempt to gain a few precious feet before sprinting away to safety. "I didn't think so—" Then my words broke off in mid-sentence.

When my boot struck an object registering as 'foreign,' I immediately stopped talking as all of my focus went into preventing the unthinkable. In a panic, I shot my other foot backward to regain my balance, but it too struck the base of the huge fan...and I busted my ass on the floor!

"Get that bastard!" Monkey-man screamed out.

Upon hearing his blood-curdling shriek, any spells of intimidation I had cast instantly evaporated into thin air. Grimacing in horror from the seat of my pants, I saw the first wave of paratroopers rushing forward with violent intent written on their faces. With barely enough time to contract my body into the fetal position, I closed my eyes and resigned myself to my brutal fate. An instant before they arrived, however, the squeaky sound of the door being thrust open became audible over the melee. Realizing hope was not yet lost, I screamed for all I was worth. *"At Ease!"*

Suddenly every sound in the room was placed on-mute as if in a vacuum. Daring to peek, I glimpsed twenty terrifying troopers—clenched fists, tight-jaws, and all—practically on top of me. They were frozen in their tracks.

Whaddya know, the shit actually worked!

Once the CQ sergeant sorted out I was the bad guy, in addition to the remainder of my fireguard, he assigned me to do Barnes' hour too. After I finished pacing the floor for ninety minutes, I was not permitted to enter the barracks for my own safety. Therefore, I was assigned to pick-up garbage, clean the latrine, and perform other crude errands until first-call. In this way, I was punished through sleep deprivation.

By seven o'clock, when Sgt. McDowell commenced his tongue-lashing from hell, I was nauseated and had a splitting headache. However far beyond that, now sober, I grasped how badly I had humiliated myself and I was deeply ashamed.

"Your military career is through!" the E-7 repeated several times, pointing in my face.

Treated like a criminal, I was even forced to eat breakfast isolated from the others. Minutes before our mid-morning formation, Sgt. McDowell told the CQ sergeant to notify the MPs. "Make sure they're here to collect his sorry ass after the commander's presentation." Then he grabbed my arm and escorted me outside like a prisoner.

Being pushed by the E-7 through the center of the assembled soldiers, all eyes were riveted on us. I felt like a leper watching soldiers scurry out of my path. This sentiment was intensified when Monkey-man and a few other of Barnes' buddies began whistling and teasing me. *This was a moment I would like to forget.* Over and over again, for the past several hours, I had reviewed every detail of each bad decision I made which led me to the predicament I found myself in.

"Company, attention!" On Sgt. McDowell's command, everyone locked-up with precision and got quiet. "Half-right-face," the E-7 continued. "Front-leaning rest position, move! In cadence, exercise…" Then he proceeded to count out twenty-five reps. In doing so he released his fury, not to mention his awful cigarette-coffee breath, into the morning air.

We were still doing push-ups when a VIP motorcade entered the parking lot.

"If I see so much as one head nod during the presentation, there'll be hell to pay! Am I clear?" boomed

SFC McDowell.

"Clear Sergeant!" The lively response reverberated.

After Sgt. McDowell ordered us to recover, he came and stood in front of me.

"Present arms!" he barked before the visitors exited their vehicles.

On his command, everyone raised their right hand until their upper-arm was horizontal to the ground. Then we gently rested our index-finger slightly above, and to the right of our right eye. We held our salutes until the dignitaries entered the building.

Minutes later, everyone was seated in the stuffy auditorium. The atmosphere was buzzing due to the unexpected presence of one of the VIPs. No one guessed that General Carl Stiner, himself, would accompany the post-chaplain and some representatives from the Soldier Support Center to greet us. Once his name was announced, everyone rose to their feet to give the post commander a standing ovation.

Seeing the war hero dressed in his Class-A uniform, the man appeared larger than life. In a trance-like state, I stared at the four silver stars decorating both shoulders of this distinguished soldier. The last thing I remember thinking was: I wonder what it would have been like to serve in a LEG unit had last night's fiasco not occurred?

Then I fell fast asleep.

This should have been a major turning point in my life. However, due to some very unusual circumstances, this change never transpired. Allow me to rewind to the point when the CQ sergeant flung open the squeaky door, just in time to save Billy's ass.

"Goddamit, someone better be dyin' in here!"

238

Pushing his way through the crowd, Sgt. Whitmore snatched me by the arm like a rag-doll, seeing I was the only one dressed in BDUs. "You the fire-guard on-duty?"

After taking me outside, he went back inside.

Seconds later, he reappeared with Barnes. "Both of you, sit here and shut-up!" he said in a stern voice while pointing at the stairs leading up to the door. "I better not hear a sound coming from out here!" Then he went inside to question the others.

Seated next to one another in the cold air, Barnes and I were quiet. With nothing else to do, I thought back to the remarks I made to Cpt. Errickson a week ago on knightly chivalry. This caused me to wipe my tears as I realized I was behaving more like the sub-standard human he accused me of being. *Maybe he was right,* I lamented. Following a few moments of soul-searching, I straightened up and made a vow: whatever punishment comes my way, I'll take it like a man. I will redeem myself!

The first thing I had to do was apologize to Barnes. Without his forgiveness nothing could be accomplished. Even though Barnes was sitting next to me, I did not say anything to him right away. Instead, I decided I would approach him *after* he reported what happened to the CQ. I felt this was the only way he'd believe my apology was sincere. To accomplish this, I ended up waiting until after first-call.

The sun was already high in the sky the next morning when Sgt. Whitmore led Barnes and his long-armed bunk-buddy to the CQ station. I followed at a discreet distance, making sure to present myself in plain view and stay out of earshot of their conversation. Along the way, I continued picking up garbage on my police-call detail. Upon arriving at the headquarters building, the sergeant pointed at a picnic table near the entrance. The CQ desk was just inside the front door.

"Sit down here, I'll be right back," Sgt. Whitmore said before he jogged up the steps and disappeared inside.

With the sergeant gone, I watched the two of them glare at me before I looked away to avoid antagonizing them. I was hoping they were going to conduct the interrogation outside.

A couple minutes later, the NCO reappeared holding a huge black notebook and joined the privates at the table. Seeing this, I plopped down on the steps of the mess hall. Situated about fifty yards away, I watched Sgt. Whitmore question both soldiers for over twenty minutes but I could not hear them. Following every statement by either private, the NCO inked their words into the black binder. When they all stood up and shook hands, I knew the meeting was over. With the facts now documented, this was the moment I had been waiting for. By the time, I approached the trio, my heart was in my mouth.

"Pardon me Sergeant but the private requests permission to apologize to Private Barnes concerning last night."

Before Sgt. Whitmore could respond, *Curious George* blurted out his opinion. "Amaru, you're full of shit! You just want Barnes to feel sorry for you, so he won't report you!"

The scowl on my face indicated what I thought about his asinine remark. However, before I could snap back, Barnes shut everyone up.

"No!" he yelled loudly.

All three of us were stunned by Barnes' outburst.

Seeing he had our attention, Barnes quieted down and resumed in his normal voice. "To be honest," he stated looking at his friend, "I thought Amaru was gonna try something underhanded myself. But when Sergeant Whitmore took us out of the barracks last night and made us sit next to each other, he never said a word. He just sat there and stared at the ground." Having explained this, Barnes pointed at me without looking my way. "At the time, I didn't think the slime-ball was sorry, just sleepy and hung-over. I mean, we're talking about the type of dude who'll belt a guy laying in bed, you know? But now..." Rubbing his chin, he turned toward me and studied my face. "Now that I saw him sitting over there watching us…" Pausing again, he pivoted back toward his friend. "Think about it, Vukovich: he was watching us when we gave our reports, it was kinda obvious what we were doing." Finished making his case, he waited an extra second to entertain any forthcoming rebuttal.

Though Vukovich appeared to remain steadfast in his opposition, he said nothing. Seeing this, Barnes glanced at the CQ sergeant before facing me.

"Amaru, if you still want to apologize, I'm listening."

"Just a second." Saying this, Sgt. Whitmore stepped between us. "Private Amaru, you *do* realize that nothing you say will affect the sworn testimonies written in these reports, right?" Displaying the dubious, black binder with 'Incident Reports' stenciled in bold white letters, he waited for my reply.

"Clear Sergeant, I understand one hundred percent."

Before granting his permission, the NCO pulled me to the side. "Amaru, come over here. I wanna speak to you in private."

Once we had walked about fifteen yards, he stopped.

"Okay, this is far enough." Turning to face me, the urgency in his face was evident. "Listen, no stupid shit, you

241

hear me?" Staring hard, he was trying to get a read on my intentions. "I swear if you fuck this up, I'll break your neck myself!"

"I understand Sergeant. And I just want to thank you for giving me this opportunity to apologize. To you too. My behavior last night was inexcusable." Admitting this, I stared at the ground.

After hearing my reply, Sgt. Whitmore led me back to where Barnes and Vukovich were waiting. When the sergeant and private-first-class walked away, it was Barnes who spoke first.

"That was a fucked-up thing you tried last night," he said in a reserved tone.

"I know it was," I agreed. And without exhaling, I spit the apology out. "Hey Barnes, you got every right to not trust me, or even hate me…" I felt so guilty it was a relief to release the heavy burden. "But I really am sorry for everything I did last night. And I have no excuse. I was wrong and I'm sorry."

The heart-felt sincerity lacing my words seemed to move Barnes.

"You know Amaru, five minutes ago, I never thought I could've possibly respected you enough to even have this conversation. But like Sgt. McDowell said, "your actions spoke for themselves last night," therefore the same rule has to apply this morning too, right?" Nodding his head to some unspoken thought in his mind, Pvt. Barnes then stepped forward and gripped my right hand in his. "Apology accepted," he stated with a broad grin.

Soon our hearty handshake extended into a warm embrace, and like teens oft-times do, we soon forgot the entire episode. Ten minutes after my teary-eyed apology, we were sitting on the steps laughing about one of his childhood memories growing up in Ontario, Canada. When Sgt. Whitmore returned, he did not even attempt to mask his astonishment.

"What the heck is going on here?"

"You Private Amaru?" asked the bulky, Caucasian soldier after he entered the office where I had been sequestered.

"Yes, umm, Private Stockman."

I was surprised the soldier sent to apprehend me was only an E-2.

"Ready to go?" Saying this, the guy grabbed one of my duffel bags and walked out the door.

With more than a little uncertainty, I grabbed the other two duffel bags and followed him. Outside, I was greeted by a staff sergeant who looked way too old to be an E-6. Nobody else was in sight, not even SFC McDowell.

"Put your stuff in the back of the jeep," the old, white-guy said. "We'll get acquainted on the ride to headquarters."

When the E-6 directed me to sit in the back of a M151 utility vehicle, which was the standard jeep before the hummer, I scratched my head thinking this was a weird arrest procedure. We were already on the road when something occurred to me: *I can scratch my head...that means I'm not wearing handcuffs!*

Studying the two Caucasians occupying the front seats, I tried to restrain my joy. Instead of the tough-looking MPs Sgt. McDowell had repeatedly threatened me with, I thought the jovial pair could pass for father and son.

"Hey Amaru," said the 'son' in a friendly tone. "I'm from San Diego. Where're ya from?"

"Shut up Stockman!" said 'pops' in a playful voice before introducing himself. "I'm Sergeant Barnaby, your new platoon sergeant. Welcome to Headquarters, 3rd of the 759th Aviation Regiment."

His greeting brought to mind a low-budget rendition of Mr. Rourke welcoming his guests to Fantasy Island. And ironically, it was in this outfit of five-jump chumps, terminees, and other assorted misfits, where my dreams would come true.

"Thank you Sergeant," I simply replied.

Although keenly aware a miracle had taken place, any feelings of appreciation quickly dissipated. After switching to a mischievous grin, which was unlike the expression of humility on my face just seconds ago, Billy rehashed his signature lie. "Yo Stockman, I'm from Philly."

And just like that, as if nothing out of the ordinary had occurred over the past eight hours, Billy was back.

Chapter 11: Don't Call it a Comeback...

"This Army Commendation Medal is hereby awarded to PFC Takuan Amaru for meritorious achievement serving as PLL / TAMMS clerk while being assigned to Headquarters, 3rd Battalion, 759th Aviation Regiment, Ft. Bragg, North Carolina. PFC Amaru demonstrated a commitment above and beyond the call of duty in establishing an initial Prescribed Load List for a motorpool still in the genesis of its creation. PFC Amaru's dedication to exceptional service and professionalism reflect great credit upon himself, his unit, and the United States Army. Signed James T. Packer, Lieutenant Colonel."

At the conclusion of the ARCOM award ceremony, held for both Stockman and myself, we were swamped by fellow soldiers wanting to congratulate us.

"Good work boys!" beamed our ex-supervisor, Sgt. Barnaby. Considered 'short' because he was due to retire in less than a month, the elderly E-6 had been replaced as the motor-sergeant five weeks ago. Standing next to him was our new supervisor.

"Tak, Stock, it's great y'all are getting the recognition you deserve for the hard work you're putting in around here. You guys make me proud to be the motor-sergeant, congratulations!" Sgt. Williamson, who everyone called 'Sgt. Will,' was still shaking our hands when another soldier joined the conversation.

"Good morning, men."

"Sergeant Major, what a surprise! I was just saying the other day—"

"No surprise." After cutting-off the old-timer's attempt to brown-nose, the hardcore vet greeted Sgt. Will before giving me and Stock his undivided attention.

"PFC Amaru, it's a pleasure to finally meet the future Heisman trophy winner in the seven-five-ninth."

"Thank you Sergeant Major, but the pleasure's all mine," I politely responded.

After shaking my hand, he stepped back to inspect my physique like a slave trader at the auction block. "Yeah, I can imagine you taking a hand-off and stiff-arming a safety in the facemask before dashing thirty yards and crashing your way into the end zone."

Watching the squat, *very* non-athletic E-9 imitate a running back's moves, I strained to suppress a grin. "Thank you Sergeant Major. But actually, I plan to play wide-receiver."

"Well, what the hell does an old GI like me know about football? Just score some damn touchdowns." Saying this good-naturedly, the senior advisor for the battalion commander shook my hand once more before stepping to my right. "PFC Stockman, heard you're one helluva mechanic..."

Times sure done changed.

My first four months in 'LEG land' were exactly what I had hoped for: an absolute get-over experience. For a slickster probing for loopholes in the system, this undemanding unit was almost too good to be true. From the college-dorm-like barracks furnished with restaurants masquerading as mess halls, to the roody-poo PT sessions which only occurred three times a week, this was heaven-on-earth compared to the oh-five.

Immediately recognizing my new unit to be exactly what it was, largely a collaboration of burnt-out soldiers and inexperienced privates, Billy also identified a few characters who did not fit the typical mold. After further investigation, I found that most of these rare robins were involved in some sneaky, extracurricular activities on the side. Drugs, outright theft, and sexual fraternization headed the list of the "on the down-low" dealings.

In spite of Billy's schemes and dreams, when I first arrived believe it or not, I tried to turn over a new leaf and be a good soldier. I even signed-up for evening classes at FSU, thinking I should start accumulating credits that would easily transfer to another university later. The courses available on-post for soldiers were limited but I found two classes that I felt would be interesting and not too demanding. Like many brothers, Spanish was a language I had picked-up organically in the streets of Camden and Philly; so I elected to take a beginner-level class and also attend a US History lecture. After all the discussions on history with Che and Colón, I figured this class would be easy too.

Even though I was intent on attending college in the future, I was turned-off by the thought of sitting in boring lectures. *I wonder if I'll cheat on exams at the university level too?* This was when it occurred to me I no longer felt any incentive to play by the rules. With this in mind, I reminisced on my time at Ft. Lee and recalled how smoothly my days went when no one knew me. This is what led me to re-enact that plan in my new unit. *Hell yeah*, I thought. *I'm just gonna chill-out in the background and see what happens.*

Still in the 'genesis of its creation,' our fledgling

company had not yet been activated. Lacking personnel and equipment, the disadvantage of being in a still-forming brigade was the excess of meaningless activities. With no official mission, the NCOs used their imaginations to manufacture the appearance of keeping everyone busy. In other words, we spent an inordinate amount of time cutting grass, digging holes, and hauling heavy furniture around Smoke Bomb Hill. In order to escape the more exhausting jobs, I learned to volunteer for the less demanding assignments. However, I soon realized my 'choosing the lesser of two evils' tactic was minor-league in comparison to one unique personality.

Specialist Leonard Wiley was a character indeed. In fact, he is the only Caucasian I've ever met who was running shit on a 'brutha level.' I will never forget my initial encounter with the redheaded rebel known as "Wile E, the Super-Genius."

"Ay Ware, when you take your *Chicken George* looking-ass back over there, grab my bag for me, will ya?" Wiley said this while he relaxed in the shade of a deuce-and-a-half truck.

I gawked at the slim, red-headed E-4 in amazement. I couldn't believe he was sitting there munching on a bucket of *Bojangle's Famous Chicken 'n Biscuits* while everyone else was working.

When Pvt. Lionel Ware, who was one of my roommates, scurried to comply with his request, Wiley yelled again. "Not right away dumb-ass! I ain't no NCO to be bossing you around like that. I just thought that since you were okay with the slave-routine around here, you might as well grab my bag on your next indentured effort. Man, you gotta learn to relax. Ya know, enjoy life a little." Smirking under his Carolina-blue, Oakley sunglasses, Wiley scrutinized Ware closely. "You know what? From now on I'm gonna call you 'Toby,' from *Roots.* You even look like LeVar Burton." Following a brief snicker he continued. "Yeah…Private Toby, the grinning manservant."

"Wiley, you're crazy man," Ware replied with a sheepish grin.

Scanning the crowd, I was disgusted seeing all the melanin-rich faces giggling at Wiley's antics. To my surprise, I also noted that most of the white privates did not find him amusing. Just as Billy finished hoping that cracka would pop that bullshit my way, his wish was granted.

"Ay Toby, is that your new roommate?" Asking this, Wiley rotated his head as if it were on a swivel before placing one hand on his hip and snapping his fingers with the other one. Then he pointed at me. "The quiet dude over there with the low-budget S-curl in his natural."

Despite his poor imitation of Pvt. Ali, the sista from Atlanta in our company, he was again greeted with gut-wrenching laughter—even from Ali herself.

"Yo Ware…" As Billy geared up for his response, a hushed silence fell over the peanut gallery. "Tell that *Raggedy Andy-Ronald McDonald* look-alike just 'cause he switched up his normal Happy Meal for some fried chicken today, he still ain't got no soul." Seeing the coyote's ears perk up, I looked back at him. "Red, *you* wanna crack some hair jokes?" Before he could reply, I turned back toward my audience. "The peckerwood actually thinks he's cool. Look at him," saying this, I summed up my observation, "with his plastic sunglasses and fake-ass afro, he's over there looking like *Heat Miser* chillin' at the beach."

Once my peers dug into their childhood memories and

compared Wiley's flaming-red, moussed-up mane to the hairstyle sported by the fiery character in the Christmas animation special, in addition to erupting into laughter, they were inspired to sing a rendition of *Heat Miser's* theme song.

"He's Mr. Heat Miser, he's getting hot...[6]" Ali started singing first before the rest joined-in on the second verse.

With the crowd both laughing and singing, it appeared the Super-Genius was getting angry in-tune with the melody; so when he stood up, Billy seized the moment.

"Yeah, bring it son...by all means, if you're feeling froggish, leap your punk-ass over here!"

I believed Wiley wanted to fight so I used my favorite battle challenge; one I had copied from Mann back in the day. As soon as the path between us cleared, Wiley stepped toward me. However, once he reached me, the specialist at once shut down any notion of a brawl.

"Amaru, what the hell're you talking about? My name's Leonard Wiley." Having regained his composure, he stated this cordially while extending his hand in a gesture of friendship. Then he glanced at the rubber-necking onlookers and added another comment. "It's a pleasure to finally meet someone in this bullshit company with some fuckin' balls!"

Like I said, the guy had character.

All-Points Bulletin: the Secret to unraveling Cracka Theology

It's simple: just let crackas know from jump street you're not going to tolerate any of their bigoted, ethnocentric attitudes. I will never forget the phrase that established my

---

[6] The actual lyrics are: *"He's Mr. Heat Miser, he's Mr. Sun..."*

relationship with Wiley: "The next time a racist-ass *Roots* reference comes out your mouth—*and I don't give a damn if you remember me saying this or not*—put your hands up or I'm gonna sneak you!"

While I admit violence may not be the answer, I do recommend keeping it plain, simple, and to the point. Although they probably won't be done testing you, it will make it much easier to stand on your square in your time of need. In my experience, I've noticed whenever this foundation of respect is *not* established, we gradually become marginalized by the passively-violent side of racism. This results in us feeling pressure to squeeze our melanin-richness into a three-dimensional box, which consequently curtails our unique abilities and forms of expression.

The Super Genius

"See you guys at the motorpool after lunch. Oh, except Stock and Amaru. You two report to Top's office at thirteen hundred."

"Ahh Sgt. B, we gotta clean those dog-gone rifles again?" Stock whined.

"Probably. All I know is, Top requested you two for the afternoon. So it's either that or lawn maintenance. Any other questions?" When no other inquiries were made Sgt. Barnaby released us for lunch. "Platoon, attention…fall-out."

Together with my motorpool mates, I sauntered toward the dining facility. As I grew weary of listening to their complaints about how 'ate up' our unit was, I heard a voice call my name from beyond their rhetoric.

"Yo Amaru!"

Looking in the direction of the voice, I was surprised to see Wiley standing outside the cafeteria. I replied by grinning and raising a fist in the air. When we reached him, he shook hands with Stock and greeted a few others before pulling me to the side to let everyone go inside the mess hall.

"Let's roll off-post and get some real food," he proposed with his sly coyote grin.

As good as that sounded, with nothing but lint lining my pockets, I had no choice but to decline. That is, until Wile E made an offer I could not refuse.

"My treat," he said.

After hitting the drive-thru window at Bojangle's, Wiley wheeled his candy-apple, BMW 325E into a nearby, upscale apartment complex. Noticing the first-class surroundings, I surmised he had sweet-talked some millionaire's daughter into falling in-love with him.

"Oh, I see...you shacking up with a rich chick, huh?"

"According to the Army records, I live in the barracks. In the building next to yours." Replying thus, Wiley shifted the transmission to park and extinguished the engine. "But unofficially yes, I really live here with my fiancé. She's in class now." Reaching in his pocket, he then pulled out a gold money-clip containing a thick wad of c-notes. "Unlike this, those fuckin' personnel records ain't worth the paper they're printed on."

Entering his lavish three-bedroom condo, I took a seat in the living room. My attention was drawn to a crystal table in the corner of the room which featured an austere, black-and-white photograph of Wiley and his fiancé. They were dressed formally. The picture caught my eye because it looked like a photo from the old west. Wiley was standing in a black, cut-away tuxedo with gray slacks. Donning a sleek fedora and holding a cigar in his left hand, I have to admit the boy looked sharp. His blonde-haired fiancé was seated in a wooden chair next to him. She was wearing a white, nineteenth century, baroque gown with a tight bodice and a long, flowing train.

"That's me and Jeannie at her brother's wedding last February," Wiley said while he turned on the air conditioner.

"Word," I said with a nod of my head. "Y'all make a good-looking couple."

"Thanks," he replied. "I'm sure you two'll meet each other soon."

Once Wiley scarfed down his last chicken wing, he announced he was going upstairs to change into a dry t-shirt. Taking advantage of this quiet moment, I ripped into the last of my Cajun Deluxe lunch set. I really relished the moment, just thankful for this rare occasion to eat seasoned food in the luxury of a nice home. Looking around at the expensive furniture, I concluded Wiley's golden-haired, fiancé's father must be swimming in dough. Considering the E-4 was sporting a beemer, a blonde, and a condo, I thought Wiley was faring quite well in the white man's world. For this reason, when he returned looking glassy-eyed with a runny nose, I was certain the white powder in the Ziploc bag he placed on the coffee table was not baking soda.

After snorting my third line, in spite of the air conditioner being on full blast, I was clammy with perspiration and the pounding in my chest was deafening in my ears. Taking a deep breath, I glanced around the room and noticed the clock. It was ten minutes to one. Recalling it had taken fifteen minutes to drive here, I exploded.

"Dammit Wiles, we're gonna be late!"

"Relax," is all he said.

"Relax my ass!" I replied, high-as-a-kite.

Looking unfazed, the genius tilted his head down, inserted a straw into his left nostril, and inhaled two more lines. To control the blast, he shook his head like a dog does when it's wet. "Damn Amaru! You're about to blow my high with your bitchin' and moanin.' You starting to sound like Tob—er, I mean Ware." Catching himself before he slipped, he recovered by divulging a secret. "Amaru, Sergeant Barnaby told you to report to Top's office after lunch, didn't he?" Without waiting for my reply, he asked another question. "You know my job is basically being the CQ runner for Top and the CO, right?"

"Yeah. So-the-fuck-what?" I was losing patience.

"So, my overly exuberant—not to mention wasted—friend, since Top, the CO, and damn near every E-5 and above are at a golf course this afternoon hobnobbing with the Alpha Company inspectors, with no NCOs around, Top put *me* in-charge of your detail."

Comprehending what he said, I flashed a grin. "Get the fuck outta here! You serious?"

"He told me right before lunch."

"Are we still in the Army? This shit's almost too good to be true!" Shaking my head in disbelief, I flopped back down on his black, leather sofa.

"Well, I can definitely say it damn sure ain't the oh-four or the oh-five."

Wiley, also a terminee from the Division, then reached over and opened a drawer on the side of the coffee table.

Pulling out his old AA patch, he held it up and we both chuckled.

As I reclined back and rested my feet on a stool, I had to confirm the good news once more. "In other words, my orders for this afternoon are to report to *you?*"

Instead of words, the sly coyote grinned his affirmation.

"Well, in that case Specialist Wile E, stop being so stingy and break-out some more yayo!"

The next six weeks were a blur of lies and chalky white lines. During this time, I was chosen for five 'random' drug-tests. Somewhere along the way, I should have been alerted to chill-out. But like the musical genius, Rick James, was quoted as saying: "Cocaine is a helluva drug!"

"So Private Amaru, you're telling me you can't give us any information on who's selling the cocaine?"

"I'm afraid not sir. I'm still new to this unit and haven't made many friends," I lied.

"What about the LSD?"

"Sorry sir." Shaking my head, I feigned regret.

"No friends huh? By the looks of this raggedy outfit, you might want to keep it that way," the CID officer added with a derisive air. "Okay, no further questions. But remember, if you hear anything, talking to us isn't snitching. Not only could you be saving one of your buddies' lives, you might be saving your own as well. Imagine the damage that could occur if one of those druggies got behind the wheel of a deuce."

To my knowledge, there were about fifteen cokeheads in our company. What I didn't know was the grapevine had designated me as the sixteenth member of this dubious group. There was, however, a significant difference between me and the majority of other users: the results of my urinalysis came back negative all five times.

For this reason when the CID officers, accompanied by the MPs, made their numerous appearances to herd what Top called the "low-life bums" into the paddy wagon, I stood in formation counting my blessings.

On the Friday night kicking off Memorial Day weekend, I mindlessly flipped through the numerous cable stations as Wiley walked across his black-and-gold carpet. He was coming toward me carrying a small, metallic case. After watching him carefully place it on the coffee table, I shut off the television and put the remote control on the sofa.

"Three more got popped on that last piss quiz, bro," he commented before gazing in my direction.

"Stock told me…and don't call me 'bro'," I responded looking back at him. "Are you the one supplying those fiends?"

"Not anymore," he coolly replied, brushing off the diss. "I stopped once everyone started getting arrested. I don't know where they're coppin' from now. Probably somewhere on Murchison Road."

Opening the case, Wiley revealed a basic chemistry set. Without interrupting his flow, he began to inspect the various flasks and test tubes. As he removed them one-by-one from the case, he asked something which had mystified me ever since I passed my first piss quiz almost two months ago.

"Tak, have you figured out how we get coked up every day at lunch but never turn-up positive?"

"Nah. But I must admit, I have been thinking about it."

"I'm a fuckin' genius, that's how!" he replied, cracking a smile. "Those amateurs can't deal with a real professional." Seeing I had no idea what he was talking about, he proceeded to clue me in. "They say coke stays in your urine for seventy-two hours, right?" Asking this, he dumped a couple grams of white powder into a vial and poured in some water.

"Yeah something like that, so what."

"They're right, that's what!" he stated with emphasis while pointing at his mini-lab set-up. "I'm a scientist, I've been running tests."

"Oh, I get it...you've been using me as your guinea pig."

"Well kind of, but I'm taking the same risk as you," he responded. "Besides, you get high for free."

"True," I grinned back.

Being a former candy man myself, I knew that weekends were the time to cash-in. For this simple reason, it had never appeared strange that Wiley always disappeared on Fridays. That is, until he had emphasized 'seventy-two hours.'

"Remember about a month ago, when you and McKnight caught me at the barracks picking up my laundry?" Wiley worked as he spoke. Now, he was using a glass eye-dropper to meticulously insert ammonia into the vial containing the cocaine dissolved in water.

"That was a Friday night, wasn't it?" I asked.

"Yeah, and of course you two wanted some blow. I didn't want to give y'all any, but once Mick said there were girls in your room, I had to hook it up."

Watching Wiley slowly stir the substance until it turned milky white, I thought he resembled a mad scientist. "Yeah, me and Mick had a good time that night! I really owe you for that." Smiling, I sat back and reclined my feet on a stool as Wiley poured the contents into a fresh beaker. Then he picked up a cylindrical container labeled 'Ethyl Ether.'

"This shit's flammable as hell," Wiley warned before adding a liberal amount, closing the top, and shaking the mixture vigorously. "Man, after y'all left, I was shittin' bricks you wouldn't get pissed on Monday." Stopping here, Wiley stared at me with a profound look on his face. "I don't know if you noticed but..."

Vibrating along the same shady wavelength, I completed his thought in unison with him. *"That was the only Monday last month we didn't get piss-tested!"*

Completely awestruck at this discovery, I was also amazed by something else. "You sayin' you purposely avoid me on weekends so I won't get busted?"

"Think about it, with the exception of that one Friday night, you never see me after Thursday's lunch. But Tak, don't get sentimental on me. Remember, I'm a business man, this is about dollars and cents. Now that you're steering guys looking to score nose-candy my way, you represent a financial investment, so to speak."

"I gotcha, it's all about dollars and having good sense."

"Yessir, that is an accurate statement."

As Wiley rattled on, I recalled being in a similar

258

conversation with Belkis. Following a few minutes of laughing at his high-falutin, Fortune 500 gibberish, I pointed at his mini laboratory. "A-ight, since you're in the mood for giving speeches, what the hell's up with the science project?"

"Tonight I'm gonna show you how to freebase…Hollywood style!" In dramatic fashion, he gestured toward his in-progress, chemistry experiment and cleared his throat. "Boys and girls, don't try this at home, or you might get your ass burnt-up like Richard Pryor did."

"Don't worry, snorting blow's enough for me," I replied rubbing my hands together like a greedy beggar. "But you know I gotta check-out how the stars get down and dirty, for educational purposes only," I added with a mocking grin.

"You gonna love this!" Wiley exclaimed, suddenly excited. "Smoking crack the 'ghetto way' can't compare to real freebasing." After siphoning off the ether with a pipette, Wiley slowly dripped what remained onto a brown plate in small piles before setting it under a lamp to dry. Then he lifted a blue plate that was next to it and carefully placed the porcelain dish in front of us. With his palm facing upward, he majestically presented the dehydrated, yellowish-white crystals resting on the plate and snarled his coyote-grin. "This is tonight's entree. If you look closely, you can tell they're dry, right? I did this batch last night. Don't expect service like this from your neighborhood crack dealer."

"Hold up a minute genius!" Like a shot, I realized we were violating his Law of Seventy-Two Hours scheme. "It's Friday night!" I blurted out.

"But Monday's a holiday—"

"But it still won't be enough time to clean out!" Using my fingers, I verified my mental calculations. Just before I was overcome with panic, Wiley cut me back off.

"Let me finish!" he yelled to quiet me down. "Since I went to the trouble of adding your name to last week's overnight detail—"

"Oh, so I have you to thank for the privilege of guarding the airfield, huh?"

"Like yours truly," Wiley continued, ignoring me, "you happen to be off Tuesday as well, remember? Top announced that in formation. And yes, you have me to thank for that." Finishing his statement, he pulled out his money-clip and peeled off a crisp Franklin-face. "Whatever you do this weekend," he stated holding the bill between his middle and index fingers, "don't go back to the barracks 'til Wednesday morning. And no more blow after tonight!" Then he handed me the c-note and his car keys. "Take your girl to a hotel and chill out," he said. "Me and Jeannie are off to the Aspen Mountains." With his hands free, the Heat Miser grabbed a small torch from the table and ignited it.

"Where the fuck's that?" I naively inquired as I happily inserted the keys to the 'Black Man's World[7]' inside my pocket. Smiling, I wondered how many hoes would be on my dick this weekend.

"Colorado," Wiley replied. "You gotta go sometime. Jeannie's already there, at their family's cabin with her brother and his wife. We're hittin' the slopes this weekend!" With this exclamation, Wiley picked up his home-made pipe, which was actually a glass tube wielded to a flask.

"Well la-di-da," I responded. "But lemme tell ya something Wiley. You may be white, but I dunno if you're 'white enough' to hang with those poguish aristocrats."

"Think so, huh?" Wiley's thought seemed to be

---

[7] Another reference to BMW

260

interrupted as he paused to concentrate on the final stages of his ACME operation. Seconds later, when he put a couple crystal-rocks in the pipe, he looked at me before expressing what made him tick. "Amaru," he said looking at me with a serious expression. "Right now as we speak, there's a whole world going on out there. It's a big-ass party that you and I weren't invited to. I don't know about you but *fuck that!* My money's just as green as any of those silver-spoon eatin' mother fuckers!" Prior to putting the pipe to his lips, he picked up a small spoon and ceremoniously tapped the silver utensil against the pipe. Then he put it down, lit the torch, and proposed a toast.

"This first hit commemorates our partnership. May we always stay two steps ahead of 'em, and make dough at all costs!" After clinking the pipe against my raised glass, he applied the blue flame to the bowl. Just prior to inhaling the white smoke accumulating in the conical flask, he made one more comment. "I'm a fuckin' genius!"

The misty clouds swirling around the transparent bong mesmerized me. In spite of this, I considered how Wiley was anything but a mastermind. Don't misunderstand me, I still appreciated being assigned to the details he was 'supervising.' However, once he revealed his father was a general in the Marine Corps, I stopped being amazed he was able to pull strings. Like he said: "No one wants to screw around with a general's son."

It took about thirty seconds for Wiley to exhale the potent vapors from his lungs. "Goddamn that feels good!" he exclaimed, nodding his head and handing me the pipe. Following a sip of cognac, he sat back and closed his eyes. It was not long before his high prompted him to talk again. "I remember when you told me about the 'pawn shop scheme' you were planning." With his eyes still closed, he began to laugh hysterically.

I started laughing too when he put his foot on the coffee table and kicked over his glass.

"Shit, Jeannie's gonna kill me!" With this declaration, Wiley jumped up and ran to the kitchen.

I was still cracking up when he returned with a roll of paper towels and wiped up the spill. Once he refilled his glass and mine, he returned to his artificial state of ecstasy.

"Where was I? Oh yeah, the pawn shop. The next day, when I saw you and your roommates lugging about seventy pounds of technical manuals into the barracks, I knew you were on to something."

"Like you said, always stay two steps ahead of them," I stated before taking a sip. "To find a loophole in their system, I had to learn it first. You can only get away with stealing behind their back for so long. That's a short-term racket."

While I spoke, Wiley refilled the bowl.

"At some point," I continued. "Either you'll get sloppy or they'll get lucky. And you only have to get caught once. So I learned the trick is to devise a profitable scheme that works in accordance with their rules and nonsense."

"I couldn't have said it better myself!" With his emphatic compliment, Wiley held the torch close and I inhaled.

Listening to the rocks sizzle, I watched the resin dissolve from the edge of the glass. Gradually, a wonderful numbness encompassed my entire body. This was followed by an unexplainable head-rush.

"Think about it…" Too coked-up to remain quiet, Wiley took advantage of my silence. "My man Harry is an ex-

GI, so he knows Bragg just like we do. When he meets you inside the supply-pickup building for the exchange, no one ever looks twice, do they?"

After blowing out the chemical mist, I proceeded to add more bullshit to the bravado. "Hell no, they don't have a clue!" I bellowed wearing a smug look. "He looks just like everyone else dressed in his BDUs. Check-it-out, even if the CID was trailing me, nothing I do would look strange. I doubt they could get any real evidence against me."

"Unless, that is, you confessed."

"Yeah imagine that!" I stated with a pompous smirk.

As we relaxed amidst the swirling vapors encompassing the living room, I actually believed we were above the law. I mean, think about it: I was nineteen years old, drinking 'top shelf' liquor and freebasing cocaine in a white man's home. According to everything I'd learned, this what it's all about.

"Let's watch some videos," Wiley said. "Turn on MTV."

I was thinking about how Wiley reminded me of a tougher version of Jeff when I flipped on the television and saw the video for my high-school buddy's favorite song, *'The World Is My Oyster.'* Before I could mention this extraordinary coincidence, the telephone rang.

"Hello," Wiley said after picking up the phone on the second ring. "How'd you get this number?" he asked following a brief pause. "No, it's cool. It's just because it's unlisted. In the future, page me okay?"

By the way Wiley was talking, I assumed the caller was one of his regular customers. Thus, when he handed me the phone, I was surprised.

"It's for me?"

"Yeah it's Mick," Wiley responded before heading toward the kitchen. "You need more ice?"

"Nah, I'm good," I replied, placing the receiver to my ear.

"What up boyee?" Mick's husky voice reverberated from the phone loud and clear. "You up in the deluxe mansion suite gettin' nice, ain't ya?" Before I could even say hello, he tried to make me feel guilty. "That's ill how you left your boy out here in the cold."

"Sheeit, you sound more fucked up than we are!" I replied in a joking manner.

"Nah, I'm just playing with you cuz," Mick responded before laughing.

Despite my eagerness to cue him in on getting stoned Hollywood style, Mick had his own agenda.

"What y'all into tonight?" he asked.

"You mean besides getting fucked up? Nothin' bro, why? What's up?"

"Roll with me to my crib," he simply stated. "Something's up back home and I don't wanna take that long-ass ride by myself."

"What? You wanna go to Michigan tonight?"

"Yes my brutha. Listen, I'll fill you in on the details when I pick you up."

Before he finished making his proposition, I remembered the car, the cash, and my four-day weekend. "Cool, I'll drop by my barracks and pack a bag. But there's one change: I'm gonna pick you up," I stated in a proud voice. "I should be at your barracks in about forty-five minutes."

"Hold up, you're gonna pick *me* up?" Mick asked in surprise. "How the hell's your no-car-having-ass gonna do that?"

"In the beemer, that's how boyeee!" Completing my statement with a pompous exclamation point, I waited for his reply.

"Oh, it's like that, huh? Well, in that case *Scarface*, bring some *yay* 'cause we got a fourteen-hour road trip in front of us."

"Gotcha. See you at your barracks in in forty-five, I'm out."

About a half hour later, I pulled into the parking lot at Mick's barracks zooted out of my mind! Pumping *Eric B and Rakim's 'Paid in Full,'* I marveled at the stares of the peasant GI population. In order to show-off even more, I made sure to park diagonally using two spaces. When I stepped out of the sparkling BMW, I felt like a movie star. While I had the attention of the crowd loitering in front of the 307th Engineer Battalion's barracks, I activated the ear-piercing alarm.

The first to publicly 'jump on the jock' were two, nasty-looking dykes with crew cuts.

"Hey, commere sugar."

"You talking to me?" I asked.

"Yeah Amaru, we're talking to you sexy," added her partner. Sensing my confusion, the tattooed lesbos hugged one other to paint a vivid picture of their intentions. "Let's make it a ménage-a-trois."

"Thanks but maybe next time, ladies."

Although I had seen both of them on previous visits to Mick's barracks, neither had ever spoken to me before that night. After declining an offered beer from their six-pack, I asked them if they had seen Mick.

"Here he comes now," the less-buffed of the two replied, pointing over my shoulder. When I turned around to greet my friend, both women loudly complained.

"Damn that's cold-blooded, Amaru! You just gonna leave us hanging like that?"

"At least hook us up with a couple lines," one of them whispered. "We cool like that, right?"

Yeah right!

Before we hit Rt. 421, Mick and I had already stopped twice to snort lines. Needless to say, we had no trouble staying awake that night.

"I got some drama back home with my baby's mama," Mick began explaining before I had the chance to ask.

"Some 'baby-mama drama,' huh?"

As an image of irate parents bickering over child-support payments flashed in my mind, I spotted a billboard: "Big P's is Fayetteville's #1 Dance Club!"

"Check this out," I said, gesturing at the large sign. "On the strength of the beemer alone, we could pull two females straight from the Big P's parking lot. Fuck needing any fake IDs to get in." Once I indirectly suggested a change of plans, Mick let me know he was not feeling my vibe.

"Oh that's fucked-up!" he complained. "You gonna sell-out on the mission first chance you get?"

"Mission? What mission? Mick, I don't wanna seem insensitive to your situation with Lorraine and Li'l O, but we got a fly-ass ride plus a hundred bucks to burn, and you want me to referee while you cat-fight with your lady?" In a loud voice, I sighed before completing my analysis. "Sorry cuz, but I wanna get some pussy this weekend."

Mick really started pleading his case when he saw me hit the right blinker and decelerate. "Why's it gotta be like that?" he chuckled, revealing his uneasiness. "Listen, there's no beef between me and Lorraine."

"Word?" I probed in a suspicious tone, "then what's up with the 'mama drama' comment a second ago?"

"A-ight here's the story," Mick hurriedly began to explain as we exited the highway. "I heard one of my boys is trying to get with Lorrie. Me and this dude go way back, damn near to when we were in diapers."

Hearing this, I reminisced on my own 'Jodie episode' with Asia for the first time in months. "I hear ya, there's no loyalty in the hood," I concurred.

Determined to hear the facts before proceeding any further, I pulled into the parking lot of a package-goods store and stopped.

"So what's the plan? You gonna knock this chump out or what?" I said, shifting the transmission to park.

"It shouldn't come to that. Like I said, we go way back, we even played varsity ball together. He ran the point and I started at small-forward."

"And nowadays, your homie's taking shots at Lorrie. Okay I get it."

"Well that still remains to be seen," Mick stated, still optimistic his teammate was not stabbing him in the back. "But lemme finish, 'cause I didn't tell you the best part yet. For you that is."

"There's more?" Releasing the steering wheel, I sat back and listened.

"Remember Lorrie's homegirl? The light-skinned chick posing with us in my year book? The one you were drooling over?"

"If you mean that sensuous, butterscotch honey, hell yeah! What about her?"

"She's staying with Lorrie for a couple weeks."

"Oh, Lorrie got her own place?"

"Yeah, she don't get along with her mother. They just can't live together. Her mother also thinks so too, so she agreed to pay half the rent if Lorrie would move out."

"So it'll be just the four of us…I mean the five of us, including Li'l O, chillin' in the apartment?"

Understanding what I was thinking, Mick started nodding with a sly grin. "That's right, playa. You'll have all weekend to kick it to her. Plus, Lorrie's mom will probably baby-sit at least one night."

The situation seemed too good to be true, so I sensed a trap. "Hmm, what's the catch?"

"Okay, you got me. The catch is: Tina moved-in 'cause she just broke up with her man." *After saying this, Mick's forehead and ears appeared to be moving ever-so-slightly.*

"I don't care about that. What else?"

"Pretty good, what're you clairvoyant? Mick chuckled. "Okay, Lorrie said Tina gained some weight."

Having collected enough information, I announced my decision. "Well as long as I'm expecting a plump chick, fuck it. Let's go check-out your corny-ass town. What's it called again? Cornflake, Michigan?"

"Battle Creek!" Mick emphatically corrected me, showing his hometown pride.

Ironically, for that weekend, this 'Cereal City' could not have been named more appropriately.

Chapter 12: The Journey begins...♀

"You ready to do this?" Asking me this, Mick sounded excited. "Here," he said after using the seatbelt's clasp to open two cold-ones.

Having returned from purchasing a case of Heineken and relieving ourselves, of course, we snorted a few more lines before hitting the road.

Checking the rear-view mirror, I slid the transmission into drive just as Larry Blackmon's lyrics started pumping through the speakers. "Word up…let's jet."

Hearing my comment precisely as the Foxy 99 disc-jockey introduced *Cameo's* hit by the same name, Mick condescendingly snickered at my attempt to blend my words with the DJ's. "Who's corny now?"

For the next couple hours, we reminisced on some of the mischief we committed in Airborne School. Laughing about the good ol' days with the last version of the City Crew eventually lead to paying homage to Stew. As we strolled back up Memory Lane to the present, I asked a question which abruptly changed the entire mood of the conversation.

"Yo, whatever happened to those holy-rollin' brothers we met at the shoppette? Jon and Curt were their names, right?"

"Damn man! Why you gonna bring them up while

we're having a good time?"

Seeing I struck a nerve, I egged him on, "Tak, praise the Lord…Jesus loves you!' That's all I heard after you got saved, that's why!"

"Seriously, can we change the subject?"

Utterly detesting the neurotic 'Negro State of Mind' which afflicts so many melanin-rich people when it comes to religion, in my impatience, I snapped. "What the fuck you so scared of? We gonna get struck by lightning if we mention 'Jesus' while we gettin' bent?" I sneered. "Chill out! Nobody's showing any disrespect toward your Christian God."

"Oh boy! Here we go again with one of your 'the Christian God is the white man's god' rants."

"Those ain't my words homeboy, I'm just repeating what the bean-pie selling brothers on the Ave. be saying," I mentioned with a chuckle.

"Amaru, you don't respect nothing, do you?"

"Come on man, you're hurting my feelings." Even though it was too dark to see my face, the sarcasm in my voice was apparent. "Nah for real," I added in a serious tone, "I think about God a lot…and my ancestors too."

"Yeah right," Mick added, sounding like he didn't believe me.

"Hold-up, don't try to change the subject. This ain't about me."

"What're you talking about?" Blurting this out, Mick feigned ignorance.

270

"Oh, you need me to spell it out? No problem." Clearing my throat, I commenced the breakdown segment. "Like I said, after you prayed with what's his name, my man Jon, you gave me a Billy Graham sermon every day for the next week. You called me a sinner, condemned me to hellfire and brimstone, and all kinds of terrifying shit. But look atcha two short weeks later…" Following the silent drum-roll, I lashed out my harsh criticism. "You over there looking like a back-slid coke-fiend!"

"First of all," Mick shot back in anger. "That was almost two months ago. But more importantly, out of everybody I know, not *you!*" Hesitating here, Mick demonstrated his own ability to utilize the empty space between phrases. "I know your lying, low-down conniving ass ain't trying to judge me!"

Curious about his 'Jesus experience' but too embarrassed to simply ask, instead I tried to extend our routine of playing the dozens into the realm of religion.

"Two weeks, two months, two years, who cares? Stay on the subject 'Jeremiah Jehovah.' For all enquiring minds that wanna know, the fiddy-cent question-of-the-day is: are you, or are you not, still a card-carrying member of a Sunday, Welch's Grape Juice and cracker club?"

"Like I said Amaru, you're ignorant…you don't respect nothing." With this declaration, Mick shook his head in disgust and looked out the opposite window.

Listening to Mick, I actually believed he thought a lightning bolt might tear through the sunroof at any moment. Fed up with what I considered to be his irrational caveman superstition, I made my thoughts known. "I'm ignorant and don't respect nothing? Why? Because I'm asking about God?

271

No Mick, the real deal is, I *do* respect God!" This last phrase exploded from my esophagus so loudly, I surprised myself. Taking a second to catch my breath, I expounded further. "As a matter of fact, I respect God so much, if I ever do get saved, or whatever you did that night, it'll mean more to me than taking a two week—*or two month*—break from gettin' high and chasin' pussy!"

"Fuck you Tak! You know damn-well I was serious that night. You were there, you saw me. I'm not perfect that's all. I wasn't ready for that type of commitment!" Pissed-off, Mick threw his bottle out the window. "You know what, I don't need this shit! Drop me off at the next town. I'll take a fuckin' bus!"

Astonished my normally calm-and-collected friend unraveled so quickly, I decided to stop prying and change my line-of-questioning.

"Chill out cuz! I just wanna know what happened in case we run into the 'Divine Duo' again. You know them fools gotta knack for showing up everywhere we go." Pleading with him thus, I handed him a beer before grabbing another one for myself. "Remember we saw them praying with some dudes in the damn Big Ps parking lot?" I resumed. "Blew my mind to see OGs wearing silk shirts, fat gold chains, and Mauri gator shoes holding hands with their heads bowed. And check this out, I was thinking about going to church a couple Sundays ago, but you'd already quit. So I wanted to get the run-down. What happened? I mean, what's the deal with them cats? They just two crooks scamming folks out of their cash, or what?" As I rattled on, basically parroting rhetoric I had picked up at the courts or from TV, Mick remained reluctant to talk about his experience at the Doorway of Christian Unity.

Nicknamed 'The Way' for short, similar to my tiny unit, this burgeoning store-front church was new to the Fayetteville community. The late comedian, George Carlin, poignantly points out how religious institutions specialize in collecting financial offerings from its parishioners. The Way was no different. They were always searching for initiates willing to tithe ten percent of their hard-earned incomes. But what separated this church from many others was their aggressive campaign to reel-in and convert 'lost sheep in the wilderness.' Our brigade, on the other hand, with its overwhelming need for a spiritual cleansing, was a match made in heaven for Pastor Bartholomew and his "Soldiers of the Lord."

Taking a peek over at Mick, he seemed to have calmed down but was still sulking. In silence, he stared out the window with a vacuous expression. I was amazed he was so upset. This is when it dawned on me I knew absolutely nothing about religion.

Being the son of a non-religious man and a Buddhist mother, my main impression of western religion had come through a confrontation with Catholicism during the 'White Flight' era. When the third, fourth, and fifth graders in our elementary school were assembled in the multi-purpose room to view 'Pope John Paul—Live!' I was held spellbound by this mysterious man because I had never heard the word 'pope' before.

Along with everyone else, I watched the Bishop of Rome as he waved to the thousands who had gathered to greet him in Washington DC on a dreary autumn afternoon. Standing in the backseat of a black limousine, his upper body was protruding from the sunroof. While he benignly smiled, dozens of men wearing dark suits and sunglasses jogged alongside the limo.

In my experience, anyone wearing a cape in October was linked to a Halloween celebration. For this reason, I assumed the old man decked-out in flowing white robes, a red cape, and a long-brimmed boater of the same fabric as his clothing was the first float in a parade. Having convinced myself thus, when Pamela Paddock, the white girl in our class with a notorious reputation for shedding crocodile tears, began bawling for the sake of attention, I suspected something was lacking in my theory. Feeling uneasy, I searched for someone to confer with; yet, I was shocked when my friends ignored me. Following a brief reassessment, I concluded anyone being taken so seriously while wearing such outlandish attire must be a spiritual leader.

Although I had been to a Jewish synagogue a handful of times, my experiences inside of a church were limited to two visits. Nonetheless, like healthy children tend to do, I had carefully studied my surroundings. Having gathered fragments of information here and there, I learned the main personality in Christianity was a white man. When I heard about his spectacular healings and other miracles, I was baffled why anyone would want to murder this 'Messiah.' However, not to be outdone, I was relieved that Jesus Christ saved his best act for last by phenomenally resurrecting himself back to life for all eternity.

"All eternity." To me, that meant Jesus was alive—in the flesh—right now.

The biblical verses I read described masses of people crowding around *Him* just to get a glimpse—exactly like the old man in the limo. Although the guy in the red-and-white ensemble was much older than the hippy in the biblical pictures, it seemed reasonable to my fifth-grade logic that

274

anyone returning from the dead might bear some marks of old-age. Aware of only one Caucasian, religious figure, I hastily jumped to the wrong conclusion: I believed we were watching the 'Jesus'…of Nazareth and Bethlehem fame.

But I was not one hundred percent certain, so I tried to confirm my findings with the boy sitting next to me. "Ay Mike, why do they call Jesus, 'the pope'?" I whispered after nudging him on the shoulder.

"Huh?" Mike did not seem to understand.

Pointing at the TV, I revised my question in a louder tone. "Is that Mr. Jesus H. Christ?"

Suddenly all eyes were on me.

Once the gut-wrenching laughter began, it took the faculty more than a few minutes to regain order. Once they did, one of the teachers, a stubby white woman wearing an ugly, light-blue dress and brown glasses accused me of being a troublemaker before sending me to sit in front of the main office until the viewing concluded.

The following day, I was interrogated by our school principal, Mr. Tucker.

"Takuan, look directly in my eyes for a moment. You were joking yesterday weren't you? When you asked if the Pope was Jesus, right?"

"What's the 'H' stand for?" Glancing around the room, I tried to avoid his intense stare as much as possible.

"Are you listening to me?"

With his clinical mannerisms, it is reasonable to believe Mr. Tucker was attempting a mild form of hypnosis. However, my classmates' explanation for our principal's soft-spoken ways was to simply label him as a 'gay guy.'

"Yup, I was Mr. *Sucker."*

"Wha- what did you say?"

"Yes, yes, I was joking. Are you happy now?" I whined.

"N-n, not that...you n-n-know what I'm talking about. What's my name?"

All the kids knew whenever Mr. Tucker got upset he would stutter. So in order to thwart his interrogation, I purposely provoked him. Although he eventually got me to pronounce his name correctly, I made sure he used every ounce of his patience to do so.

"The night I prayed with Jon..."

The earnestness in Mick's raspy voice snapped me out of my daydream and I looked over at the slouched silhouette in the passenger seat.

Mick sat up and turned down the music. After shifting in his seat to face me, he exhaled sharply before resuming. "Tak, it was crazy. I still can't believe I did it. That night, I really thought I had changed into a 'better me' forever." After murmuring this he deliberated for a second to collect his thoughts.

In my peripheral vision, I saw him lick his lips like Cool J does in his videos.

"Tak, you might not believe me, but Jon had me convinced I was cleansed in the blood of Jesus."

"Why wouldn't I believe you? Like you said, I was there. And don't forget, his boy Curt was kicking the same game to me too."

Hearing this, Mick started laughing. "Word? I meant to ask you about that, 'cause I remember just before I prayed, you walked over to me looking all serious. Cuz, I'll never forget the surprised look on Jon's face when you said you were going in the store to buy some beer." When Mick lightly elbowed my arm, I smiled but I did not laugh. "Then," he continued, "after you asked me if I wanted a forty, you turned toward Jon and said, 'No disrespect'." Saying this, he busted-out laughing again.

"Ay, when they introduced themselves, the first question Jon asked was, 'why did we come to the shoppette that night?' And what did I say? I told them straight-up: we came to get drunk!" I declared self-righteously. "When Curt was breaking down Christ's message, even though I wasn't interested, I listened to everything he said. When he finished talking, there was nothing else to listen to, that's all. I don't think that was being disrespectful." Saying this in a defensive tone, I wondered why Mick found my actions so amusing. With the tension lifted, I dared one last inquiry.

"So after that night, did you go to their church?"

"Yeah. Why?"

"Because I wanna know what it's like to hang out with the Caped Crusadin' Christians?"

Smiling, Mick took a sip of his beer. "All I know is, it definitely wasn't what I expected."

"Whaddya mean?"

"Put it this way, I always thought of church as being an indoor activity," he began. "You know, some singing, some hand-clapping, and maybe a little dancing. But mostly, I expect to sit down, read some biblical verses, and hear a sermon."

"Really? That's it? What about all those Reverends I hear about that're always begging for money? Or the crazy folks jumping up-and-down screaming about catching the Holy Ghost?"

"Shut up and listen! Yeah, they got all the normal, church stuff going on too but that ain't what I'm talking about. Cuz, they do this shit called 'witnessing'."

277

"What's that?"

"It's what Curt and Jon are doing every time we see them." Sensing my uncertainty, Mick explained further. "Those dudes, along with their entire church, literally pull out maps and pinpoint areas to deploy their forces."

"To do what?"

"To strategically spread God's word: to be His witness. And the shit actually works."

"How do you know?"

"'Cause I watched those muthafuckas in action, that's how!" Eager to back his claim, Mick then revealed more than just witnessing the witnessing, he had actually taken part himself.

"You weren't embarrassed?" I asked.

"At first I was," he admitted. "Until I watched Jon and Curt do their thang. Cuz, they made me proud to be a black man! No joke, them two be breaking fools down like Malcolm X!"

"Get the fuck outta here!"

Having already met this dynamic duo, I knew they were different from the Five-Percenters, Nation of Islam, or even MOVE members; i.e. the other proselytizers of 'the truth' I had the pleasure of meeting thus far. When Herb and I used to trek through West Philly, we often encountered some of these outspoken, street prophets. However, we adamantly ignored representatives of the run-of-the-mill, Christian denominations; especially the pain-in-the-ass Jehovah's Witnesses!

My disdain for Christianity had little to do with the tenets of their belief system. Rather, it was their ungodly appearance. Up to that point, every Christian I had met, black or white, had been a dork wearing polyester slacks, a knit sweater, and thick-soled Buster Brown shoes. Or a wrinkled suit. With their bland personalities, I found it amusing these nerds wasted their time trying to persuade complete strangers they represented an omnipotent, all-perfect God. My logic was: if they were really cool with *Him*, *He* would never allow them outside looking the way they do. Particularly as His spokesperson. I was more willing to chop-it-up with members of other religions, especially the NOI, because I could relate to what the brothers were saying. That said, any effect their words had was fleeting at best.

My talk with Curt and Jon was different. Although I did not pray right away, we spoke in that parking lot for three hours and they had my attention the entire time. Simply put, these two were masters of elocution when it came to spreading Christ's Gospel. What set them apart from the aforementioned messengers began with their physical appearance. Whether in BDUs or civvies, they always looked sharp; and their body language exuded confidence. Being 'white-man educated' brothers from around the way, they knew how to transcend both worlds using a combination of wit, charm, and intelligence. In my opinion, had their message been from the prophet Muhammad, or about Buddha's divine love, they would have been no less dynamic a duo. Representing the heart and soul of the Way, this 'twin energy' was successful in sharing God's Word with everyone from teenagers to high-ranking officers.

"I got paired up with Curt on my first deployment," Mick said after opening another Heineken and taking a healthy swig. "That guy's hard-charging...he don't give a fuck!"

"Whaddya mean?"

"He really believes he's the Son of the living God. He

279

repeats it out loud all the time. My man Curt," Mick took another sip, "he'll witness anywhere. Cuz, he took me to a whorehouse and started handing out Christian leaflets to dudes going inside. Yo, and guess who showed up out there?"

"Who?"

"Lloyd," Mick answered in a matter of fact tone.

"Lloyd? You mean the Lloyd who flunked out of Jump School, Lloyd?"

"You know another Lloyd? Remember when Parnell and Chavez told us Lloyd was a regular at the hoe houses on Murchison Road…and the VD clinic too?" Mick added with a chuckle. "Anyway, after the third, horny customer ran down a taxi trying to get away from us, this real evil bitch started yelling at Curt."

"Did she come from inside the house?"

"Exactly! That's what I wanted to know." With the sun threatening to break through the horizon, I could barely make out the stunned expression on Mick's face. "Word is bond, homegirl appeared out of nowhere like a witch. She scared the shit outta me!" Mick exclaimed.

"So what'd your boy do?"

"That muthafucka didn't bat an eyelash," he replied taking a sip. "After Curt glared back for a couple seconds, he walked toward her and stuck his face inches away from hers. Then he said, 'We ain't going nowhere!'"

"Word? What'd the witch do?" I asked excitedly.

"When *Broomhilda* started screaming again, he stuck his head even closer and repeated it louder. 'Nowhere!' After that, home-girl got ghost with-the-quickness! So to answer your question, I don't know where honeybuns came from, but I do know she funneled her narrow ass back inside through the front door. And peep this…" he piqued my interest before trailing off.

"What's that?" I asked through my laughter.

"After that, not one, not two, but *three* 'would-be Johns' prayed with us and joined the Way. Two of those guys were still there when I left."

"Just a guess, but I imagine your boy Lloyd wasn't one 'em, huh?"

"Hell no! Not that nasty-ass heathen!" Mick exclaimed before adding with a smirk, "And he ain't 'my boy' either."

Thinking the conversation had reached its conclusion, I reached down and turned up the radio just as *'I'm Bad,'* by LL, which was Mick's personal anthem, was coming on. To my surprise, he promptly re-muted the music.

"Hold-up, I ain't get to the best part yet." Smacking his own leg in laughter, Mick seemed to be visualizing something. "After we left the whorehouse, we met-up with four other groups at that movie theater on Bragg Boulevard. You know, the one that's been showing *Lethal Weapon* for the last couple months."

"Y'all met inside of a movie theater?"

"No dumb-ass, outside in the parking lot. And you know I was *not* happy about that. Walking around Fayetteville had been bad enough, but I was sure to see folks I knew at the movies. And guess who I saw?"

"Who?" I asked.

"That married chick, Amy. You remember her? She was there with her husband."

"Nah, don't think so," I said thinking back.

"Stop frontin', you remember. That hoe with the big titties you were fingering in the back seat of my car while her friend was sucking my dick."

"Ay, I didn't know she was married 'til later," I insisted.

Ignoring my plea of innocence, Mick got back to his story. "So while we were standing outside waiting for Jon and a few others, one of the church members named 'Dennis' came running up to us yelling something. Cuz, at first I thought Jon was in a fight."

"What'd he say?"

"He said Jon was inside the theater. And get this, he was witnessing."

"Inside? Get the fuck outta here!" Dumbfounded, I used the only expression that seemed appropriate.

"When we went inside and Jon was nowhere to be found, I just thought he was in the latrine taking a leak," Mick continued. "But Curt knew the deal right away. He said Jon had been talking about how many souls could be saved at a blockbuster movie like *Lethal Weapon* ever since it started showing. Since it was playing in two different rooms, we split-up to cover both possibilities. Of course, I went with Curt's group," he said before pausing to burp. "And sure enough, when we opened the door, I heard Jon's voice loud and clear. But Tak, check this out: homeboy was preaching a sermon to the whole room."

"What?"

"Right, that's what I thought too!" Mick took a break to laugh at my hysterics and take another swig. "Check-it-out: the movie had ended and all the lights were on. Jon was standing on the stage, in front of the screen. Not only did he give a five-minute sermon, my man gave a brief Q & A when he was done."

"That muthafucka's crazy!"

"Hold up, I ain't finished. Then he asked if anyone

wanted to redeem their soul right then and there. When he gave the altar call, six people ran down the aisle to pray before the cops showed up."

"Get the fuck outta here!"

With the morning sun blinding me, I gritted my teeth from the passenger seat. Glancing away, I spotted a sign. It read: 'Welcome to Michigan! Great Lakes and Great Times!' It was almost ten o'clock. Although hours had passed since our conversation ended, my mind never quite abandoned the images of Curt staring down the hooker, or Jon's on-stage, theatrical performance. Somewhere around the Ohio-Indiana leg of our trip, Mick had assumed the driving duties. At that point, both of us were tired, so we turned off the radio and stopped talking. As a result, when Mick suggested we stop at *Denny's*, he startled me.

"It ain't as dope as *Shoney's*, but they got a decent breakfast menu," he said while turning into the parking lot.

"You really feel like eating?"

"Hell no, but that don't matter because we're only about two hours from the crib so we gotta eat something."

"Oh yeah, we gotta sober up before meeting your folks."

Following three, heaping servings of eggs, pancakes, grits, and hash browns, we both recalled our declarations about not being hungry and cracked-up laughing. Subsequent to our lavish meal, we drove to a nearby car wash to polish up our appearance. As I discarded empty bottles and other evidence of our dysfunctional activities, Mick hosed off the grit, grime, and dead insects which had accumulated during our high-speed flight through the chilly, Midwest morning.

"That's good enough," I said after vacuuming the inside. "Throw me the keys, let's jet." Saying this, I approached the driver's side of the still-dripping BMW.

Looking disappointed, Mick protested, "Aw come on cuz, you ain't gon' let a brother floss in his own hood?"

Like many, we were convinced an expensive car defined our manhood. It mattered little whether the vehicle was borrowed, rented, or even stolen. *Just so long as we were being seen in it.* Realizing had the roles been reversed, I too would want to push the beemer in my hometown, of course I let him drive.

"Oh yeah, my fault."

Minutes later, I dozed off. When Mick woke me up, I looked out the window and rubbed my eyes.

"We're almost at the spot," he said with a yawn.

"This is Battle Creek?" Greeted by green lawns, shrubbery, and loads of children playing in their yards or at well-kept parks, it looked like a great place to settle down and raise some kids. "Yo cuz, I thought you said your neighborhood was hard?" I teased him.

"Still talking shit?" he asked while looking at me with one eyebrow raised. "Don't forget, I know your ass ain't really from Philly. I seen your mail, remember? What's the name of that li'l, rinky-dink town you're from again?"

Once Mick had carefully parallel parked in front of a duplex apartment, we got out and popped the trunk to get our bags.

"Mmm-mmm, who's that fine brutha getting out the beemer?" said a girl from the balcony.

"Wait a minute, is that Orlando?" countered another

female while sucking her teeth. "And look, he brought a cute friend with him too!"

Although their catcalls were flattering on the surface, it was apparent the two girls were mocking us. Checking out the second-story terrace, I glimpsed both teenagers giggling under their breath. Mick, also looking up, responded with his own joke material.

"Tak, the tall, goofy girl on the right is my sister, Melissa. I don't know who the other chickenhead is."

Just then, another female voice could be heard in the distance. "Orlando, don't you come here starting no trouble! You hear me?"

I deduced the unseen person was Mick's mother.

Seconds later, a woman holding a baby joined the teens on the veranda. Although she did not appear much older, I knew the three of them were not peers. All three of them wore scarves over their curlers and were donned in jean-shorts and t-shirts.

"Nah ma, I'm just playing," Mick pleaded before turning to me. "Tak, that's my mom. And the baby she's holding is my son, Li'l O. Oh, and the other girl is my cousin, Janice." Then he returned his eyes to the terrace. "Mom, this is the guy I was telling you about."

"My name's Takuan," I greeted the foursome. "Nice to meet y'all."

After carrying our bags upstairs, Ms. McKnight made us wait outside as the three ladies hurriedly straightened up the apartment. Fifteen minutes later, she opened the door and loudly complained.

"Un-unh, how you gonna show up without calling us—and bring a friend?" Despite this, she was obviously happy to see her son.

285

Thirty minutes later, we were treated to a hearty lunch comprised of leftovers, plus some turkey-burgers Missy fried up. In spite of downing a huge breakfast a couple hours before, like many on-the-move teenagers, we had no trouble making room for more food.

"Mom, you know why Orlando didn't call before he came, don't you?" Despite Ms. McKnight seeming to ignore her daughter, Missy volunteered the information anyway. "He's trying to catch Lorrie out there with another guy."

Sitting there, I was amazed at how she knew Mick like the back of their hand. When the three women started laughing, I snickered along lest they start taking shots at me, too.

"Shut up Missy!" Mick scolded his little sister before appealing to his mother. "Nah, that ain't the reason—"

As I wondered if Mick appeared as unconvincing to them as he did to me, his mother put the matter to rest.

"Boy, after nineteen years of catching you in lies, don't you know you can't get over on me yet?" After Ms. McKnight busted his chops, Janice sampled some sweet revenge on her older cousin.

"Takuan, if you ever notice Orlando's ears wiggling when he's talking to you—" At that point, Missy grabbed her cousin's arm and they busted-out laughing over their secret. Seconds later, following a series of deep breaths to compose herself, Jan was able to complete her statement. "That means he's lying." Barely getting this out, the two cousins began giggling again.

Her words somehow rang a bell. I may have noticed this little idiosyncrasy, I thought. Before I had an opportunity to think about it further, Ms. McKnight offered me another helping of food.

"Yes please. Thank you," I replied holding out my plate.

Compared to the hum-drum life of a GI, sitting around the living room with Mick's family was crazy fun. Once Mick and I finished off another 'mythological grub-session,' within minutes, the two of us became drowsy. We soon retired to the larger of the two bedrooms and fell fast asleep.

The sound of a crying baby woke me up. Opening my eyes, I yawned but I did not dare move. For almost a minute, I laid still until Mick's baritone vocals erupted over the din of the television in the next room. His voice was followed by the laughter of many women. Using these hints, I was able to piece together the details of our journey. Feeling a sense of relief, I sat up and glanced out a nearby window. It was getting dark outside and the street lights were already on.

I switched on a lamp and spotted some bath towels at the foot of the bed. I also saw a clock on a night stand; it was a few minutes past seven thirty. Standing up, I stretched my limbs and tried to eavesdrop on the conversation going on in the living room. Although I could not hear what was being said, I was able to distinguish two new voices. Following a moment of deliberation, I imagined they belonged to Lorrie and the butter-scotch honey. Since I wanted to make a good, first impression, I grabbed the towels and walked into the connecting bathroom.

Seconds after I got in the shower, Mick walked into the bathroom. "Glad you found the towels I left out for you. You need anything else?"

287

His sudden appearance startled me. Coughing up a glob of phlegm, I spit it down the drain to clear my throat. "Nah, everything's cool, thanks," I replied.

"Well, I already shit, showered, and shaved so take your time," Mick said in a joyful tone.

Once the tepid water hit my face, I perked up. This prompted me to comment further. "But on to more important topics, where's the party at tonight?" When Mick did not reply, I pulled the shower curtain back a few inches. This revealed his smiling face. It was smeared with so much lipstick, Mick resembled a friendly clown. "I see somebody's happy to see you. I just hope her name's Lorraine."

"And you know that!" replied my hyped-up friend.

Beyond the normal frills and thrills, a homecoming like this provides for any young GI, Mick, being reunited with his girlfriend and son, appeared more at ease than I'd ever seen him before. As I tried to analyze this metamorphosis in more detail, he broke through my mind chatter.

"Lemme be the first to congratulate you on the fine piece of ass you're about to sample tonight."

Although I wanted to hear more, I had to chastise him for messing up my chances to get naked. "Shhh...keep it down! They're in the next room, right?"

Hearing this, he looked at me like I was stupid.

"Oh, I see," I continued, "now that your pussy cat's in the bag, you gonna forget your playa instincts."

"Nah cuz, I'm on-it-dog-onnit. I sent them home to wait for us," he said using an authoritative tone.

"Oh, it's like that? Excuse me, you must be the man!" I shot back before finishing my witty satire. "Because only a true pimp could send *two* women home—not to mention a baby—to get barefoot in the kitchen."

"You damn skippy!" Mick replied in a cocky voice. "And check this out homeboy, if you weren't here, I'd be dickin' them both down tonight. Believe that!"

"Yeah right!" Before either of us had a chance to laugh at the absurdity of his statement, we both detected the sound of two snickering girls.

"Missy, get outta here!" Yelling this, Mick ran out of the bathroom and chased his sister and cousin back to the living room.

Ten minutes after stepping out of the shower, I was dressed in a red-and-white Todd-1 sweat suit, white-on-white Reeboks, and a matching white, baseball cap. While I fixed both beds, I could hear Mick in the next room. He was still snitching on his siblings. Listening to him and Missy argue, I imagined this was an everyday event when Mick was in high school. The final touch to my preparations was applying a dash of Polo cologne, made famous by *Slick Rick, the Ruler.* With one last look into the gold-trimmed, oval mirror on the wall, I exited the bedroom.

Once I was in the hallway, I sensed a lot of anxiety coming from the living room. Because the atmosphere reminded me of a courtroom, I remained silent, careful not to interrupt the proceedings. Entering the living room, I took a seat in the chair nearest to the hallway but in spite of my attempt to be quiet, the judge, the plaintiff, and both defendants looked my way when the plastic furniture cover on the chair I sat in crackled. Following a brief pause, without saying a word, the three women busted-out laughing.

Needless to say, I was thrown off my high horse.

Fearing a huge blotch of black ink had stained my Todd-1, I stood up and glanced at the full-length mirror propped near the front door to scan my reflection from head-to-toe. While confirming my appearance was still cold-crush, I caught a glimpse of the two juveniles. Both girls had their arms extended in a semi-circle, in front of their stomachs; it looked like they were hugging an imaginary person. I also noticed they had their cheeks filled with air like Dizzy Gillespie does when he's blowing the horn.

"Oh I get it." Saying this, I sat back down and pointed at Jan and Missy. "Y'all calling somebody fat. The only question is: who?"

"You two mind your business!" No longer smiling, Ms. McKnight reprimanded the adolescents before they could say anything. "I'm serious, we don't talk about people behind their backs like that," she warned. Then, having restored her grin, she looked at me. "My, don't you look nice…you must have a big date tonight, huh?"

Lacking any sincerity in her voice whatsoever, I suspected she was more concerned with camouflaging the awkward silence which had developed. While I considered this, the girls began giggling again. In spite of Ms. McKnight's stern warning, Missy and Jan were in rare form that night; they refused to remain quiet.

"No mom, it's not a 'big' date, it's called a 'heavy' date. If Takuan goes out with that fat pig tonight, he'll be on a *heavy* date with a real heavyweight." Then, she hi-fived her cousin as if to complete their tag-team effort.

"The overweight lover's in the house!" Janice screamed pointing at me. "Forget *Heavy D,* Takuan's the real *Overweight Lover!"*

With that, the room exploded in laughter. And if that was not enough, everyone pointed at me and began singing the chorus of the popular hit song.

"The Overweight Lover's in the house! The Overweight Lover's in the house…in the house!"

Seeing both girls wopping their heads, shoulders, and arms to the silent beat, Mick and his mom couldn't resist getting caught-up in the hilarity of the moment. Soon everyone, except me, was on their feet dancing and chanting the chorus. This lasted for the next five minutes, until Mick and I were on our way out the door. When Mick kissed his mother on the cheek, the four of them were still breaking out in snickers here and there. With a smile on my face, I chuckled along good-naturedly the entire time. In spite of this, once we got in the car, my mood shifted.

"Mick, whatever you do tonight, don't leave me alone with *Ms. Piggy."* I knew my demand was ridiculous, so I continued talking before he could complain. "Just 'til I fall asleep. Then you can go get romantic with Lorrie. Word is bond, if y'all roll-out while I'm still awake, I'm jettin' to a hotel and I don't know my way back here, so you'll have to catch a bus back to Fayetteville."

"What? You're joking right?" Seeing I was not, Mick flipped. "Cuz, you gonna let Missy and Jan get in your head like that? Yo, those two chickenheads are just 'boy crazy.' They probably got a crush on you, that's all. But don't let it go to your head playa, 'cause they sweat all my friends like that."

"Cut the bullshit! How fat is she?"

"Honestly, she looked thick to me. Not fat." Then Mick flashed a queer expression my way. "Unless you one of them brothers with a fetish for bony white women."

Just as I was feeling some sense of relief, I noticed Mick's ears appeared to be vibrating ever-so-slightly. "Aw cuz, you lyin'!"

Determined to hurdle this minor impasse, Mick expressed his disgust. "Tak, you acting real corny right now! Especially since we already had this discussion, remember?"

In spite of my inability to argue, I was determined to stand by my previous declaration. "Like I said, if you and Lorrie disappear in the bedroom, I'm out."

Knowing how stubborn I could be, Mick relented. "Okay, okay *son.* I'll babysit until you fall asleep."

Happy to get my way, I went right along with his joke. "Thanks pop."

Our next stop was at a liquor store. Even though Mick could easily pass for twenty-one, he balked at my suggestion that he try to get served. "They got a lotta undercover cops working inside these joints," he assured me. "It's better to pay a homeless person a few bucks to hook it up." With that, we exited the BMW and stood there for a few seconds to scrutinize the people loitering in front of the store.

"They look bummy enough to me, whaddya you think?" Mick asked.

"Let's go," I agreed, nodding my head.

Since this was Mick's town, he took the lead as we approached one of the street folk. The unshaven, melanin-rich man was dressed in jeans, a faded BDU field-jacket, and a dirty Detroit Tigers baseball cap.

After promising the man, who was undoubtedly a Vietnam vet, we would give him a few dollars, we handed him our money and watched him enter the store. It only took him a few minutes to return holding three pints of Bacardi rum and a twelve-pack of Molson Golden. Mick and I were so pleased we let him keep the nearly five bucks of change.

"Good-looking-out, young bloods!" the ex-soldier gleefully cried out, placing the money inside his left, breast pocket. When he did so, I noticed the Airborne wings stitched on his jacket.

"You're jump qualified?" I asked in a friendly tone, happy to find something we all shared in common.

Far from pleased, my question seemed to upset the man. Instead of answering right away he stared at us for a few seconds before making his own inquiry.

"Y'all doing time in Uncle Sam's war, ain't ya?"

"Yeah," Mick and I responded simultaneously, understanding he was asking if we were GIs.

"Lemme give you a piece of advice—"

"No thanks old-timer," Mick interrupted in a cold tone. And without further ado, we grabbed the bags, turned around, and walked away.

However, the down-on-his-luck elder remained undaunted; he was determined to be heard. Raising his voice, he drilled his stern warning into our backs as we crossed the street. "The only way there can be a 'just war' is if y'all turn your guns against the cracka-man, himself! Never trust him! He's a liar all the way down to his wicked core! You need to understand this, and get out while your minds are still intact!"

Arriving at the car, we glanced back. The raving madman was standing in a spread-eagle pose, with both arms fully extended. In one hand, he held a bottle sheathed by a brown paper-bag. It appeared he had been holding that pose, waiting for us to turn around. Once we did, he quaked in a loud, troubling voice. *"Look at everything he did for me!"*

For the remainder of the drive, I was unable to leave behind the disturbing image of the transient. That is, until we arrived at Lorraine's apartment and two heavy-set women bounced outside to greet us.

Thinking they could easily pass for the *Weather Girls,*

I imagined they were about to sing their hit song, *'It's Raining Men...Hallelujah!'* Seeing both of them dressed in bright, pastel colors, I felt like I was watching the video; the only thing they were missing was their trench coats. In order to disguise my emotions, I froze a polite smile onto my face. Before I got out of the car, I remembered Mick's previous comment about skinny girls. I now understood my homie liked his ladies a little thicker than me.

After Mick introduced me, both women gave me a hug. Judging by the way the bigger of the two squeezed her humongous breasts against me, I knew she was down for whatever.

"Hi Takuan, I'm Tina," she revealed with a flirtatious wink.

Around my way, we called fast-chicks like Tina 'skeezers.' In all honesty, I never was convinced Tina was the same girl I saw in Mick's yearbook. Aside from her general complexion and dark features, she did not resemble the pretty girl in the photograph at all. Nonetheless that photo was over two years old; and since that time, according to Mick, Tina had been the recipient of several beatings at the hands of her boyfriend not to mention three abortions. Considering this, I imagined it was possible for a girl to become depressed enough to cut her hair off and start pounding-down Tasty Kakes.

But don't get me wrong, Tina was not butt-ugly. In fact, I'll go on record and say she was *almost* cute—in a chubby sort of way. For one thing, she had a fly hairstyle. Bobbed and neatly parted to the side, it was blown-dry for smoothness and cropped perfectly to fit her round face as it rested in layers along her puffy cheeks. Tina resembled a lighter-complexioned *Ms. Sofia,* played by Oprah Winfrey in the movie, *'The Color Purple.'*

Upon entering the single-family home with my plastic smile still on display, I was glad to see Li'l O. When the three adults left the living room, leaving the two of us alone, I walked to the sofa and picked him up because I needed a distraction.

"Hey little man," I said raising the child toward the ceiling. Orlando Jr. started laughing. "You like that huh? Well, I don't wanna get you too excited." Saying this, I took a seat on the couch and set the boy on my lap. He looked back at me and smiled. "What am I gonna do?" I asked in a soft voice, hoping anyone—even a baby—could help me strategize an excuse to leave.

Gazing into Li'l O's face, I noticed he was the splitting image of his father. The same wide eyes and flat nose, he even had the extra folds of skin on the back of his head which had prompted Wilkins, back in Jump School, to joke that Mick stored water there.

"That's why Mick ain't never thirsty after PT!" Wilkins had yelled as we cracked up.

With the boy on my lap, I felt relieved. Not knowing who went where, I was content to play babysitter—*all night if need be.* When the doorbell rang, I was startled to see a middle-aged woman open the door and let herself in.

"Oh excuse me, young man. I didn't mean to frighten you, I'm Lorrie's mother," said the woman in a kind voice.

The lady was wearing a black camisole sweater over a modest, gray one-piece dress. Due to her conservative attire, I missed seeing the obvious family resemblance. Like Lorrie, the woman had an oval face with deep-set eyes. A bit on the hefty side, her coffee-colored complexion bore little traces of make-up, unlike her daughter.

"Good evening ma'am," I replied matching her polite tone. "My name's Takuan. I'm Mick's—I mean Orlando's friend." It was strange to refer to Mick in this way. "I think Lorrie's in the kitchen."

Hearing this, the lady scanned me from head to toe. "Oh yes, of course. Lorrie said Orlando brought a friend home with him," she continued in her pleasant tone. "Welcome to Battle Creek. My, my, you're just as handsome as my son-in-law. Well, future son-in-law that is."

It was not difficult to pick-up on the vibe that Lorrie's mother was uncomfortable with the out-of-wedlock dynamics which had created her grandchild. Sensing this, I wanted to steer the conversation back to the whereabouts of Mick and Lorrie. Before that became necessary, the kitchen door swung open.

"Hey mama." After affectionately greeting the older woman, Tina hooked her thumb toward the door at the end of the hall. "You know where those two are. They're in there getting *re-acquainted.*"

"You see Takuan, that's how all this got started in the first place," Lorrie's mom looked at me and said this in a complaining tone.

Beyond suspecting the witty comment reflected her honest opinion, I also noticed Lorrie's mother was ignoring Tina.

"Hey mama." When Mick and her real daughter emerged from the bedroom holding hands, everyone noticed Lorrie's clothes were disheveled; it appeared Lorrie had rushed to get dressed.

"Girl fix your blouse!" the mother admonished her daughter. Then, she pointed at Mick. From this point, the nice lady from a few seconds ago looked and sounded like a

completely different person. "Orlando, it's nice to see you." Although the words were cordial, her voice sounded much colder than before. "But take it easy, okay? And make sure to use the condoms I gave Lorrie 'cause we can't afford no more little ones. You hear me?"

"Yes ma'am," Mick responded.

Then, without a hug or a handshake, she walked toward me and snatched Li'l O from my lap.

Watching my alibi for the evening vanish before my eyes, I sprang from the couch to intercept Lorrie's mother before she could reach the door. "Ma'am," I said using my most polite tone, "please, don't trouble yourself. I'd be happy to watch the boy tonight."

Easily seeing through my chicanery, she pointed behind me. "What kind of grandmother do you take me for?"

Looking over my shoulder, I caught a glimpse of Mick and Tina smuggling the liquor we bought into the kitchen. Seeing this, I was deeply embarrassed. By the time I turned back around, she was already walking out the apartment. Once outside, Lorrie's mother hesitated for a second. Wearing the wickedest frown I had ever seen, she stared right through me.

"You better get right with God!" she screamed before slamming the door.

With this eerie premonition fresh in my mind, along with the foreboding words of the wino, I spotted the car keys lying on the coffee table and placed them in my pocket.

"You going somewhere?" Lorrie asked in a mocking tone after she walked to the door and locked it.

Before I could respond, the high-pitched sound of a blender shearing through ice got our attention. Hearing this, Lorrie seemed to remember something.

"I'll be right back," she declared once the noise subsided. "Make yourself at home." Then she slipped into the kitchen with the others.

Five minutes later, Mick beckoned me to join them.

"Yo Tak, the party's going on in here. Where you at?"

Although I knew it was set-up, I felt helpless to escape. Considering I knew nothing about Battle Creek, where could I actually go? Having no options, I dejectedly walked through the kitchen door only to be greeted by three people toasting wineglasses in the air.

"We're waiting on you playa, the guest of honor!" announced Mick in a celebratory tone. Right on cue with Mick's declaration, Tina extended a glass of dark liquid, mixed with crushed ice, toward me.

"Un momentito," she said once I grabbed the glass. "I have to finish mixing it." Then, she placed a small spoon into my glass and stirred it three times.

Afer receiving the mixed concoction, I stared at it for a second. Then I sniffed it.

"This is my favorite drink," Tina said with a lusty grin. "It's called 'Mi Amor.' That means 'love' in Spanish."

"Actually, it means 'my love,'" I corrected her, eager to disagree with anything she had to say.

"Takuan, welcome to Battle Creek!" Lorrie said, clinking her glass against mine. "And baby, welcome home!" she added, turning toward Mick and tapping his glass before kissing him on the lips.

After everyone touched glasses, I took a seat at a small table and gawked at the numerous mixers and cocktail ingredients laid out before me. There were various fruit juices, liqueurs, soda, and a big jar of honey.

"Mmm mmm, see I told you girl," Tina remarked to

Lorrie. "Takuan's a *Porto-Rican!*" she said, cracking a smile. "Takuan, you can you speak Spanish, can't you?"

"Hell yeah!" Mick responded before I could say anything. "Tak can speak three or four languages. Come on y'all, let's go back out there, *Bamanos!*" he uttered in his badly pronounced Spanish while pointing at the kitchen door.

Once everyone was in the living room, I walked toward the lone chair at the head of the coffee table and sat down. I did this so Mick and Lorrie could sit together on the couch. This was also to distance myself from Tina.

"Lorrie, put in a movie," Mick suggested.

"Y'all seen *Return of the Living Dead?*" Lorrie asked reaching for the VHS tape on the coffee table. "I just rented it yesterday".

"We're in the Army, we ain't seen shit!" Mick stated in loud voice.

Once I assured Lorrie I had not seen the movie either, she walked over to the television. Squatting down, she inserted the the tape into the VCR, which was located under the TV.

"Hold up a sec!" Mick declared, jumping up and running into the kitchen. In less than a second it seemed, he reappeared with four beers. Passing me two of the bottles, he winked. "This is to wash down Tina's drink. It's a little sweet. Whaddya think?"

"I like it!" Lorrie vehemently responded even though his question had been directed to me.

When everyone looked my way, I had to say something.

"It's okay," I commented looking at the dark liquid. "The jury's still out."

"I was just kidding, Tina," Mick assured her. "Your

299

drink, what's it called again, 'Mi Amor,' it's the shit! Tak knows he likes it too. He's just stubborn like that." Then he addressed his girlfriend. "Lorrie, turn off the lights, we wanna feel like we're in a movie theater."

"Thank you, Orlando," Tina showed her gratitude.

The light banter continued after the lights were dimmed and the movie started. Twenty minutes later, Tina stopped the movie and disappeared into the kitchen. At that time, I was already feeling light-headed.

"Damn! What's in this stuff?" I asked to no one in particular.

Even though she was in the kitchen, Tina heard me. In a flash, she returned holding a pitcher and answered my question. "It's a love potion, *mi amor!* Do you like it? I saw how fast you drank your first glass."

Still reluctant to admit the drink was tasty, I half-heartedly nodded. *That was good enough for the skeezer.* With a huge smile etched across her face, she refilled my glass.

"Thanks," I said before returning my attention to the television screen when Mick restarted the flick.

Before long, I heard the sound of liquid being poured into my glass again. Looking to my left, I noticed Tina was now sitting on the floor next to me. Because my plan was to get drunk and fall asleep, I figured her pouring my drinks would work in my favor. Nevertheless, the Coca-Cola in the mix had other ideas. I guess it's not called 'coke' for nothing. Knocking back glass-after-glass, I completely underestimated the power *any* loose woman has over *any* heterosexual man under the influence of alcohol. About an hour later, Lorrie paused the video.

"I gotta use the ladies' room," she declared. "Tina,

what about you?"

"I gotta go too," Tina answered. "Let me go first."

After the two women left the room, I stood up and stumbled badly.

"You alright cuz?" When Mick rose to his feet to turn on the light, he too appeared wobbly.

Man, was I lit up! And to my dismay, I was wide awake without a hint of drowsiness. I wanted to leave but I knew I was way too drunk to drive through a strange town at night. On the other hand I realized if I remained in Lorrie's tiny, two room apartment, I would have to sleep in the same room with Tina. Either in the living room or the bedroom. With this in mind, I decided it was better to sleep in the car.

"Mick, I'll be right back," I said, stepping toward the door.

Before Mick could reply, Tina ran back into the room.

"Where you going baby?" she asked, positioning herself between me and the door. "Come sit with me on the couch," she coaxed in a sweet voice. When I opened my mouth to reply, she put both of her hands on my shoulders and began giving me a massage. By doing this, she got me to sit down on the couch.

"Listen Tina, I got something to say—"

"Shhh, try to relax baby," she cut me off in a gentle voice. Instead of sitting next to me, Tina walked around to the back of the couch. From behind me, with her mouth just inches from my ear, she started massaging again. "I got something to tell you too," she purred in an even softer tone. "Ladies first, okay?"

I figured under the circumstances, it was the least I could do.

Once Tina saw my head nod, she slid her hands from

my shoulders to my chest before eventually squeezing my biceps. "Mmm, you have such a nice body," she whispered.

With the VCR on pause, her words were easily overheard by Mick. "Umm, it's getting kinda hot in here," he joked. "Tak, you need a beer?"

"Nah, I'm cool," I replied.

"A-ight, I'll be right back," Saying this, he stood up and excused himself. After he left, I spoke first, but Tina interrupted again.

"Thanks for the compliment but—"

"Takuan!" she cried out before giggling like a schoolgirl. "Wait a minute, I'm not finished yet. It's not so easy for a girl to tell a guy one of her intimate secrets."

I wanted to get this over with so I resolved to be quiet until she was done.

"Do you feel like we met somewhere before?" Tina asked between snickers. When I did not respond, she decided to cut to the chase. "Okay, I'll just say it. Did you see the jar of honey in the kitchen?"

"Yeah," I replied nonchalantly.

"Well," she giggled again, "there's no honey in *Mi Amor,*" she hinted before getting to the point. "The honey's for you."

"What?"

Seeing I was slow to grasp her erotic meaning, Tina added some detail to the picture. "I had a dream last night. Actually it was a fantasy. It was about you Takuan, I know it was. I'm so embarrassed!" Appearing far from ashamed, Tina made her case for me to stay the night. "In my dream, I was on my knees giving a sexy, Porto-rican man a blowjob." Then she reached down and grabbed my penis. By this time, she was breathing so deeply, she was almost moaning. "He was so big…and so hard. Just like you, *mi amor.*" Following a few caressing strokes, Tina reached inside my pants and started giving me a hand-job. Satisfied she had my attention, she resumed her narrative.

"When you grabbed the back of my head and rammed your cock down my throat, it felt so good I had the biggest orgasm…then you came too," she said, exhaling in huge gusts. "Your cum tasted just like honey. It was so good I licked every drop of it!" Utterly lost in her x-rated vision, her story finally reached its climax. "Takuan, I want to suck your dick…I want you to cum all over my face. Can you do that for me, baby?"

This was the precise moment when Tina magically mutated from nasty-fat-nasty to thick, rich, and sexy!

"Uh-umm," Mick cleared his throat. "I hope we're not interrupting anything."

"Yeah!" Lorrie exclaimed wearing a mischievous grin. "What's going on in here?"

Even had they not spotted Tina hurriedly removing her hand from my inside my pants, it was obvious the room's atmosphere was now charged with lust.

"How you love-birds making out?" Mick rephrased his previous comment into a question.

"Yo cuz…" I responded after a lengthy pause. "If you and Lorrie want to be alone, it's cool. I understand."

"Let's Get Ready to Rumble!"

"Where's my homie *O* at?"

The sound of a man's voice woke me up. The instant I regained consciousness, I saw someone reaching toward my blanket. Snatching the stranger's wrist in midair, I glared at the intruder through the dimness.

"Oh my fault cuz!" he said in a loud voice. "I thought you were O."

Before I could respond, Mick ran in the room and placed a brown paper bag on the floor. It looked like a six-pack of beer.

"What up fool?" Mick yelled.

Hearing this, I let go of the guy's arm.

"What's happenin' Army-man?" replied the unknown visitor. And the two friends hugged.

After releasing the stocky guy, Mick turned on a light and removed his jacket.

"I knocked but no one answered. Since the front door was open I came in," the stranger explained with a grin. "When'd y'all get here?"

"Yesterday," Mick said, clicking on a second lamp. "I just ran to the corner-store for some brews." Saying this, Mick picked up the bag and removed the six-pack. Looking at me, he extended a bottle in my direction.

By this time, I had sat up and placed my feet on the floor. Once I grabbed it, Mick likewise gave one to his friend. As he did this, I watched him scrutinize his buddy's box-fade haircut along with the rest of his body.

"I got two words for you," he resumed with a mocking grin, *"Jenny Craig!"*

Hearing Mick mention the popular weight-loss company, I imagined he was teasing his friend about putting on a couple pounds.

Following a few seconds to chuckle at his own joke, Mick finally got around to introducing us. "Tak, Benji. Ben, this is my dawg from Ft. Bragg, Takuan." As Mick gestured back toward Ben, I jumped in.

"He was on your high school, basketball team, wasn't he?"

"Yeah, how'd you know?" They both replied in astonishment.

After hearing their question, I realized I had no idea how I had known this. "Because...because you talk about him sometimes," I said looking at Mick.

"Yeah but you never saw a picture of him. How'd you know *this* was Ben?"

It was true. I had never laid eyes on this *Amos 'n' Andy-like* grinning caricature before in my life. But for some reason, I was reluctant to admit this simple truth. Fortunately, a more suitable option came into view.

"Not true," I dissented, putting on my glasses. Then I pointed at a newspaper clipping on the wall and half-guessed. "That's him passing you the ball, right?"

"Hell yeah, that's us...the Fighting Tigers, boyee!" Ben replied first. "That there's the state championship game."

"Mick, you didn't tell me y'all took the states," I said impressed.

"We lost in the final seconds on a bullshit call by the ref," Ben again replied.

"Hold up, lemme get this straight," I snickered looking at Mick. "You gotta a photo up on your girl's wall, caption and all, about a game y'all *lost?*" Although my challenge was directed toward my friend, you-know-who responded first.

"You don't know what the hell you're talkin' about stranger! O showed his ass that night, didn't you cuz?" After glancing at Mick, Ben pivoted back toward me. "When O took Terry Mills—the six-foot-ten, MacD All-American—to the hole for the three-point, play-of-the-day, the crowd went ballistic!"

"Maybe so, but it damn sure wasn't the 'play of the day' because y'all got beat!" I stated, stubbornly rejecting any reason to reminisce on a losing effort.

To me, winning was everything. Even though I had quit my high school football team before the season ended, since one of the managers had a crush on me, she took the liberty of ordering a state champs jacket bearing my name and presenting me with it as a gift. In spite of not really earning it, I sported it with all the confidence of a blue-chip athlete simply because our team had won.

While Mick and Ben recalled various highlights from their hoopin' hey-days, I realized I did not like Mick's ex-backcourt mate. Not yet linking him with the backstabber trying to date Lorrie, I credited my agitation to the way he woke me up. For this reason, I ignored my instincts when they warned Ben was hiding something behind his nice-guy grin.

Looking out the window, I was surprised to find it was already dark outside. Earlier that afternoon, when I woke up, Tina was gone. After Lorrie made us lunch, Mick and I went to a shopping mall so I could buy a pair of jeans. It was then we both realized how sleepy we still were; so we decided to return to Lorraine's for a power-nap.

"Come on y'all, hurry up and get dressed," Ben amiably persuaded. "It's almost nine and there's a party at the rec-center tonight. Javvy and them are deejayin'," he added.

"Mick, where's Lorraine?" I asked.

"At work. You know my woman got to have my money on time!" he joked.

Seeing he was not going to be serious, I gave up

asking.

Following a shower and a quick stop at McDonald's, we drove to a remodeled house in the middle of the hood. With most of the surrounding buildings looking abandoned, we appeared to be in a district slated for gentrification.

"Welcome home O!" yelled a voice from the porch. Then, one-at-a-time, three of Mick's friends walked down the steps to greet him with a hug and me with a handshake. Following a brief introduction, we went inside the refurbished, two-story home.

"I been waiting for a good reason to break this open," said one guy as he displayed a fifth of Absolut Vodka.

After seating ourselves in the living room, we began throwing down chilled shots while we became acquainted.

"Tak, that your ride?" Ray, who was the owner of the house and the only guy I felt an instant liking for, asked this peeking through his curtains.

"Hell no!" Mick interjected. Speaking loudly, he told his version of the story. "That's one of my hoe's rides, so you might as well say it belongs to me." Seconds after he slapped hands with Ben, his ex-teammate displayed his turncoat potential.

"Stop lying!" he yelled. "Tak already told me it was his boy's when you were in the shower."

Wanting to avoid a debate, I decided it was a good time to search for the bathroom. Upon seeing me departing, one of Mick's friends commented. "You see homie don't wanna answer no questions about it."

And the entire room fell-out laughing.

Ray, it turned out, fancied himself a connoisseur of high-performance automobiles. For this reason, when I returned from the bathroom he begged me for a test-drive.

"Yo Tak, is it cool if I drive the car around the block real quick? I wanna check her out. Plus," he continued, "it ain't safe to park no *bimmer* on the street after dark, especially one with Carolina plates."

"Bimmer? What the fuck is a 'bimmer?'" When Mick asked this, everyone chuckled at Ray's strange pronunciation. "You mean 'beemer?'" he added.

"No muthafucka, I understand English better than your stupid ass! For those *not* in-the-know, BMW started-out making motorcycles. And everybody called their bikes 'beemers.' Later, when they started producing cars they couldn't use the same nickname, so instead they called them 'bimmers.' I'm talking about outside of the US, you dig? Y'all ready to go?"

"Well here in America, especially in black-ass America, they're called beemers. But thanks for the history lesson professor," Mick said in a patronizing tone as we walked outside.

"I didn't know that," I said in amazement. "Is that true?"

"Hell yeah. I wouldn't say it if it weren't," Ray replied with a smile. "Does that mean I can take her for a spin?"

"Yeah, do your thing cuz." Saying this, I tossed him the keys.

"And when I'm done, I'll park her in my garage," Ray said, snatching the key chain out of the air with one hand.

"Cool, thanks."

"Hold up, hold up, what're y'all talking about?" Ben protested. "O, you gotta make your return-appearance in the beemer, cuz!"

Unwilling to debate with this guy, I walked across the

308

street to take another piss. *The brews and the vodka were really running through me.* By the time I walked over to Mick, 'Judas' had piled in the car with the others, leaving Mick and I alone.

"So what's up with you and 'Dimples Bee?' I asked wanting an update on what was going on. "Is he the guy trying to get with Lorrie?"

After laughing at my comical reference to Ben, Mick responded. "Oh my bad, I forgot to tell you. Yeah, he's the dude another friend of mine told me was tryin' to get with Lorrie but I don't think it's true."

"Why not?"

"Me and Ben talked about the rumors floating around when you were in the shower."

"And?"

"Like I said, nothing but a bunch of rumors." Saying this, Mick turned his head to spit. When he resumed talking, he never looked at me. Instead, he gazed down the street, in the direction Ray had sped off. "It turns out Ben and Lorrie go to the same junior college. To save gas, they carpool to class together. A couple heads probably saw them together and boom, next thing you know, some chickenhead looking to make headlines started clucking gossip."

"And I guess he showed up at her apartment today to study for exams, right? Come on cuz, if you believe that story, you're slippin'."

"Nah, he went there looking for me," Mick insisted. "He said some of the fellas saw us when we drove into town yesterday. People tend to notice bright red BMWs with out-of-state plates." Then Mick completed his petition to convince himself. "Tak, he's my homeboy. I mean, where else would I be?"

Before I had an opportunity to debate his bullshit rationale, the revolting sounds of *MC Shy D* got my attention. Seeing the 'Battle Creek Boyz' had returned from their spin around the block, I reluctantly surrendered with one final comment. "Yo, before we leave Michigan, make sure we put your homies onto some *KRS* and *Rakim.*"

Once Ray backed the Bavarian Motor Works, German-made automobile inside his garage, Mick, Ben, and I got into his '84 Supra while two of the guys started walking to the rec-center. Ten minutes later, Ray stopped in front of a dilapidated, one-story structure. Being the first person to exit, I was greeted by a bunch of unfriendly stares until the homecoming king stepped out and flashed a grin.

"Why all the serious faces?" Mick yelled. "Let's get this party started!"

"Is that O?"

While some mumbled their uncertainty, two humongous bouncers rushed forward. After this behemoth two-some hugged their friend, they gave me a pound.

"Damn cuz, when'd you get home?" inquired one of the giants while they escorted us toward the building.

"Yesterday," replied Mick in between hugging and shaking hands with numerous, unknown characters in the crowd. "And yo, this here's my homie, Takuan." Then he looked at me. "Tyrell and Hakim were the center and power-forward on our squad."

"Any friend of O's is a friend of mine," Tyrell assured me.

"Same here," concurred his partner. "Come on, let's go inside."

Our short stay in Battle Creek revealed Mick had been immensely popular in high school. Furthermore, once our

Army status was revealed, everyone treated us like visiting heroes. Generally speaking, I notice this trend to exist among country folks; they really love guys in the military. In Jersey, on the other hand, joining Uncle Sam's ranks was largely viewed with contempt, while attending a reputable college ranked as the only post, high school endeavor that mattered. I can still recall my eccentric, eleventh grade English teacher repeating to us time and again that, "Attending a recognized university hints a youngster may be stumbling onto the road to success."

Please shut the fuck up!

Although I was initially uncomfortable with the celebrity-like prestige, after only one day, the bigwig treatment had gone to my head. Through my intoxicated lens, I forgot these strangers were showing me respect because I was Mick's guest. Instead, I started believing it was simply because I was 'the man'…of course.

Inside the rec-center, the dance floor was mostly empty. Most of the folks had not arrived yet or were still outside. After Mick introduced me to a few more people, we approached two fine, caramel-coated honeys. Before we could sit next to them, *Rob Base* expressed the exact vibe I was feeling.

"I wanna rock right now!"

Once the lyrics blasted out of the speakers, the four of us stepped toward the dance floor along with a bunch of other people. Following a couple minutes of watching this seductive sista in motion, I winked my appreciation at Mick. After he grinned back, he disappeared behind three other couples dancing near us. Now alone with my beautiful dance-partner, I grabbed her hand and pulled her close.

"I'm Takuan, what's your name?"

"Amber," she replied with a shy grin.

"Did you go to school with O?" I asked, not knowing what else to say.

"Yeah. Orlando's like a brother to me." Saying this, Amber revealed two rows of perfectly straight-teeth.

"Well, we have that in common then," I said, moving my hands to her slim waist. "Me and O are stationed together at Ft. Bragg."

"I know," she replied as a matter of factly. "I told Orlando I wanted to meet you tonight."

Her words were precisely what I wanted to hear! There was no doubt about it: Amber was fine enough for a solo return-trip to Battle Creek. By the time we decided to take a rest, I was on cloud nine. With her hand in mine, I led her off the dance floor. We walked around until we found two seats near the back of the room. Sitting down together, Amber and I were all giggles and grins; everything was perfect. Then, a group of dark, foreboding clouds congregated over our picnic.

"Hey baby, did you miss me?"

The unfamiliar female voice startled me. Nevertheless, within seconds, I was outraged when the chubby stranger walked over and sat on my lap. By the time Amber, who seconds ago had been playing with my hair, rolled her eyes and excused herself to the ladies room, I was nearly in hysterics.

"Wait a minute Amber," I pleaded with her. "I don't even know this girl!" Although this was true when I spoke, my brain soon caught up to the visuals being presented to it. Having assured me she would never show up at any "childish" rec-center function, I had deleted running into Tina as a possibility that evening.

Watching her rhythmically gyrate her hips to the sounds of *DJ Debonair* and *Tricky D*, her smile indicated she was pleased her actions had chased away her competition. However, once Amber disappeared from view Tina's countenance at once shifted. Snapping her fingers and sucking her teeth, she actually had the nerve to push my forehead with her index finger.

"I knew it," she said glaring at me, "just another sorry-ass nigga! Oh, you don't know me when I'm wearing clothes, huh?"

"What the hell are you talking about? Is this some kind of joke?" Infuriated, I shoved Tina off my leg and stood up. "Get your fat-ass off me!"

With both of us standing, Tina switched tactics. Perhaps she realized I was not the type to be chumped by a girl in public. Smiling, she stepped forward and gently placed both arms around my waist. Then she drew me closer and purred in my ear. "Baby, you know I can't let none of these hussies steal my man before you leave tomorrow."

The only words that registered were 'my man.'

When I realized she was referring to me, I almost vomited. "Umm…I'll be right back, I gotta take a leak," I said trying to escape.

Apparently, this was not the first time for Tina to get dissed by a guy. Before I could walk away, she snatched my wrist. *The last time I felt such a vice-like grip, Hawk was saving my ass in the P.X.*

"Muthafucka," she started to threaten, "if you embarrass me in here tonight, I'll—"

"What!? Embarrass *you?"* I exploded back at her. Then I calmed myself and smiled, "What you gonna do?"

"Oh, you wanna test me?" Completely unfazed, Tina

313

completed her threat. "I'll tell my brother and them to kick your conceited ass, that's what!"

Hearing this, I arrogantly chuckled before ripping my arm out of her grasp. "Bitch, get the fuck off me!" Following one final glare, I walked away from her.

Entering the men's room, after relieving myself and washing my hands, I looked in the mirror. "Damn I'm fucked up!" Saying this, I splashed some water on my face. As I did so, I blamed Tina for our heated exchange. "That scandalous hoe gonna slip me a mickey so she can suck my dick, then expect me to act like she's my lady? She done lost her mind!" I exclaimed out loud before realizing two guys were behind me using the urinals.

Perhaps our fates were not sealed until I dissed Tina; but it seems foolish to blame my karma on someone I just met.

After exiting the lavatory, I searched for Mick and Ray. Scoping-out my surroundings, I was amazed to find the huge room was nearly filled to capacity. As to be expected in such a large crowd, I was unable to spot either of them anywhere. While contemplating my next move, I took a sip from the pint of Bacardi in my pocket before deciding to look for the sexy sista whose name I had already forgotten.

Stepping through the crowd, I checked my rear flank several times to ensure Tina was not following me. A couple minutes later, I spotted some tight-fitting jeans and a white, cut-off t-shirt which revealed just enough cleavage. Squinting my eyes in the hazy darkness, I had little difficulty recognizing those luscious lips and sensuous hips. Since she was talking to someone, I found an empty space along the wall and leaned against it.

Five minutes later, I was growing impatient. I was certain she was aware of my presence as she sat chatting with a guy sporting a box-fade haircut. In order to get her attention, I pointed at the dude's raggedy Pro-Keds. The fact my rival was wearing dirty canvas sneakers at a jam automatically labeled him as 'wack' in my book.

When she covered her mouth to suppress her laughter, I knew she could see me. At that point, I pointed back-and-forth at the other guy and me. My message was clear: I wanted her to choose.

From the standpoint of being a visitor in a strange town, there are so many things wrong with this picture. And I mean erroneous to the point of mortal danger. Somehow I had concluded this guy's outdated apparel meant he was soft. When, in reality, it is usually the other way around. Generally speaking, guys who are forced to wear beat-up hand-me-downs are more aggressive simply because they have a whole-lot-less to lose and much to gain. My next mistake was even more stupid. I assumed that being Mick's guest somehow guaranteed me a fair fight. In my intoxicated arrogance, I forgot a cardinal rule of the streets: *never try to shine when you're far away from home.* This edict holds even more weight if you're by yourself. This is the kind of situation where I've seen guys who were normally laid-back, I mean really calm dudes, just flip-out and get 'the rams' to hold a stomp party.

"Oh, I know your out-of-town ass ain't over there disrespectin' *me!*"

All of a sudden, my adversary was standing in front of me, about fifteen feet away. Although his facial features remained veiled in darkness, by the angry sound of his voice, I understood he was pissed-off. In my drunken stupor, I failed to notice when the guy moved. Once I did, I left little doubt as to whether or not I was being disrespectful.

315

"True, true, I'm from out of town," I calmly responded, nodding my head. "But homeboy, your wack-ass gear is *out of style!*" Then I busted-out laughing at my own joke. Before I could nail the guy with my next punch line, he stepped into the light. *"Ben?"* Although I easily recognized him, I was stalling in order to adjust my attitude. "My fault cuz, I didn't recognize you in the darkness—"

But it was too late.

"Nah, fuck that! I'm sick of watching you and O walk around here like you're better than us. This is *my* city muthafucka!" Then Ben got what he really wanted to say off his chest. "First, that bastard goes behind my back and steals Lorrie, and now he got the nerve to come back here with your faggot-ass!"

In spite of his insult, I never considered fighting Ben. I was still chalking this up as a misunderstanding. In fact, I was trying to apologize until he stated he had a beef with me too.

"So what you think? I'm just gonna let you fuck my sister, then diss her in front of her own people?"

Reflecting on Tina's threat to call her brother, I was flabbergasted to find she was talking about Ben. "Yo cuz, Orlando didn't tell me she was your sister."

"Benji, fuck him up!" This is what Tina yelled as she pushed her way to the front of the crowd that was forming around us.

Seeing them together for the first time, their resemblance was striking. Beyond being mere siblings, I thought they might be twins. I was aghast at this turn of events. Before I could think of an excuse, Ben surprised me again.

"And on top of that, you gonna try and steal my

316

girlfriend, right in front of my face!"

I immediately suspected his claim of being Amber's boyfriend to be a lie. Not only did she tell me she didn't have a boyfriend, she was way too carefree with me earlier, especially when we were holding hands. She never would have allowed that if her boyfriend was here. With this understanding, I scanned Ben's features and realized his resentment had nothing to do with Tina. Ben was jealous. Jealous of Mick for his relationship with Lorrie; and probably upset I had been dancing with Amber too. Having arrived at this conclusion, I responded according to my hood ethics.

"What a bitch!" I scoffed with a grin. "So what you wanna do Guy-Smiley?"

In spite of my swagger, I was hoping Mick would show up. However, once Ben brought the confrontation to my doorstep, there was no time to think about anything but defending myself. As soon as I put my hands up, at the moment *before* we clashed, everything went black.

To this day, I don't remember those initial impacts. Nonetheless I do recall being overwhelmed by a deeply fatigued sleepiness, almost like I had been drugged. As I desperately struggled against gravity to remain upright, Ben stepped forward and splattered my nose with an overhand left.

According to Ray, who later described what happened, he said so many dudes punched me at the same time I never had a chance to fall. "That was the only reason you didn't go down, Tak. Because they stole the shit outta you from your blind-sides. At least three dudes hit you and few more missed. Word is bond, you were knocked out on your feet!" He went on to say that when Ben hit me, he thinks it jolted me back to semi-consciousness. "But I gotta give you some dap," Ray said before clearing his throat. "When those fools didn't drop you—and instead you ran at them—they were scared as hell!"

All of a sudden, I had no idea where I was. I tasted blood and heard all around me that someone had gotten "sucker-punched." Even after hearing this, it never occurred to me those remarks were about me. Following my instincts, I scurried away to avoid being trampled in *someone else's* fight. As people ran to the corners of the room, it was complete mayhem by the time Mick finally showed up. And he could not have come at a better time because I was completely surrounded.

"Whoa, whoa! What's going on here? He's with me!" Mick screamed, blindly running into the conflagration. He assumed this was a big mistake so he was completely unprepared to defend himself. "Tak, you alright?"

Still in a daze, I watched Ben pivot and deliver a vicious, roundhouse punch. The awesome impact of bone colliding with flesh caused Mick's blood to erupt like puss exploding from a ripe pimple. As Mick's body collapsed like a broken lawn chair, a blotch of red fluid sprayed across my face and jacket, snapping me out of my trance. Seeing Mick on the ground, I realized we were in a fight and I rushed to clear the hyenas away from my fallen comrade. At this point, this was my only concern.

Still dizzy and unsteady on my feet, I staggered forward and almost fell. Ray said this stumble was a blessing in-disguise, claiming it caused me to inadvertently duck under a few punches aimed at my head.

Pandemonium had erupted on the dance floor. Once the bystanders deserted the area, I was able to identify my enemies. Charging toward the dark silhouettes with reckless abandon, I threw a bunch of wild punches. Although I never hit anyone, seconds later, the area around Mick was clear and I reached down to pick him up. In that instant, the lights came on.

Once I helped Mick to his feet, I stared in horror at the cascading, red liquid gushing down his chin like a crimson waterfall. *His lips were split open like a ripe pomegranate.* With the lights illuminated, both bouncers rushed over, pushing several scavengers out of the way. Recalling our warm welcome a couple hours ago, I still harbored the possibility of getting some revenge. Then, to my surprise, the two giants grabbed *me.*

"Get off me!" Before I got the words out, Ray appeared with four guys I had not met. Even though their arrival caused the bouncers to let me go, I was convinced they were attacking us. This time however, I was determined to throw the first punch so I ran straight at Ray. Before I could reach him, his four henchmen combined their efforts and tackled me.

"Chill, chill!" Ray screamed, "he thinks we're his enemies. Let him go!"

Drunk, scared, and confused, once they released me, I squared-off against one of Ray's cousins. After he easily dodged my two attempts to decapitate him, the disciplined fighter stepped backward and exposed his hands in a gesture of peace. His unorthodox actions caused me to take notice of everyone around me. Spinning around, I noticed Ray, Mick, and the other unknown strangers were also frozen in a similar pose. Having formed a circle around me, they were standing just beyond my reach. With the music now turned off, Mick's words boomed in my ears.

"Tak, chill the fuck out! They're on our side!"

When Mick was sure I had stopped fighting, he

stepped toward me. Then, about ten more guys ran through the entrance and surrounded Ray. Once Ray's defenders were sure I was calm, they ordered the bouncers to leave; they even threatened them with violence if they did not move quickly enough.

Watching the frightened behemoths scamper out the exit convinced me Ray's cohorts were indeed on our side. *Thank God!* They continued proving their worth as allies by frightening everyone with violent intentions away. One of them even gave Mick a bandana to stem the blood oozing from his mouth.

"Tak, we're safe," Mick spoke to me, holding the cloth against his face. "These are Ray's folks...his disciples."

Although the word 'gang' was never mentioned, there were numerous hints which indicated these dudes were a cut-above the average, street posse. For one thing, they were adorned in black bandanas, with most of them sporting a single glove, or one pant-leg rolled up to the knee. Most importantly, they were following Ray's commands to a tee.

"Come on, let's jet outta here!" Ray boomed in a loud voice.

Before taking a step, I scanned the area for potential danger and realized our enemies were not among the remaining spectators. Once outside, we spotted Ben walking away with his crew. There were about six of them. When I glanced at Mick, he was already breaking into a jog. Then I heard Ray shout.

"O stop! That fool'll shoot you!"

But Mick and I were already in full stride. Ben, seeing us coming, turned around to confront us.

"Yeah muthafuckas, come get some of this!" While he was yelling, his crew fled in all directions.

When Ben reached into his pocket, this should have warned us to be wary. Yet, we never thought he had a gun; the only thing we saw was an opportunity for some pay-back.

After all, it was 1987. Still over a year before the release of 'Colors,' the Los Angeles based, gang movie that introduced the American public to the idea of a melanin-rich gangster, this motion picture also marked the timeline for the escalation of weapons and drugs to be dumped into the hood by the cops and the FBI.

"What you fumbling in your pocket for punk? A knife?" Mick taunted. "Hold up Tak, let him pull it out so we can use it to carve our names in his face!"

Listening to Mick ridicule Ben's uncoordinated efforts, I noticed he was whistling whenever he said any words containing an 'S' sound. The blow he received must have jarred his teeth, I reflected.

"Freeze!" Screaming this, Ben pointed a .22 caliber handgun at us. For a moment, he stood there wearing a sardonic grin before issuing another command. "Step back or I'll blast you!"

Watching Ben, he appeared to be talking in slow-motion. For some reason, I was convinced he was bluffing. With this in mind, I suddenly rushed forward…only to get tackled for the second time that evening.

"What the fuck is wrong with you?" Mick yelled from his position on top of me. "He has a gun!"

"Get off of me!" I protested. "That bitch ain't gonna shoot nobody!".

By the time we stood up, Ben was nowhere to be found. Hearing the sound of approaching footsteps, we both wheeled around. When Mick and I realized it was Ray and a couple of the guys wearing black bandannas, we relaxed.

Ray ran up to me, grabbed both of my shoulders, and shook me. I guess he wanted to ensure I was totally conscious. "Listen Tak," he stated in an urgent tone. "You can't fight Ben with your hands. If you really want to get him, come with me." Gesturing toward his car, he flashed a sinister grin. "Let's even the odds, cuz!"

Our first priority was to stop at a convenience store because we needed some ice and bandages. Ray stayed in the car when Mick and I entered the 7-Eleven. During that time, in so many words, Mick revealed Ray's high-ranking status with a neighborhood organization. Although I do not remember their name, I have a vivid recollection of their appearance. How could I ever forget the image of twenty, ominous figures cloaked in black waiting for us at Ray's house. *Beyond surreal, the scene was eerie!*

Mick and I stood by and waited until Ray was finished greeting his soldiers with handshakes, embraces, and phrases which represented their esoteric order. Formalities concluded, once they determined Ray was unharmed, Mick and I were given permission to follow him into his home. While we walked up the steps leading to the porch, I noticed Ray's disciples were assuming strategic positions along the street.

"What's all that for?" I asked once we had entered his living room.

"They think Ben might strike back because I interfered. Sit down here," Ray said, pointing at the dining table. "There are some towels in the bathroom. Use as many as you need. I'll be right back." Saying this, he walked into one of the back rooms.

As soon as he left, Mick and I began nursing our injuries.

Staring at my bloodied jacket, for a split second, I

visualized the streaking scarlet stains as a form of abstract, graffiti-art. I almost showed it to Mick, thinking the tie-dye design looked cool. Then I recalled scoffing at the photo in Lorrie's bedroom and understood this was certainly not a moment to memorialize. Grabbing a pair of scissors, I promptly shredded the jacket into strips. Even if we did not use them in our doctoring efforts, the Todd-1 was finished forever.

"Well I'll be damned!" Upon his return, Ray surveyed our first-aid station with both hands on his hips. He appeared to be impressed. "Y'all some muthafuckin soldiers after all, I like that!" Then he folded his arms and got right down to business. "So I'll assume y'all fired a *Roscoe* before. But this ain't gonna be like shooting at no pop-up targets," Ray said, making eye contact with us. "I'll lend y'all the *burners,* if that's what you want. But since this ain't 'folk business,' I can't be involved."

"Understood," Mick replied without thinking.

"A-ight then, step this way," Ray said gesturing down the hallway.

The three of us walked toward the only room that was lit-up. Entering it, we all stopped at the foot of the king-sized bed to marvel at the sight before us. Neatly displayed on a black and silver comforter were various caliber rifles and pistols; there were about twenty-five lethal instruments in all. Standing there, I was impressed at Ray's vast arsenal.

"Tak, how about this .357 Magnum?" Ray asked, wearing a grave expression.

The metallic-grey pistol he was holding in the air was way too bulky, I thought. Ignoring his recommendation, I picked up another weapon. "Lemme get this Beretta."

Being an M-60 machine-gunner, I also had to qualify

at the firing range with these hand-held, 9 mm models. Since I did not want to miss, I chose a weapon I was familiar with. That's when it struck me like a bolt of lightning: *I don't want to kill this guy!* To be honest, at this point, I just wanted to get something to eat, take a shower, and hit the sack. With this in mind, I opened my mouth to speak but nothing came out. Checking out the grim expressions in the room, I realized I was more afraid to admit this, than to shoot Ben.

After Mick selected the Magnum,we returned to the living room and changed into the t-shirts we bought at the convenience store. Our preparations complete, Mick and I carried our ice packs, burners, and bandages to the BMW while Ray consulted with one of his lieutenants. Before I unlocked the door, Ray yelled over to us before pointing at his car.

"O, Tak, get in my car. I'll explain later," is all he said.

Seconds later, Ray waved good-bye to his lieutenant and the three of us drove away. After braking at a traffic light, he glanced back-and-forth between the rear-view mirror and the passenger seat.

"I know I gave y'all a speech back there about how this ain't none of my business, but fuck that! If y'all gonna put a slug in that *mark,* I wanna be there! I'll drive, y'all buck. Cool?"

After we agreed, I heard Ray peel the government seal off a bottle of liquor.

"Here's to all my folks who've went out like soldiers!" Declaring this proudly, Ray poured a small libation out the window. Then he took a healthy swig before passing the bottle to Mick.

Sitting alone in the back seat, I continued to stare at Ray's eyes through the mirror. As I contemplated how to break the news that I was hungry—*and that I wanted out*—in my indecision, I drank over half of that bottle. From that moment, everything appeared grayish and blurry. It felt like I was watching a black-and-white movie without my glasses on. About ten minutes after entering this dense fog, Ray sighted Ben's yellow Hyundai.

"There he is!" he suddenly yelled out.

Once the chase began, there was no turning back.

Shots rang out as we tailed the compact car around the small city. Running red lights with reckless abandon, we endangered the lives of hundreds of innocent bystanders. During one intense segment, both drivers entered the freeway on an exit ramp. By this time, I cannot remember if I was shooting or not because my head was swimming in nausea. Despite Ben's daredevilish effort to dodge cars driving in the opposite direction, it was apparent his beat-up Sonata had little chance of out-running Ray's sleek, high-powered Supra.

Once we entered the expressway the cars were slowing down due to the congested traffic. Within minutes, we saw the truck ahead of us coming to a complete stop. At this point, it was total gridlock—even the shoulders were blocked. When the yellow hoopty skidded to a halt, we imagined Ben and his crew were making a stand.

This was it.

As Ray expertly screeched his car alongside the smaller vehicle, he was screaming over his shoulder. *"Tak, peel that muthafucka's wig back!"*

While the car was still skidding, I stuck my head and arm out the window, aimed at the hazy outline, and squeezed the trigger. But nothing happened. In a panic, I squeezed it two more times. I don't know if the gun jammed or what but nothing came out. Squinting my eyes, I focused on the fuzzy shadows in the other car.

"That ain't Ben!" I yelled. Seconds after making out the petrified image of a Caucasian man and his son ducking down in fear, I passed out.

Chapter13: Post-fight Aftermath

With its novelty worn off, the BMW became just another car neither of us wanted to drive. Sulking and depressed, Mick and I purchased a case of beer and stayed drunk until we reached North Carolina. As crazy as it might sound, the drive back might have been the most dangerous leg of the trip. Whenever Mick was behind the wheel, beyond the challenge of sleeping in a car moving in excess of a hundred mph, I was tormented by images of a child's head exploding into a thousand, crimson-colored fragments, like a bloody firecracker.

Did I kill those people?

The first time I awakened from this nightmare, the thought the events of this trip had only been a bad dream occurred to me. Then I yawned. Once intense pain shot through every fiber of my being, I knew the ass-whipping I received over the weekend was not imaginary. When I looked over at Mick, I had to grimace. Beyond his left eye being swollen-shut, that entire side of his face was purplish and puffy. His lips, appearing stapled-back-together, featured one huge gash which bisected his head; plus he had an assortment of other scars.

"My mom's probably still laughing," whirred Mick in his newly-acquired manner of whistling his s's.

Our last stop before hitting the interstate had been at Mick's home. Even though my duffel bag was already in the trunk, I had to thank Ms. McKnight for her hospitality; so I listlessly followed Mick inside the apartment. In all my years of enduring 'Jap jokes' and losing at the dozens, I never felt as humiliated as I did once Ms. McKnight looked at us and started laughing. To sum up her candid comments: "Two, tough paratroopers came to little ol' Battle Creek and got their asses kicked by a bunch of townies!"

"Yeah, she was cracking up," I concurred. "I'm just glad Missy and Jan weren't there."

"Who you telling?" Mick added.

These were the last friendly words Mick and I shared until I contacted him as a reference for this book. That was twenty-five years later.

A far cry from the brash tandem who had arrived days ago, we limped out of Michigan with our tails between our legs. With shame stabbing at our pride, we argued for half of the trip about who was to blame for our beat-down. As Mick labeled me a 'big-mouthed show-off,' I winced watching him adjust the ice pack he held against his eye.

"I mean, of all people, how you gonna diss Ben?" he said. "You met him face-to-face. You knew he was my homeboy!"

Due to Mick's new habit of chirping his s's, I tried to not laugh. That is, until he described Ben like they were still cool; this ticked me off. "Your homeboy? Mick get a grip, and take a good look in the mirror," I advised. "We look like Sugar Ray Leonard and Thomas Hearns after their first fight for god's sake! Ben's *not* your friend!" I exclaimed before taking a sip of beer. "I agree someone in this car is stupid. But it damn-sure ain't me!"

Seeing he had opened a can of worms, Mick tried to interrupt. "If you wouldn't have dissed him—"

"Fuck that!" I shouted, silencing him. "Even if that was true, how do you explain that all the guys we were fighting were dudes you introduced as your homeboys? Maybe they know something about you that I don't?"

"Now you're exaggerating."

"Am I? I don't think so. You just don't wanna face reality. The truth is, outside of Ray and your family—*and I'm only talking about those in your blood-line*—the rest of them muthafuckas can eat a dick!" With hostility lacing my tone, I expressed my contempt with a series of unfair statements. Our friendship would not survive this tongue-lashing.

"There's no need to disrespect my baby's mama like that."

"What?" Believing I had done a good job of venting without specifically bringing her up, I was blown back he tried to defend her. "You're showing disrespect right now by using that stupid-ass title. I already met her, remember? Her name is Lorraine. But let's be honest, if you really respected her I'd be calling her *Mrs.* McKnight. In case you ain't heard Mick, it's called marriage. And it's the path respectable adults take *before* they have children!"

"Oh I see, just 'cause you ain't got no kids, that makes you better than me? Fuck that, I take care of Li'l O! I ain't no dead-beat dad!"

"Mick, what're you talking about? Snap out of it! Your whole conversation's irrelevant. Lorrie sold you down the river and that's all there is to it. I mean listen to you, I've heard of 'whistling while you work,' but damn cuz, you're whistling while you talk!"

Since neither of us was in any condition to fight, we settled for bitching and moaning until both of us stopped speaking altogether. The only exception being: "It's your turn to drive, wake me up in an hour."

"Three Days Later...Go See the Doctor!"

Beyond rocking the airwaves that year, *Kool Moe Dee's* song highlighting teenage, sexual promiscuity proved useful in a more significant way. It educated me. By explaining the symptoms of 'the clap' in detail, my panic was reduced because I knew the nasty infection was curable. What's more, the title was accurate. Exactly three days after being seduced by the tubby temptress and her tantalizing tonic—*plus that devilish jar of honey*—I felt filthy, dirty, and diseased; i.e. violated.

My first hint something was amiss came at around two o'clock in the morning. I felt a slight stinging sensation while I was urinating. This prompted the playful instrumental to begin looping in my inner ear, kinda like background music. However by first-call, not only were the lyrics mixed-in, *Moe Dee* was turned up full-blast: *"Woke up fussin', yellin' and cussin'...drip, drip, drippin' and puss, puss, pussin'..."*

Once I finished taking the most painful piss of my life—it felt like I was peeing fire—I brushed my teeth, got dressed, and went to formation. As you can probably imagine, I was embarrassed so I decided to keep my condition a secret. With my swollen lip and other assorted scrapes and scratches, I figured I had the perfect pretext to go on sick-call. Nevertheless, just in case anyone was suspicious, I contrived a dramatic tale about being fouled while soaring-in for a tomahawk dunk.

"Sergeant B, you should've been there, I was in a

zone!" I boasted in my usual manner. "They couldn't stop me so they started hacking."

"Well, hold on to some of that enthusiasm until the brigade's basketball season starts, okay?"

After my NCOIC approved the sick-call request, I continued my 'down-low' approach at the Troop Medical Clinic. In the event it became necessary to explain my presence at the TMC, I brought along a large manila envelope stamped 'Official Documents' on the outside. Walking in the entrance, I picked up a copy of the boringly biased, Army newspaper *Stars and Stripes* to hide my face. Once inside the Sexually Transmitted Infection unit, my covert mission instantly faced a bump in the road when I was forced to check-in with a very attractive receptionist.

PFC Fields, a beautiful red-bone with green eyes, was way too fly to be wearing BDUs, let alone dealing with STI patients. After mumbling my reason for being there, she made me repeat my symptoms in a loud voice before directing me to write them on a medical form.

Damn Shorty! If I gotta write them anyway, why the hell did I have to say 'em too? Complaining thus in my mind, I filled-out the form and handed the clipboard back to her. Then I grabbed my newspaper and turned toward the crowded waiting area.

Following each weekend, particularly one extended by a holiday, STI clinics were filled to the brim with sex-depraved GIs foaming at the mouth in anticipation of receiving that infamous shot in the butt. Before joining the forty-plus losers, I had to suppress a grin because I noticed almost every one of the seated soldiers was hiding behind a copy of *Stars and Stripes.* Seeing this, I decided to leave my newspaper at the front desk.

Finding an empty seat near the back, I sat down and relaxed. As I watched random GIs open, close, and adjust their periodicals like they were reading, I began feeling drowsy. Once my eyelids got heavy, the room resembled a moving black-and-white collage. Fearing if I fell asleep, I might miss hearing my name being called, I sat up and stretched my arms. When my eyes rested on another non-reading soldier, initially, I suspected his smile indicated he likewise was amused by the spectacle of phony readers. Nevertheless after I broke eye contact, I was perplexed when the brown-skinned, private called out my name.

"Amaru? Is that you?"

Fuck! I thought while glancing at the floor to ignore the guy. Too late, he was already on his feet walking in my direction.

"Aw shit, I knew it was you!" the private stated triumphantly. "And a first-time customer, I presume, by the way you're trying to play me off."

Tilting my head upward, I looked at his smiling face, pretending to notice him for the first time. "Ssup Lloyd," I gave him a pound without standing up. "It's been a long time. Since Jump School, right?" Faking a yawn, I placed my 'Official Documents' envelope on my lap, in plain view.

He ignored my effort.

"Fuck the small-talk, home-slice," Lloyd replied. "Was she fat? Tell the truth Amaru, she was fat wasn't she?" Before I could say anything, several soldiers seated nearby began to snicker.

Glancing at them, I raised the envelope higher so everyone could see it. "Nah cuz, I'm here to deliver this." Watching Lloyd's grin swiftly broaden across his face, I instantly wanted to take my lie back.

"Get that bullshit outta my face!" he snapped, smacking the envelope out of my hand. "If I had a dollar for every first-timer who told me they were here on some 'official business,' I'd buy my own whore-house...and VD clinic too! You don't think I tried that when I first came in here?"

"Seriously man—"

"Shut up!" Lloyd scolded as I reached down to pick up the envelope. Once he realized I was doggedly sticking to my plea of innocence, he shook his head in disgust. "Okay tell me this Amaru," he began, "if you're here to deliver that package, then why is your dumb-ass sitting in the waiting room, huh?"

When several soldiers burst-out laughing, I felt perspiration dripping down my back. Seeing I had no reply forthcoming, Lloyd playfully slapped me on the shoulder.

"My brutha, you ain't gotta be embarrassed about getting burnt, it's just a natural part of being a dog. But what you *do* need to be embarrassed about homeboy, is how fat and sloppy that bitch was that did it to you!"

With the majority of the waiting room now in an uproar, I was relieved when a male nurse walked in and reprimanded everyone to keep it down before calling my name. As I rose from the chair, Lloyd grabbed my wrist.

"You see 'brown sugar' over there?" he said referring to Fields. "I tore that pussy up too so you ain't gotta be bashful in front of her neither. And check this out Amaru, I kid you not, if she stands up you'll see the fattest ass on Bragg! But yo, before you take that penicillin shot in yours, admit it cuz: the hoe that burnt you was a big ol' heifer wasn't she?"

Snatching my arm out of his grasp, I almost ran away

from Lloyd and his cackling audience. Upon reaching the male nurse waiting to escort me, I noticed he was trying to stifle a grin of his own. With my head down, I followed behind him along two dimly lit passageways until we entered an examining room.

"Good morning, Private."

"Good morning, sir."

After our greeting, the Chinese doctor politely told me to get undressed.

While Captain Zhang performed his duty, I closed my eyes thinking this was the lowest a human being could possibly sink to. Desperate for real change in my life, from this moment, I was determined to seek God. As this single idea dominated my thoughts, it was interrupted by one other: *How the hell did Lloyd know she was fat?*

The Crux of Cracka Theology

"People smile in front of your face and talk behind your back..."

In their second *Message,* known as *'Survival,'* *Melle Mel* and *Duke Bootee* lyrically illustrate that modern society is founded upon exploitation. The powers-that-be have used theft, deceit, and murder to enslave the masses through a manufactured condition called 'scarcity.' Long-story-made-short, the name of the melanin-deficient game is to hoard all the Earth's natural resources. This includes her original inhabitants too.

Since the creation of the asinine slogan 'black-on-black' crime, a primary function of media outlets has been to mass-produce evidence of "minorities" committing atrocities

334

against themselves. This is not only happening in the US but all over the globe; especially in so-called 'developing' countries. Whether in the form of drug abuse, violence, or other crime, the origin of these problems is *never* investigated or addressed. This strategy of 'blaming the victim' allows a smooth transition to the next phase of neo-colonialism.

While the cameras are rolling, representatives of powerful governments show up with window-dressing remedies disguised as charity. Yet, behind the scenes, these parasitical entities are stealing, raping, and performing other forms of exploitation. Through the media, they mask their greedy intentions with righteous claims of helping impoverished, war-torn, or disease-infested areas. *The very conditions they themselves created.* Having mastered the art of subterfuge, their favorite disguises are medical assistance, religious piety, or what is perhaps their most creative deception of all: a 'peace-keeping' mission.

Likewise, since religions have been dumbed-down with false doctrine and degraded by several centuries of biased, ecumenical conferences, even the most righteous of the flock are doomed to be sucked into the whirlpool, propaganda campaign aimed at an imaginary guy named 'Jesus.' Considering the multitude of mind-control devices in operation, it is virtually impossible for the masses to distinguish authentic, worship practices from the synthetic, distorted imitations masquerading as spirituality.

END

If you enjoyed Book II, please consider leaving a review here:
https://www.amazon.com/review/create-review?asin=B01AQT38V2&ie=UTF*&#

Thank you so much!

In Book III, Takuan is true to his word; he seeks out God and finds Him—in the flesh. In accordance with the scriptures, God is forgiving as He takes Tak under his angelic wing. For the next several months Tak dedicates himself to nothing but training his mind, body, and spirit. Exercising in the gym by day and scouring the Bible at night, in time, he becomes one of Pastor Bartholomew's "Soldiers of the Lord." However, right when life seems on-point and intact his whole world collapses; this leaves young Tak with only one way to achieve his 'Quest for Christ Consciousness.'

Acknowledgements

First and foremost, I must give praise and respect to the entity called "God"—but also known by many other names. I want to thank my family and everyone I was ever cool with in the Army. To all drill sergeants past, present, and future. Especially Drill Sergeant McDowell, Drill Sergeant Asuncion, and Drill Sergeant Baker. To the Black Hats and Air-Assault cadre; and to every NCO that has ever taken time out of their busy day to school a hard-headed private. That means you Sgt. Queen, Sgt. Will, Sgt. Watlington (who also was a drill but I knew him as a supply sergeant) and many others…

Another big shout to all my dawgs in training or permanent-party: Tazewell, Odom & Dunbar, McCown, Lumpkin. To my bunk-buddy and big brother, Jackson, and of course the Hawk…thanks for being there! Can't forget my tutor in AIT, Housen, the guy who took on the nickname 'Corny' with pride. McBride, Womack, and Shockley, we really kicked it in Jump School and Ft. Bragg. Atkins & Quincy, Chill, Wade, Stock, "Ragu," Johnson, Howard, Ware, Carrington, Douglass, and Wiles thanks for the memories!

ABOUT THE AUTHOR

Takuan Amaru is an accomplished writer, teacher, and youth advocate. He is the author of over 100 articles ranging on such diverse topics as popular culture, music, history, ancient spirituality and philosophy. Takuan borrows from his former occupations as a soldier, social worker, mental-health specialist, athlete, music artist, and high school teacher / coach to connect with readers on an intimate level. He makes his home in Nagoya, Japan. For more information, please email him at: takuanamaru@gmail.com. Or, connect via Facebook.

Glossary of Terms, Historical Figures, and Events

(3 Volumes)

A – B

ACAP is the abbreviation for: Army Career and Alumni Program

Affirmative Action is a policy that seeks to redress past discrimination practices through measures to ensure equal opportunity in education and employment

Air Jordan is a nickname for Michael Jeffery Jordan (1963 -), who is considered by many to be the greatest basketball player of all time

Air-ball is a shot attempt in basketball that misses both the backboard and rim *(see Brick)*

Akashic Records: According to *Robert Bruce* (2009), it is a frequency that permeates all dimensions. An interdimensional broadcast containing records of all past events and future probabilities (pg. 277)

Akitu (or *Akītum*) means: cutting of barley; it was the Sumerian spring festival in ancient Mesopotamia

Albert Hofmann (1906 – 2008) was the Swiss scientist credited for synthesizing the psychedelic effects of LSD

Alfred is the butler and father-figure to the famed Marvel Comics super-hero, *Batman*

All the Way Live! Refers to: an exceptionally cool vibe at a party; popularized by a 1978 single by Lakeside

Alvin Ailey (1931 – 1989) is the choreographer who is credited with popularizing modern dance

Amazing Grace is a Christian hymn written by poet and clergyman John Newton in 1779

Amazon Warriors were called *Oiorpata* in the Scythian lexicon. According to Greek mythology, they were a nation of all-female warriors

Amen (also *Amon, Amun*) is an ancient Egyptian god who, together with his spouse Amaunet, rose to the position of patron deity of Thebes during the 11th dynasty of the Old Kingdom (c. 21st century BC). The name itself signifies the 'hidden one,' and according to Dr. Muata Ashby (2000-2001), the concept of Amun is the central theme of every world religion – and of modern physics as well (p. 77)

American: Until the 19th century, *Negro, Indian, Colored, Black,* and *Moor* were used interchangeably with *American;* Caucasians were referred to as 'Europeans' or 'settlers' (in their history texts)

Amos 'n' Andy: In the 1920s - 1950s, two Caucasians in *black-face* portrayed 19th century, racist stereotypes on radio and television shows

Angkor Wat [អង្គរវត្ត] is a vast temple complex built by Suryavarman II, the Khmer King. It was dedicated to the god, Vishnu. It is still the symbol of Cambodia and appears on its present day national flag

Anomaly: Deviating from what is standard, normal, or expected; i.e. an inconsistency

Anubis is also known as *Anpu.* This ancient Egyptian god is the 'opener of the way' into the Underworld

Apollo Theater: Reference to: the *World Famous Apollo Theater;* located on historical 125ᵗʰ Street in Harlem, NYC

Apostle-hood: In classical Greek, *Apostle* means: one who is sent away; this is what the disciples were called after Jesus' death

ARCOM is an acronym for: Army Commendation Medal

Area J: A rugged training area located on Fort Bragg, NC

Aretha Louise Franklin (1942 -) is one of the best-selling female artists of all time; known as the 'Queen of Soul'

Arizona Brown is marijuana from Mexico that is rumored to be smuggled into the US through Arizona

Arms Room: a secure area for stocking military armaments

Army Slogan: "Be All You Can Be!" was the official Army slogan from 1980 – 2001. It was featured on a commercial with another popular phrase: *"We do more before 9 am than most people do all day!"*

As the sound of many waters is a quote in Revelation 1:14-15. It states: *His head and his hairs were white like wool as white as snow; and His eyes were as a flame of fire; His feet like unto fine brass as if they burned in a furnace; and His voice as the sound of many waters*

Asiatic: the Original Man; we have existed for aeons preceding anything documented in western history books. The Noble Prophet, Drew Ali, referred to black, brown, red, and yellow people as *Asiatics*

Assata Olugbala Shakur (also known as JoAnne Chesimard) (1947 -) is a former member of the Black Panther Party and Black Liberation Army. Between 1971 and 1973, Shakur was accused of several crimes and was the subject of a multi-state manhunt. In May 1973, Shakur was involved in a shootout on the New Jersey Turnpike. She was wounded while BLA member, Zayd Malik Shakur, and New Jersey State Trooper, Werner Foerster, were both killed in the incident. Assata was accused of murdering the officer and assaulting fellow Trooper, James Harper. Between 1973 and 1977, Shakur was indicted on many charges. Some of which included: murder, attempted murder, armed robbery, bank robbery, and kidnapping. (Note: it is documented fact that many of these crimes occurred while Shakur was in legal custody. Many claim this illustrates she was being framed by the state of NJ). The charges resulted in three acquittals and three dismissals. However, in 1977, she was convicted of the first-degree murder of Officer Foerster, and of seven other felonies related to the shootout. Shakur was incarcerated in several prisons in the '70s. This includes serving time in a men's prison where, as a "cop killer", she was subjected to regular vaginal-and-anal strip searches. *Is this equivalent to saying she was repeatedly raped?* In 1979, she escaped from prison, and is now in Cuba, where she has been living in political asylum since 1984. Since 2005, the FBI has classified her as a 'domestic terrorist' and offered a $1 million reward for assistance in her capture. In 2013, the New Jersey Attorney General doubled the reward for her capture to $2 million. Shakur is the first woman on the FBI's Most Wanted Terrorist List. According to Ms. Shakur herself, she is a "20th century escaped slave"

ASVAB is the initials for the Armed Services Vocational Aptitude Battery. This entry test is administered by the United States Military Entrance Processing Command. It is used to determine qualification for enlistment in the US Armed Forces

Ate up is military slang meaning: far below the accepted standard; i.e. bad, terrible, fucked up

Awesome God is a contemporary worship song by Rich Mullins on his 1988 album, *Winds of Heaven, Stuff of Earth*

AWOL is a military acronym for: Absent Without Official Leave; i.e. a deserter

Baba Dwame Ishangi (1934-2003) the artistic director of the world renowned Ishangi African Dancers is also an accomplished African folklorist, dancer, percussionist, choreographer, lecturer, storyteller, sculptor, yoga instructor, nutritionist, poet, family counselor, spiritual advisor, and teacher

Babbit is marijuana with very low levels of THC; i.e. bad weed

Back Slide is Christian term meaning: to return to a prior state of sinful living; i.e. to regress

Baller is slang for: basketball player; it later adopted attributes of street hustling and womanizing

Balls: This term makes reference to the testis. It means: courage, brashness, boldness. "Having balls' is military slang for: having the nerve to do something

Bama means a southerner (from Alabama) trying to blend in up north, but is so obviously 'country'

Bar-Mitzvah is a Jewish coming-of-age ritual. It is akin to the female version, *Bat Mitzvah*

Barrio is a Spanish term for the *Hood*. In the US it is the Latino equivalent of *Ghetto*

Battle Creek, MI is the home of *Kelloggs;* a multinational manufacturer specializing in breakfast cereal products

B-Boys is terminology for: a participant in the Hip Hop culture of the early '80s; there were also *B-girls*

BDU is the initials for: Battle Dress Uniform. It is the olive-drab, camouflage uniform

Be Down: This phrase is questioning if a person is worthy to be included. It's a shortened form of 'down by law'

Bean Pie: A pie often sold by representatives of the Nation of Islam

Beating Meat is slang for: masturbating, i.e. jerking off, choking the chicken, etc.

Beef: 'Having a beef' is slang for: holding a grudge against someone and wanting to fight them

Beemer is a nickname for: Bavarian Motor Works; BMW

Beethoven: [ˈluːtvɪç fan ˈbeːt.hoːfən] (1770 – 1827) was the son of a Moorish woman. Most people have no idea that one of the most famous composers of all-time was, in fact, a 'black-a-moor'

Benjamin Banneker (1731 – 1806) was an astronomer, mathematician, inventor, author, farmer, engineer, and social critic. This African man was an internationally known polymath who lived as a 'free man' during the chattel-slave era of the Americas. A few of his many contributions include being the original publisher of the *Farmer's Almanac,* the architect who laid the plans for Washington DC, and inventing the modern clock. For this reason, according to Dr. Booker T. Coleman, the clock in London is called 'Big Ben'

Bensonhurst: This section of southwest Brooklyn is predominantly populated by the descendants of Italian immigrants

Bent: 'To get bent' is street terminology for: getting intoxicated / high

Bento [弁当[: refers to: a lunchbox

Big Gulp: A super-sized 20-64 ounce soft-drink introduced in 1980

Billy Bad-Ass was my shit-talking alter-ego. He is not to be confused with the Beast, who rarely spoke

Binghi: The *Nyahbinghi Order* is the oldest of all the Rastafari mansions and was named after Queen Nyahbinghi of Uganda, who fought against European invaders in the 19th century

Bite or Bitin' is the act of intentionally trying to pass another artist's lyrics off as one's own in a plagiaristic context

Bite out (someone's) Back is a phrase meaning: talking negatively about someone in secret; i.e. talking behind someone's back

Black: Beyond denoting a race or color, this term symbolizes many things (see Melanin, Moors, Negro)

Black Hawk is a nickname for the UH 60 series of military, utility helicopters

Black History Month is held annually in February to celebrate important people and events in the history of the African diaspora

Black Man's World is another reference to BMW

Black Ops is a loose reference to government, covert operations with negative overtones

Black Panther Party (for Self-Defense) was a revolutionary socialist organization promoting the Black Power movement in the US from 1966 to 1982

Black Sheep is an idiom for: an odd or disreputable member of a group; especially within a family unit

Black-and-White is slang for: police car

Blazing is street slang for: high-level; it can refer to anything from a beautiful woman to very potent cannabis

Blessed are the pure of heart, for they shall see God is a quote from Matthew 5:8 of the New Testament

Blow is one the various street-names for cocaine; i.e. *yayo, nose-candy, snow white, etc.*

Blue Devils is the nickname for: Duke University athletic teams

Blue Light Special: In a US department store named *Kmart*, a flashing blue light is turned on to indicate a short-term discount

Blues (or Dress Blues) are the Air Force dress uniform; i.e. their version of the Army's Class A uniform

BMO is the abbreviation for: Battalion Maintenance Officer

B-More is the nickname for: Baltimore, Maryland

Body-Boxing is a brutal form of boxing wherein punches to the legs, abdomen, and chest are thrown as hard as possible

Bogart: 1. The act of shoving someone out the way. 2. Cutting in front of someone. 3. Taking more than one's fair share

Bokuto [木刀] is a wooden sword commonly used in *Kendo*

Bon-odori[盆踊り] is a dance commemorating the Buddhist custom of honoring the spirits of one's ancestors

Bonaparte: A comical reference to Napoleon Bonaparte becoming a tyrant due to his 'short man' complex

Bones is slang for 'dollars'

Box is a street name for: a large portable radio/cassette player; whites labeled them "ghetto blasters"

Brainiac is a term for: studious individuals

Brick: In basketball, this is a bad shot that bounces hard off the backboard or the rim

Brickhouse is jargon for: an irresistibly sexy woman; made famous in a song by the Commodores

BRM are the initials for: Basic Rifle Marksmanship

Broomhilda is a comic strip by Russell Myers depicting a man-crazy, cigar-smoking, beer-guzzling, 1,500-year-old witch. In ancient times, the Celtic people had an entirely different image of the witch, or 'crone'. She was revered as the 'dark mother', the healer, the wise woman. The buffoonish images of women, or those of the 'wicked witch', are wholly concepts created by western society

343

Brother: Many ethnicities and groups use 'brother' to address its male members. However, 'a brother' or 'a sister' typically refers to melanin-rich people

Brown-Round is the Army's nickname for: a drill sergeant's hat

Brown-nose is Army slang for: ass kisser; supposedly, these individuals 'kiss ass' so often, they have brown, fecal residue on the tips of their noses

Brown People are generally Latinos, Indians, and dark-skinned Asians

Bruce Lee: [李小龍] *Lee Jun-fan* (1940 – 1973) this Hong Kong fighter and filmmaker, who founded *Jeet Kune Do,* is perhaps the most influential martial artist of modern times. Bruce Lee's widow, Linda Lee Cadwell, asserts that Bruce created the concept for *Kung-Fu* (with himself as the star) before Warner Brothers outright stole the idea. It is believed that David Carradine was inserted because of opposition to a Chinese man being cast in the role of a hero

Brut is a brand name by *Fabergé* for a line of men's cologne

Buck is slang for: firing a gun

Buddah is a nickname for marijuana because THC is known to cause a deep level of meditation

Buggin' out is slang for: having fun or acting crazy; popularized by a 1985 song by Whistle entitled *Just Buggin*

Bumming (something) is slang for: receiving something for free

Bumple-stiltskin is a comical reference to the imp-like creature in the German fairy tale, *Rumplestiltskin*

Burner is another reference to a handgun

Bushido [武士道]: is the samurai's moral code emphasizing frugality, loyalty, and honor unto death

Bust (someone's) Balls is Army slang for: to embarrass or humiliate

Bust a Nut means: male ejaculation; i.e. to cum

Busta is slang for: an uncool person; i.e. a nerd

Buster Brown is a comic strip character created in 1902 by the *Brown Shoe Company*

BX is an acronym for: Base Exchange; these are huge retail stores for Air Force personnel and their families (similar to PX)

C – D

Cadre means: the military personnel in charge

Cammied-up is the act of using camouflage paint and clothing in order to blend into the surrounding environment; i.e. a guerilla

Candy Shop: A metaphor for: a place where illegal drugs are sold

Carl Wade Stiner (1936 -) is a retired US Army, four-star general

Caught Out There is slang for: getting caught doing something wrong plus the consequences that go along with it

344

Chakra is a *Sanskrit* term. Often thought of as 'spinning wheels of energy', they represent the seven subtle energy centers aligned from the base of the spine to the top of the head. In Hindu metaphysical and tantric/yogic traditions, it is believed that when all seven chakras are in alignment, a person's life force *(kundalini)* can travel up the spine to the crown of the head

Challenge-Password is Guard Protocol. A question is posed to the oncoming party who must provide a valid answer to be authenticated

Chaptered (Out): Army Regulation manual 635-200 covers all types of less-than-honorable discharges

Charlie Chan: This Chinese-American detective, created by Earl Derr Biggers, is viewed as a racist stereotype by many Asians

Charlton Heston: John Charles Carter (1923 – 2008) was an actor known for his portrayal of *Moses* in *The Ten Commandments*

Cheeba is a street name for: cannabis or marijuana

Cherry Blast: is the nickname for the first parachute jump after Airborne school; i.e. the sixth jump

Chi; or *Qi* [氣] is an active principle forming part of any living thing; frequently translated as 'natural energy', 'life force', or 'energy flow', it is the central underlying principle in traditional Chinese medicine and martial arts

Chicken George: A reference to the subservient, fearful character in *Roots,* played by Ben Vereen

Chill-Guill was my nickname for Perez. It was also to honor one of *Doug E. Fresh's* deejays named *Chill Will*

Chink was originally a British slur for Chinese. Nowadays, this pejorative refers to Asians in general

CIA: On August 18, 1996, the *San Jose Mercury News* published the first installment of a three-part series of articles concerning crack cocaine, the Central Intelligence Agency, and the Nicaraguan Contra Army

CID are the initials for the Criminal Investigation Command. This unit investigates crimes within the US Army; akin to Internal Affairs

City of Brotherly Love is a nickname for Philadelphia; i.e. Philly

Civvies is military slang for: civilian clothes

Clap is a nickname for: Gonorrhea; a sexually transmitted infection (STD)

Clinton Eastwood, Jr. (1930 -) is another icon actor for white masculinity

Clockin' Dollars is a euphemism for: making money; i.e. working around the clock

Cloud 9 is an idiom meaning: a feeling of euphoria; i.e. floating on clouds

Clowning (someone) is slang for: making fun of; to ridicule someone

CO are the initials for: Commanding Officer

Coca-cola: Prior to the 20th century, cocaine was a legal ingredient used in this popular, carbonated soft drink

Cold Lamping is an alternate form of *chilling* or *cold-chilling*

Colored: An outdated Jim Crow reference meaning: black or African-American

Colt: A horse in its infancy stage is actually called a 'foal'

Columbian Gold is a a native strand of marijuana grown in Columbia. It is known for its golden hairs and powerful psychedelic effects

Commie is short for 'communist', but really meant anyone not agreeing with US policy during the Cold War. This code word for 'the enemy' was changed in the 21st century to *Terrorist*

COMMO is the Army abbreviation for: the communications platoon

Conan the Cimmerian is a sword and sorcery hero created in 1932 by Robert E. Howard

Concertina Wire is sharp, barbed wire that is formed in large coils. Also called 'Dannert Wire'

Confucius [孔子] (551 – 479? BC) was a teacher and philosopher who emphasized human morality; he is credited with being the first to write the *Golden Rule* and is the author of many famous texts including the *Five Classics*

Cool Jay is a shortened form of LL Cool Jay

Cop is slang for: a police officer. Or a verb meaning: to receive something by either purchasing or stealing it

Coqui 900 is a malt liquor brew by *Pabst Brewing Company.* It was popular in Philly for its potency

Cowardly Lion is a reference to the timidly fearful character in the 1939 musical-film, *The Wizard of Oz*

Cowboys and Indians: In this make-believe ritualistic role-play, children re-create the massacre of the original Americans

CPA: Certified Public Accountant

CQ is an abbreviation for: Charge of Quarters; the NCO in charge overnight

Cracka is a term used to identify the class of societal slave drivers; i.e. the foreman who *cracks* his whip

Cracka Theology is my way to express the system of white supremacy. Dr. Neely Fuller and **Crackhead** is slang for: a person addicted to crack-cocaine; it also suggests poor personal hygiene and kleptomaniac behavior

Crazy Horse: Thašúŋke Witkóɔ (1840? - 1877) was an American hero who defended the territories and way of life of the Oglala-Lakota branch of the Sioux Nation; he earned a reputation for being 'untouchable – un-killable' amongst the invading 'pale-face' soldiers

Crib is slang for: a person's house. According to Dr. Francis Cress Welsing, we unconsciously equate the bed of an infant with our home due to being reduced to 'child status' (minority) by white supremacy

Cum is slang for: semen

346

Curious George: Comical reference to the monkey in a popular children's book by Hans Augusto Rey and Margret Rey

Dap: Slapping hands or exchanging pounds (bumping fists); it is a sign of respect or group solidarity

Darth Vader is the main villain in George Lucas' *Star Wars* saga. After turning to the 'dark side', he evolves into a menacing character known for punishing his subordinates' mistakes with death

Daruma: *Bodhidharma* was a dark-skinned man born in the Indian state of Tamil Nadu during the 5th/6th century CE. Credited as being the transmitter of *Ch'an* to China, he also began the physical training of the *Shaolin* monks that led to the creation of *Shaolinquan*

Debarge: A family, music group that was revered by females who adored the light-skinned, wavy hair type of guy

D-Day refers to the Normandy landings of the Allied invasion. It occurred on June 6, 1944

Delta Force: 1st Special Forces Operational Detachment-Delta (1st SFOD-D) is one of the four secretive, tier-one counter-terrorism and special mission units

Deuce and a Half: The M35 series of trucks are large utility vehicles in the 2 ½ ton weight class

Dick-down is slang for: having sex

Diesel is short for *cock-diesel,* which is slang for: an extremely muscular physique; i.e. like a body-builder

Dime-piece or Dime is a metaphor for: a rating of 10. It is used to describe a good-looking female. Or, it is $10 worth of marijuana

Dimples Dee is the emcee moniker for Crystal Smith

Dissed is Hip Hop terminology for: being disrespectful toward someone

Dixie is the brand name of a line of disposable paper cups

Dizzy Gillespie: John Birks Gillespie (1917-1993), is one of the jazz pioneers credited with ushering in the 'Be-Bop' era

DJ Cash Money: Jerome Hewlett is a Philadelphia-based *turntablist* who is well-known for winning deejay contests worldwide

DJ Chuck Chillout: Charles Turner (1962 -) was a featured deejay on NYC's 98.7 *Kiss FM*

DJ Debonair & Tricky D are two progenitors of Miami Bass music in the late '80s

DMZ are the initials for: Demilitarized Zone. In spite its name, this area, which runs across the Korean peninsula, is the most heavily militarized border in the world

Dog Star is the brightest star in the night sky. Many believe *Sirius* is the original home of melanin-rich people

Don is loosely derived from Italian and Spanish; we used it to mean a cool guy with the girls – i.e. a playboy

Dove Sack is drug-dealing terminology for: a bag of marijuana or cocaine

347

Down by Law is slang for: having respect in the streets. It was popularized by MC Shan's 1987 album entitled, *Down by Law*. In the '90s, this expression was eclipsed by *Keep it Real* as the preferred catchphrase in Hip Hop

Dr. Dunkenstein is a moniker created by Darryl Dawkins to describe his thunderous, backboard-shattering dunks

DRF are the initials for: Division Ready Force. Combat brigades rotate in the planned deployment sequence of readiness

Dr. Ben: Dr. Yosef A.A. Ben-jochannan (1918 – 2015) taught us about many of Africa's ancient civilizations as a professor at numerous institutions including Cairo's University of Al-Azhar and Cornell University. A fellow historian and contemporary, Dr. Asa Hilliard III, described him as "fearless, audacious, and driven." He claimed that *Dr. Ben* did not "merely ask us to accept his testimony" but rather "put the primary evidence for his conclusions before us."

Dr. Frances Cress Welsing state that a system is practiced by the global white minority, on both conscious and unconscious levels, to ensure their genetic survival by any means necessary. Accordingly, this system attacks people of color (particularly people of African descent) in nine major areas: economics, education, entertainment, labor, law, politics, religion, sex, and war

Dr. J: Julius Winfield Erving II (1950 -) is the player credited with launching the modern style of playing 'above the rim'; the *Doctor* is considered one of the best dunkers of all-time

Dr. John Henrik Clarke (1915 – 1998) was a pioneer at Cornell University and Hunter College. Beyond revealing the truth about black people's history, he was famous for confronting and defeating western historians in public debates, most notably Wellesley College European classics professor Mary Lefkowitz. According to Dr. Clarke: "the first light of human consciousness and the world's first civilizations were in Africa." He taught us that the so called Dark Ages were dark only for Europe

Dravidian: Due to their dark skin, the original descendants of India have been relegated to a low-caste called *Untouchables*

Drop: the command to get down and do push-ups. Or, it means: a knockout (KO) in boxing

Drop Dime is street vernacular for: snitching or ratting

Dropping Knowledge is terminology for: teaching; usually by lecturing

Dumbed Down: This form of mental exploitation contains elements of *misinformation* and *disinformation*

Dun is a Moorish title; similar to El, Bey, Ali, AL, Dey, etc.

E – G

Earth, Wind, and Fire is one of the most successful bands of the twentieth century; *EWF* was one of the first black groups to claim a spiritual lineage in ancient Egypt

Eating out the palm of your hand is an idiom meaning: to have someone under a spell which leaves them helplessly gullible

Edward Leo Peter McMahon Jr. (1923 - 2009) was famous for being the set-up man for Johnny Carson

Egg McMuffin is the signature breakfast sandwich sold by McDonalds

EIB are the initials for: Expert Infantryman Badge

Elaine Brown (1943 -) the former Black Panther Party chairperson (and mistress of Huey Newton) is a prison activist, writer, and singer

Elvira: *Elvira, Mistress of the Dark* is a comedy horror character created by James Signorelli

Embed Miltarism: Since the 1980s, embed militarism in movies has been funded by a taxpayer subsidy through the military and its contractors. This process of Pentagon-Hollywood collusion includes military officials producing, collaborating on screenplays, line-editing scripts, and even changing plot and dialogue in order to guarantee the film is pro-military (Sirota, 2011)

Emotional Pain Body: As explained by Dr. Umar Johnson: an EPB is a "chip of self-hatred" that is suppressed in the subconscious of a person and can be activated suddenly and without warning if she/he is put in a stressful situation

End of Cycle Test (EOCT): is the final examination in basic training

Enquiring Minds is a reference to: the gossip tabloid newspaper, the *National Enquirer*

Enterprise is a reference to a spacecraft commandeered by *Captain Kirk* in *Star Trek*; i.e. the USS Enterprise

Ernest "Ernie" Eugene Barnes, Jr. (1938 – 2009) was an artist. His piece entitled *Sugar Shack* became famous on the sitcom, *Good Times*

Ernesto 'Che' Guevara (1928 - 1967) was an Argentine revolutionary, physician, guerrilla leader and author

ETS is the military abbreviation for: Expiration Term of Service

Everclear is a brand of rectified alcohol distilled from grains; it is bottled at 190-proof (95% ABV)

Extra Sensory Connection was a classic 'slow-jam' radio program broadcast on WDAS

Eye for an Eye: In Exodus 21:23-24, it is written: *And if any mischief follow, then thou shalt give life for life, eye for eye, tooth for tooth, hand for hand, foot for foot*

Failure to Adapt: AR 635-200, chapter 11, states the measures for dismissing personnel due to 'failure to adapt to the military environment'

Fart is slang for: flatulence; i.e. breaking wind

Fayette-nam was a nickname given to Fayetteville in the '60s by protesters of the Vietnam war

Field Negro: As explained by Malcolm X, in slavery, the 'house negroes' worked inside as butlers and maids while the others performed manual labor outside (see House Negro)

Fire Guard is a night guard-duty for trainees only; i.e. the soldier must stay awake and patrol the barracks while others sleep

Fireman's Carry is a technique for a person to carry another person without assistance by placing the body across their shoulders

First Call signals the start of the day; i.e. wake up

Fishers of Men and Women is written in Mark 1:17 in the New Testament

Five-O is slang for: police; it is derived from the TV drama, *Hawaii 5-0,* which aired from 1968-1980

Flat-line: To register as having no brain waves or heartbeat on an electronic monitor; i.e. dead

Flower Child was a nickname for idealistic young people during the 1967 Summer of Love

Fly Girl is Hip Hop slang for: a fashionably sexy female

Forties (40s) is terminology for: a 40-ounce bottle of malt liquor

Fortune 500 is a magazine which annually lists the top ranking corporations by their gross revenue

Foxy 99 FM: WZFX is a radio station in Fayetteville, NC

Fresh Fest: The first major Hip Hop tour; it featured the hottest names of '80s Rap

Frogmen was a nickname for the SEAL trainees

Front or Frontin' is Hip Hop jargon meaning: to assume a phony or disingenuous stance

Front-Leaning Rest is Army terminology for: the push-up position

FSU are the initials for: Fayetteville State University

Ft. Leavenworth is the US Army installation which serves as the military's corrections complex. The Department of Defense's only maximum security prison is located in Kansas

FTX: is the abbreviation for: Field Training Exercise

Furious Five: Joseph 'Grandmaster Flash' Saddler (1958 -) is the pioneering deejay who is credited with inventing the 'cross-fader.' His five emcees: *Melle-Mel, Mr. Ness, Raheim, Kid Creole* and *Cowboy* formed this pioneering Hip Hop group from the South Bronx

Gaijin [外 人[is a bigoted word originally reserved for Portuguese, Dutch, and other Europeans sailors; i.e. non-human, barbarian, savage. In modern Japan, it has become a pejorative to signify any non-Japanese person

350

Ganja is slang for: marijuana; derives from *Ganjika* in Sanskrit

Gasface is 80s slang meaning: to make a stupid face to show disrespect toward someone you don't like. It was popularized in a song by *3ʳᵈ Bass*

General Order: Orders to Sentry is the official code of conduct governing guard duty in the US armed forces

Gentrification: the Urban renewal (1949 Housing Act), or 'slum elimination,' is a mechanism of racial discrimination used to force a change of residence upon people who lack resources to cope in a biased housing or business market. Once the people are removed, upscale neighborhoods, resorts, freeways, or golf courses are erected. According to James Baldwin (1963): "Urban renewal means Negro removal" (Standley, 1989, pg. 42)

Get Ghost is slang for: disappearing from the scene, i.e. to leave

Get Jacked means being a victim of a car-jack or a strong-arm robbery

Gettin' New is the act of being two-faced or phony in a new environment or social situation

Gettin' Nice: Slang for the 'high' feeling one gets from marijuana or liquor; i.e. a mild euphoric state Gettin' Puffed is slang for: getting high on marijuana

GI is the abbreviation for: Government Issue; sometimes it is short for GI Party

GI Bill: A range of benefits including cash for college. GI's in the program donated $100 bucks a month and received payments after being honorably discharged and enrolled at an approved institution

GI Party: Soldiers collectively cleaning the barracks on the weekends or before an inspection

Globe Trotterish is a reference to the *World Famous Harlem Globetrotters* – most notably Marques Haynes

Go [围棋; 圍棋; 囲碁; 바둑[: literally means: encircling game. It is a board game involving two players that originated in ancient China more than 2,500 years ago. In antiquity, it was considered one of the four essential arts of a cultured scholar.

Golden Rule: The traditional maxim stated: 'One should treat others as they would like to be treated'; however, the contemporary version has become: 'The man with the gold makes the rules!'

Goliath: In 1ˢᵗ Samuel 17, *Goliath of Gath* was a giant Philistine warrior who was defeated by *David*

Good Times is a popular sitcom portraying the projects of Chicago, Illinois; it aired from 1974 - 1979

Good Hair: Part of the *Willie Lynch Doctrine* states that non-Caucasian hair textures are 'bad hair.' A documentary by Regina Belle, entitled: *My Nappy Roots: A Journey through Black Hair-itage* explores this subject in detail

GP Mediums have been the most used 'general purpose', canvas tent in the US armed forces since World War II

Grapevine: An unofficial source of rumors, news, or gossip spread by spoken communication

GrandMixer D.ST: Derek Showard is the deejay credited for establishing the turntable as a fully improvisational music instrument

Grasshopper refers to a *Kung Fu* flashback scene in which *Master Kan* says to Caine as a boy: "Grasshopper, quickly as you can, snatch the pebble from my hand". After Caine tries and is unable to do so, the master replies, "When you can take the pebble from my hand, it will be time for you to leave".

Great White Hope: John Arthur "Jack" Johnson (1878 – 1946), nicknamed the 'Galveston Giant,' became the first 'colored' champion in 1908. This was at the height of the Jim Crow era. Ever since then, every few years, a new 'great white hope' (i.e. a white man or group who can defeat the 'black threat') surfaces in the media

Grimace is a large, purple character in a fantasy world used by McDonald's to attract children, called *McDonaldland*

Grinch refers to the comically heartless character created by Dr. Seuss in 1957

Gringo: Similar to *Gaijin* and *Toubob (West Africa),* this is the pejorative term used by Latinos to describe the melanin-deficient invaders of their country

Grittin' on (someone) is the act of staring at a person with the intention of provoking a fight

Grizzly Adams is the main character in a movie about a California mountain man / trainer of wild animals; i.e. an updated *Tarzan*

GURU: Keith Edward Elam (1961 – 2010) became known as *Gifted Unlimited Rhymes Universal* with his partner, DJ Premiere

Guy-Smiley: A game-show host character on *Sesame Street* who is known for his broad smile

H – K

Haile Selassie I (1892 – 1975) was the Emperor of Ethiopia from 1930 to 1974. He was the heir to a dynasty that traced its origins by tradition from *King Solomon* and *Queen Makeda (also known as the Queen of Sheba)*

Half-Klick is an Army slang for: half of a kilometer. One klick equals a kilometer

Hanafuda [花札] are Japanese playing cards used for a number of games; it literally translates as 'flower cards'

Happy Face: A popular picture-design used on blotter sheets of LSD

Hard Rocks: tough guy or hoodlum; this term evolved into *thug* in the '90s and was popularized by Tupac Shakur

Harriet Tubman (1820 - 1913) Nicknamed *Moses* due her role in orchestrating rescue missions to free people from slavery, ironically, she actually had to threaten many 'dumbed-down' negroes to get them to leave their bondage. *"Live North or die here!"* This was the phrase she used while pointing her double-barreled shotgun in their faces

Heat Miser's Lyrics: The actual lyrics are: *"He's Mr. Heat Miser, he's Mr. Sun..."*

Hee Haw is a reference to a 1970s television show featuring country music; *i.e. redneck, hillbilly, or honky*

Heisman Trophy: the annual award given to the most outstanding player in collegiate football; i.e. college football's MVP

Hi-C is a neighborhood emcee

High Speed is Army slang to describe extreme people or situations. It can be either positive or negative. It is also used for cool stuff in order to express the cutting-edge greatness of it

Hitting the Pipe is street terminology for: smoking crack

Hoagies are a popular torpedo-shaped sandwich in northeast US cities; also known as a *submarine*

Hombres is Spanish for: men

Homegirl: In '80s Hip Hop slang, it means: a female friend who is almost like a sister; there were also *homeboys*

Honkie is a nickname earned by Caucasians in the early 1900s. Especially during the 'depression', many melanin-rich women were forced into prostitution. This is what the families of these women called the European men outside their homes honking their horns at all hours of the night

Hood is short for: neighborhood. However, since black people don't live in actual communities, the result is a *hood*. And according to Dick Gregory, "a hood is something you put over your head to hide something you're ashamed of"

Hood Ethics: The dictated customs which are created in a volatile, aggressive environment in order to survive

Hoopty is slang for: a car in poor condition; i.e. beat up, busted, etc.

Hoosiers is the nickname for: Indiana University athletic teams

Houdini: Erik 'Harry Houdini' Weisz (1874 – 1926) was a Hungarian stunt performer billed as an Escape Artist

House Negro: this label refers to people who disown their own racial identity to please Caucasians

House Nigger: The slave who imagines himself as being closer to his master than the field hands because he lives inside the house

Housing: Military service members with a spouse receive extra money as part of their allowance for living quarters

Howitzer is a type of 105 mm, anti-aircraft cannon

Huey Percy Newton (1942 – 1989) Dr. Newton formed the BPP along with co-founder, Bobby Seale

Hustle: This popular disco dance became the name of its own song in 1975

Hustler is a pornographic magazine published by Larry Flint

ICU is an abbreviation for: Intensive Care Unit at a hospital

Ijime [苛め[is a form of bullying someone deemed different from the group; it is very popular in Japan

Iron Mike: 1. A statue of a paratrooper. 2. A forward lunge exercise. With legs shoulder-length apart and hands on hips, a person steps forward with one leg at a 90 degree angle, then pushes back to the start position and repeats the process with the other leg

Iron Mike Tyson: Michael Gerard Tyson (1966 -) was perhaps the most dynamic KO artist of all-time. He dominated the heavyweight division similar to how Jack Johnson, Joe Louis, and Muhammad Ali reigned during their time as champion

Jabber Jaw is an idiom for: a person who talks too much

Jack Frost was an actual baller from my hood. This guy's reputation for dunking on people rivaled Jo-Jo's KO fame

Jackie Robinson (1919 – 1972) Jack Roosevelt Robinson was NOT the first African / Black to play professional baseball alongside white players. He wasn't even close. Blacks played for decades following the Civil War. Incidentally, in 1944, 2nd Lieutenant Robinson was assigned to the *761st Tank Battalion (nicknamed the "Black Panthers")* at Camp Hood, Texas. He was court-martialed for refusing to move to the back of the bus after being ordered to do so by a Caucasian bus driver

Jack is short for 'jack shit', it's slang for: nothing; i.e. diddly

Jam is street terminology for: a party

James Arthur Boeheim (1944 -) is the head coach of the men's basketball team at Syracuse University

James Clavell: Charles Edmund DuMaresq Clavell (1924 – 1994) was a novelist best known for his Asian Saga series

Jammy: Slang for: gun

J'd: Street terminology for: smoking a joint

Jegna is an Amharic (Ethiopian) word meaning: a brave person, elder. Note: Jon instructed me to *never* refer to him or Curt as a 'mentor'. This was because the duties of a 'mentor' were derived from the mythical Greek character who educated *Odysseus'* son, *Telemachus.* Jon said that a significant part of *Mentor's* role was to introduce the boy to a pederasty lifestyle (i.e. men raping children)

Jehovah's Witness are a modern spin-off Christian denomination created by Charles Taze Russell

Jenny Craig is the name of a weight loss, weight management company founded in 1983 in Melbourne, Australia

Jesus Christ Superstar was a musical staged on Broadway in 1971

Jewish American Princess is a Jewish girl. The term sometimes incorporates a stereotype implying materialistic, selfish behavior

Jim Crow are laws that mandated de jure racial segregation in all public facilities; i.e. apartheid, open racism

Jimmy is short for 'Jimbrowski'. This is a comical euphemism for 'penis' made popular by the *Jungle Brothers, KRS-1,* and *De La Soul*

John Brown (1800 – 1859) electrified the nation after he and his gang of 21 killed several Caucasians – including Mayor Fontaine Beckham. Believing he was the instrument of God's wrath for the sin of owning slaves, he was a heroic martyr and a visionary. His response to being sentenced to death: "Had I so interfered in behalf of the rich, the powerful, it would have been all right".

John Wayne: Marion Mitchell Morrison (1907 – 1979) was an actor who epitomized white masculinity in his movies

Johnnie Law is slang for: the police

Judas is a reference to *Judas Iscariot* (Hebrew: יהודה איש־קריות). One of the twelve disciples of Christ, he is infamously known for his kiss and betrayal of Jesus, for a payment of 30 silver coins

Juice: 'Having Juice' is equivalent to being respected; i.e. down by law

Jump Street is slang for: the beginning of any sequence; i.e. the starting point

Kata: is a fundamental martial arts stance with the feet placed shoulder-width apart. Also called a 'horse stance'

Kayumanggi: In *Tagalog,* this means: brown

Kelloggs Sugar Smacks is the name of a children's breakfast cereal by the Kellogg's Company

Kent State University: On May 4, 1970, the Army National Guard opened fire on this campus at an anti-war protest killing 4 students and wounding 9 others

Kick Game is slang for: to woo; i.e. to enchant or seduce

Kickin' it is a phrase meaning: to hang out with, or spend time with. Or, it is synonymous to 'Kick Game'

King David: According to the bible, he was the second king of Israel, and an ancestor of Jesus

Kissing the Sky: This phrase is taken from the lyrics of Jimi Hendrix's song, *Purple Haze*

Kiwi is a brand of shoe polish commonly used by US Army personnel

Knight's Creed: The Code of the Knights is: *'Protect the weak, defenseless, helpless, and fight for the general welfare of all'*

Knock It Down is street vernacular for: having non-romantic sex with a girl; i.e. hit it

Kodak Moment: A priceless moment that is captured by a photo, or should have been. This phrase is attributed to the Eastman Kodak Company

Kool Herc refers to: Clive Campbell (1955 -) This Jamaican-born deejay

355

is the first in the recognized 'Trinity of Hip Hop Architects' along with *Afrika Bambaataa* and *Grandmaster Flash*. Note: it is debatable as to whether other deejays such as *Grandmaster Flowers, DJ Hollywood, Pete DJ Jones,* and others preceded them

Kool-Aid is the name of a soft drink known for its mascot: an anthropomorphic grinning pitcher

Ku Klux Klan: A highly advanced secret society. Although the KKK is infamous for 'rednecks' and public lynchings known as *pick-a-niggers* (which later became *picnic),* many people fail to realize this white supremacist group has its roots in Moorish science. Nowadays, it is believed by many the Klan has disrobed to become the *Tea Party* (Booker T. Coleman, *Hidden Colors 2*, 2012)

Kumbaya is a reference to a children's spiritual hymn from the 1930s

Kundalini: Literally meaning 'coiled power,' it is believed that awakening this primeval energy results in evolving to higher levels of consciousness

Kurombo [くろんぼ[is a racial slur for: dark-skinned peoples; akin to the word *nigger* or *sambo*

Kwai Chang Caine is the main character in the television series, *Kung Fu*

L – M

Laid: 'Getting Laid' is slang for: having sex

Land Speeder: An anti-gravity craft featured in *Star Wars*

Land of Make-Believe refers to the *Neighborhood of Make-believe,* which is an imaginary town for puppets on the show, *Mr. Rogers' Neighborhood*

Larry Davis (1966 – 2008) later changed his name to Adam Abdul-Hakeem. He gained nation-wide notoriety after winning a shootout with NYC Police officers in November 1986. Davis's defense attorneys claimed that the police were trying to murder him because of his knowledge of the involvement of corrupt police in the drug business. After escaping unscathed, Davis was the target of a 17-day manhunt. *The Larry Davis Story,* a documentary directed by Troy Reed, alleges the NYPD was involved in narcotics trafficking, and claims that the shootout came after Davis backed-out of a drug deal. Incidentally, Adam Abdul-Hakeem was the first person in US judicial history to be found innocent by reason of self-defense in a police-shooting case

Larry, Moe, and Curly: are known as 'the Three Stooges'. This are a famous 20th century, American vaudeville, slapstick comedy team

Latin Rascals: In 1981, Tony Moran & Albert Cabrera began splicing together hit songs on a NYC dance radio station, WKTU

LEG: This condescending term is used by paratroopers to describe non-

Airborne personnel. The letters stand for: Lacking Enough Guts (similar to POG)

Lemon is an idiom meaning: unsatisfactory or defective; i.e. a hoopty or a piece of junk

Len Bias: Leonard Kevin Bias (1963 – 1986) was a basketball player drafted in 1986. He died two days later from cardiac arrhythmia induced by a cocaine overdose

Lone Wolf McQuade: In this 1983 film, J.J. McQuade is a tough-guy who prefers to work alone; he lives in a dirty trailer with a wolf

Lotta-Mo: 'I got a lotta-mo' is a phrase popularized by Mr.T in the movie *Rocky III*

LSD: Lysergic Acid Diethylamide

Lunch is modified terminology for: missing a sure opportunity; i.e. out to lunch

Lyndon B. Johnson (1908 – 1973) was President of the US from 1963–1969

Mac and Tosh are an animated cartoon duo created by Warner Bros. They are known for their over-exaggerated, polite gestures

Make Money was Curt's way of saying: to make significant gains in a chosen endeavor

Make Way for the Bad Guy is a *Scarface* quote by the character *Tony Montana,* played by Al Pacino

Malcolm X (1925 – 1965) changed his name to **Al-Hajj Malik El-Shabazz** (الحاج مالك الشباز). He was a Muslim minister and spokesman for Black Nationalism; he is noted as one of the greatest Americans in history

Man's man: A rugged leader; according to some, what all men should aspire to be; akin to the concept of the *Alpha Male*

Manzai [漫才] is a traditional style of Japanese, stand-up comedy involving two performers

March Madness is the official nickname for: the Division I college basketball tournament held each spring

Mark: A person identified as an easy target; i.e. a sucker

Mason-Dixon Line: Surveyed by Charles Mason and Jeremiah Dixon in the 1760s, it became the border between the North and South

Master Jay is a deejay moniker. He spun rap on WKDU long before it was accepted on mainstream, Philly airwaves (not to be confused with *Jam Master Jay,* of *Run-DMC)*

Mayari: In *Tagalog* mythology, she is the lunar goddess. The daughter of *Bathala,* the king of the gods, she is revered as the most beautiful deity in Bathala's court

McGuire Air Force Base is located in South Jersey, near Wrightstown and New Hanover Township

Medal of Honor is the USA's highest military honor. It is awarded for personal acts of valor, above and beyond the call of duty

357

Melanin: Derived from the Greek *melanos,* which means 'black', this is the most important, the most complex, and the most perfect molecule in the human body. This biological living light-source, which connects organisms to the universe, is influenced by the electro-magnetic field, light waves, and sound vibrations. Because of its magnetic properties, according to Anthony Browder (1989), "People with higher concentrations of melanin in their bodies are more in tune with nature...more spiritual".

Melanin Challenged: Scientific research has shown that some 85% of people with high concentrations of melanin in their skin produce 'melatonin', while only 15 percent of people lacking melanin cannot produce this spiritually inducing substance (Browder, 1989, pg. 94)

Melanin-Deficient refers to the state of lacking a functioning pineal gland; in scientific terms: the absence of the polymerization of oxidation products of tyrosine and dihydroxyphenol compounds. Note: Melanin deficiency has been connected with various genetic abnormalities and disease states

Melanin-Rich: In this book, this term is synonymous with 'black' or 'brown' people. Popularized Dr. Frances Cress Welsing and Yaffa Bey, it represents the condition of a healthy, functioning pineal gland; i.e. uncalcified

Melle Mel: Melvin Glover (1961 -) is an original member of the Furious Five. He is credited with coining the term 'MC' for 'Master of Ceremony'. Simply put, he is one of the greatest of all-time.

Messy Marvin is a reference to a sloppy boy in a popular, *Hersey's Chocolate* syrup commercial

Miami Vice was a television crime-detective series that aired from 1984 - 1989

Michael Joseph Jackson (1958 – 2009) is recognized as the most successful entertainer of all time. A global figure in popular culture virtually his entire life, he is often referred to as the 'King of Pop'

Mickey: 'To slip someone a mickey' describes surreptitiously slipping drugs into a person's drink

Midas Touch: In Greek mythology, the God *Dionysus* granted *King Midas of Phrygia (modern day Turkey)* the power to transmute whatever he touched into gold

Midnight Oil is an idiom referring to: studying late into the night; i.e. pull an all-nighter

Mighty Mouse is an anthropomorphic, superhero character created by the Terrytoons Studio in 1942

Miles Dewey Davis III (1926 – 1991) was a jazz musician, trumpeter, bandleader, and composer; widely considered one of the most influential musicians of the 20th century

Military-Industrial Complex: The aggregate of a nation's armed forces and the industries that supply their weapons and materials

Mind-Control is a systematic method to manipulate others' thought patterns

Money Mike is where my street-ball moniker came from

Monie-Love: was my nickname for Monica. Coincidentally, the identical moniker was made famous by Simon Gooden a couple years later

Moolie: Derived from Italian for *eggplant,* it's a pejorative for a dark-skinned person; akin to *nigger*

Moor / Moors / Moorish: Until the 19th century, *Negro, Indian, Colored, Black,* and *Moor* were used interchangeably with *American;* Caucasians were referred to as 'Europeans' or 'settlers' (in their history texts). Many people know the Moors ruled Spain from 711 to 1492, and are credited with bringing Europe out of the Dark Ages. However, there's much more. According to Hakim Bey, the Moors are the aboriginal / indigenous inhabitants of North, Central, and South America, including all of the adjoining islands. The Moorish empire extended from Africa & Europe to the Americas; which was known in ancient times as *Amexem*

MOS is an acronym for: Military Occupation Specialty

Moses: Arabic [موسى] Hebrew [1 [מֹשֶׁה. According to the Qur'an, Baha'i scripture, and the Hebrew Bible, he was a religious leader, lawgiver, and prophet. 2. Nickname for: Harriet Tubman

Mozart: [ˈvɔlfgaŋ amaˈdeus ˈmoːtsaʁt] (1756 – 1791) *Is it possible the most prolific composer of the Classical era was taught by an Austrian Moor?* Angelo Soliman (1720-1796) was a native of Central Africa. Kidnapped as a child, he was presented to the imperial governor of Sicily in 1734. By adulthood, Soliman was known to be an expert in many fields. As a renowned musical-composer, it is said he had a large influence on the young prodigy while serving as Prince Georg Christian's confidant

MRE are the initials for: Meal Ready to Eat; they are self-contained field rations

Mr. Magic was the moniker for John Rivas (1956 – 2009). He hosted the *Disco Showcase* on WHBI, which later had its 'world premiere' as the *Rap Attack* on WBLS. Marley Marl was his deejay, and the first member of the legendary *Juice Crew*

Mr. Magoo is a near-sighted cartoon character created in 1949 that, by luck, avoids disaster after disaster

Ms. Piggy is an animated pig-like puppet played by Frank Oz on *The Muppet Show*

MTV is a popular US cable and satellite music video channel

Muhammad Ali (1942 -) was known as Cassius Marcellus Clay before he embraced Islam and changed his name. Recognized as 'The Greatest', he'll always be remembered for his famous quote when he refused to fight in the Vietnam War: "Ain't no VietCong never called me 'nigger'. They ain't my enemy – *you* my enemy!"

Mushroom: Psilocybin or "magic" mushrooms are fungi that contain psychoactive indole alkaloids

Musk: The aroma obtained from a gland of a musk deer. Believed to have originated in ancient Egypt, Queen Cleopatra was known to wear this oil

Mustangs are one of the first-generation Ford Mustangs; known as a 'pony car'

N – P

NCAA Championship: The 1987 NCAA Finals was held on March 30, 1987, at the Louisiana Superdome in New Orleans. The Finals are the culmination of March Madness

Noriega: Manuel Antonio Noriega Moreno (1934 -) This Panamanian leader is one of the many publicized enemies who was either inserted into the leadership position by the US, or was known to be a collaborator of the CIA. Noriega has been serving sentences in various prisons since surrendering to US troops in 1990. Other notable 'public enemy' types fitting this criteria are: *Mohammed Reza Pahlavi (the Shah of Iran), Saddam Hussein,* and *Osama bin Laden*

Nappy is a description of: natural African-textured hair

Nathaniel Turner (1800 - 1831) was a prophet who saw visions that prompted him to lead one of the most effective rebellions in US history. Stating he was "Intended for some great purpose", although there were many such revolts, his ignited a culture of fear amongst Caucasians which still exists today

Nature: It is reported that many indigenous people called the planet 'mother'. However, the ancient Egyptians referred to the land as a male deity, *Geb*. His wife, *Nut,* was the goddess of the sky

NCO is the initials for: Non-Commissioned Officer

NCOIC are the initials designating the Non-Commissioned Officer in Charge

Negro denotes 'black' in Spanish. In contemporary usage, it means: a dark-skinned person manufactured in the likeness of a European (see Black)

Neo-Colonialism is a policy whereby a major, world power uses economic and political means to continue ruling its former colony from behind the scenes; i.e. the puppet master

New Yorkers are very thick, stylish laces made popular in NYC Hip Hop culture in the early '80s

Newbie means an inexperienced newcomer; i.e. noob

Nigger: Since colonial times this has been the main ethnic slur directed at peoples of African descent. Most believe it is synonymous with 'ignorant person'. However, the origin of this word is debatable. Some claim it derives from the Sanskrit and Pāli word: *Nāga*. This is a god taking the form of a great snake; specifically the king cobra. It is found in Hinduism, Buddhism and Jainism. Still, others believe it comes from *Negus;* meaning King, or Ruler in Amharic. The scholar, Taj Tarik Bey, teaches that Caucasians were the original niggers, in the form of the *Troglodyte Niger.* This is a type of pale-face chimpanzee

Nippon [大日本帝國] was a world power before the inhabitants of the *Land of the Rising Sun* became *Japanese* in 1947

Non-Commissioned Officers (NCO) are military personnel in positions of authority (E-5 – E-9), but not in positions of 'command' per-se. All commanders must be commissioned officers (O-1 – O-10)

Nori [海苔]: refers to: seaweed

North Cackalackee is a nickname for North Carolina

Northern Lights is a pure *indica* strain of weed with bud crystals that glimmer, i.e. the resemblance to the northern lights sky

Nose Wide Open is a term usually for a male who is crazy in love or lust over a girl, and as a result will focus his total attention on her, ignoring his friends; maybe a hint she is exploiting him

Nubia: The Kingdom of Kush (the Land of Gold) was located on the Nile River, to the south of *Kemet* (ancient Egypt)

NVG is the initials for: Night Vision Goggles

NWA: This group from Compton, California is considered one of the seminal acts of 'Gangsta Rap'. The original group also featured *Arabian Prince*

Nyquil is a brand of cold medication containing alcohol

Occipital Lobe: Located at the rear of the brain, it is the main visual processing center

OCS are the initials for: Officer Candidate School

OG are the initials for: Original Gangster; this street terminology shows respect for an older hustler

Ol' E is an abbreviation for: a 40 ounce bottle of *Old English 800* malt liquor

OPFOR is an acronym for: Opposing Force; this unit represents the enemy during war-game scenarios

Orangemen is the nickname for: Syracuse University athletic teams

Orgone Energy is a hypothetical universal life force closely associated with sexuality. It was proposed in the 1930s by Wilhelm Reich

Original People is a reference to: the indigenous people of the planet; i.e. Asiatics

Othello is a tragedy about the *Moor of Venice,* by William Shakespeare. It is based on *Un Capitano Moro,* by Cinthio

Oxy 10 is a skin cream for acne

PAC is an acronym for: Personnel Actions Command

PAL is an acronym for: Police Athletic League

361

Parris Island is a military installation used for the Marines' basic training. It is located in Port Royal, South Carolina

Pathfinders are covert soldiers who set up helicopter landing sites in hostile territory

PATS is an acronym for: Program for Academically Talented Students

PCS is the abbreviation for: Permanent Change of Station

Peeping Tom is a person who gets pleasure (usually sexually related) from secretly watching others; i.e. a voyeur

Perpetrating means: the act of faking something or being phony; it was a popular idiom in '80s Hip Hop

Peter Brian Gabriel (1950 -) is a musician most known as the lead vocalist of the rock band, Genesis

Peter Edward Rose (1941 -) Nicknamed 'Charlie Hustle', Rose is the MLB all-time leader in hits. Ironically, he is not in their hall of fame due to being accused of illegally betting on games

Peter Tosh (1944 – 1987) was a Jamaican reggae musician; he was a core member of *The Wailers*

PHAT is an acronym for: Pretty, Hot, And Tantalizing

Phenom is short for: phenomenon. It is slang for: a person or thing of outstanding abilities or qualities

Pig: Derogatory slang for: police; it was commonly used in the '60s and '70s

Pinocchio: is a fictional protagonist in the children's novel *The Adventures of Pinocchio* (1883), by Carlo Collodi. This animated wooden-puppet's nose grew longer whenever he told a lie

Pirates is the nickname for: Seton Hall University athletic teams

PLF is the abbreviation for: Parachute Landing Fall. This is the landing technique taught at Airborne School. Properly executed, it allows a paratrooper to land without sustaining injury

PLL are the initials for: Prescribed Load List

POG, or Pogue, is an acronym for: Personnel Other than Grunts. This condescending term is used to describe weak soldiers

Po-Po is an acronym for: Police Officer

Point-Man: means to assume the first and most exposed position in an advancing combat formation

Police Call is a brief reconnaissance / clean-up mission

Popeye: *Popeye the Sailor* was a comic strip character created by Elzie Crisler Segar in the 1920s

Post Traumatic Stress Disorder (PTSD) is a severe anxiety disorder that develops after being exposed to extreme psychological trauma

Postwar Japan refers to: the period immediately following the end of World War II in 1945 to the present day

Pothead is slang for: a habitual cannabis smoker

Pound: Also called *dap* or a *fist pound;* Caucasians later adopted it and

362

called it a *fist bump,* and by many other names. This hand-gesture, which is a symbol of respect, is commonly used by athletes to celebrate with teammates

POV is a military acronym for: Privately Owned Vehicle

Predator: Also called 'Yautja,' these extraterrestrial hunters use advanced technological weaponry to hunt any being they consider a worthy opponent

Presidential Unit Citation is awarded to units of the US Armed Forces for extraordinary heroism. It's on par with the Medal of Honor

Prima donna means: the leading woman soloist in an opera. However, sports writers adopted it to label vain, star athletes

Prodigal Son: In Luke 15:11–32, a wayward son squanders his inheritance but returns home to find his father has forgiven him

PT is a military acronym for: Physical Training

Pu-tang is slang for: vagina; i.e. pussy

Public Enemy: Consisting of *Chuck D, Professor Griff, Flavor Flav, Terminator X,* and the *S1Ws, PE* is famous for their Black Power charged lyrics and criticism of the establishment

Puerto Rico: The ancient name the *Tainos* used was *Borinquen,* which means 'Land of the Valiant Lord'

Pups was a nickname for the SEAL trainees

PX is an acronym for: Post Exchange; these are huge retail stores for Army personnel and their families (similar to BX)

PYT are the initials for: Pretty, Young, Thing. This is a song by Michael Jackson on the album, *Thriller*

Q – S

Quiet Storm is a nationwide, late-night radio program featuring love songs

Quincy's: A buffet restaurant in Fayetteville, NC

Rainbow Coalition: This is not to be confused with Jesse Jackson's diluted organization. The original coalition was led by Chairman Fred Hampton, and comprised of several extremely radical melanin-rich groups. When Hampton was assassinated by Chicago Police, this multi-cultural assembly was on the verge of creating a rival to counter the racist ruling class in the Windy City

Rangers are the elite infantry unit of the US Army

Rastaman is terminology meaning: an adherent of *Rastafari*

Ray Charles Leonard (1956 -) this 1976 gold-medalist was named *Boxer of the 1980s*

Ready Rock is street terminology for: crack rock; i.e. cocaine that is ready to smoke

Red Alert: Fred Crute (1956 -) was a deejay for the *Almighty Zulu Nation* before gaining popularity on KISS FM; he is credited with popularizing dance hall music on the radio

Redneck is a nickname for: Caucasian slaves who spent an extended amount of time working in the sun

Red Wolf: This North American canid was once the alpha-predator in the woods throughout the Southeastern states

REM 4: Rapid Eye Movement is the deepest stage of delta sleep

Replacement Centers are temporary living quarters for personnel until they process into their new unit; i.e. a reception station

Rev. Albert Greene (1946 -) is famous for singing both gospel and (secular) soul music

Rev. Dr. James Cleveland (1931 - 1991) Crowned as the 'King of Gospel', this singer/composer popularized the modern gospel sound

Richard Franklin Lennox Thomas Pryor (1940 – 2005) Perhaps the funniest stand-up comedian of all-time, he was known for his social examinations of racism while consciously probing history; most notably, ancient Egypt

Richie Cunningham is a character from the sitcom *Happy Days.* He was a pip-squeak, redhead with freckles

Richie-Rich is slang for: a person who grows up in a wealthy family. It originates from the 1950s cartoon

Rick James: James Ambrose Johnson (1948 - 2004) popularized funk music in the late 1970s and '80s

Riddler: is a comic book super-villain appearing in *Batman* comic books, published by DC Comics

Roach: the remains of a joint, blunt, or rolled-up cigarette after most of it has been smoked

Robert Ludlum (1927 – 2001) was an author of suspense novels about governmental conspiracy theories

Robert Montgomery Knight (1940 -) is a retired Indiana University basketball coach

Roberto Clemente (1934 - 1972) was a pro baseball player from Puerto Rico. Arguably the best right-fielder of all-time, he died in a plane crash on New Year's eve while delivering aid to earthquake victims in Nicaragua

Rock is street slang for: a basketball. Or, a cluster of cocaine

Rockin' the Cradle is a crass reference for: having sexual relations with a person deemed too young; i.e. statutory rape

ROK is the abbreviation for: Republic of Korea; i.e. South Korea

Roody-poo is a combination of the word 'rude' and 'poo'; i.e. a lame, easy, soft, cowardly, etc.

Roots is a best-selling novel by author Alex Haley; it was later aired as a historical TV drama in 1976

Roscoe is a nickname for: handgun; i.e. gat, heater, etc.

ROTC: The Reserve Officer Training Corps prepares students to be a commissioned officer

Rubber to hit the Road is an idiom meaning: the most important point; i.e. the moment of truth

Rumble in the Jungle is a reference to: the *Rumble in the Jungle* boxing match on October 30, 1974, in the Democratic Republic of Congo, between George Foreman and Muhammad Ali

Run-DMC: Joseph 'Run' Simmons, Darryl 'DMC' McDaniels, and Jason 'Jam Master Jay' Mizell comprised this influential rap group

Running a Train is a ritualistic re-enactment of slave owners raping one slave; i.e. post-traumatic slave behavior

R&R is an abbreviation for: Rest and Relaxation

Sakura [桜] means: cherry blossoms

Salem Witch Trials: In Massachusetts, between February 1692 – May 1693, 14 women and 5 men were executed after being accused of doing witchcraft; i.e. the "devil's magic". Hundreds more were imprisoned resulting in many more deaths

SAT: The Standardized Admissions Test was the most widely accepted college admissions test in the US

Sayonara [さようなら] means: Good-bye

Scared Straight: The act of abandoning a life of crime due to stark fear, this phrase was popularized by a 1978 documentary

Scarface was originally a 1932 film portraying the life of gangster Al Capone. The 1983 remake about a Cuban immigrant turned drug dealer is more well-known

Scarlet Letter: In this 1850 sadistic work by Nathaniel Hawthorne, a European community humiliates a woman by forcing her to wear a scarlet 'A' on her dress as a punishment for allegedly committing adultery

School Boy: This belittling term meaning *nerd* is also the name of a style of frames

S-Curl: Reference to the *Luster* hair-care product that slightly straightens 'nappy' hair into curls and waves

SEAL is an acronym for Sea, Air, and Land Teams; they are the special operations force of the US Navy

Sell-out is slang for: A person who betrays his people to promote his own personal advancement

Seminoles is the nickname for: Florida State University athletic teams

Senioritis is an informal term referring to a reduction of academic focus characteristic of some high-school seniors, especially after they've been accepted into a university

Sensei [先生] is defined as: teacher; literally, it means a 'a life before another'

Sent-up is street terminology for: getting sent to prison

Separate Rats is short for separate rations. Service members with a spouse receive extra money as part of their allowance for meals

Serpentine Fire is an indirect reference to a song by Earth Wind and Fire. In Sanskrit, *Prana* [प्राण] means *Kundalini Energy*

Sess: Meaning high-quality, female cannabis; this is a shortened form of the Spanish word, *Sensimilia*

Setting-Up Camp is slang for: the act of preparing for rulership or leadership in any significant venture

Sev is an abbreviated form of *7- Eleven*. It was also Takuan's street-hustling moniker. Tak's friends called him this due to his proclivity for shoplifting

Seventh Heaven means: a state of intense happiness or bliss. The number 7 is prevalent all throughout Creation. From the number of notes, the days of the week, to the number of orifices on the human body, there are numerous examples. Accordingly, many spiritual systems profess there are 7 heavens, with the 7th being the highest

Shakespeare, William (1564-1616): It is rumored the famed poet either assisted in the compilation of the King James version. Or, he and the king are the same person

Shammer is military slang for: a person who shirks his duty; i.e. lazy or shiftless

Shibumi: This novel, by *Trevanian,* incorporates the philosophy of the Japanese game *Go* to create the 'perfect assassin'

Shirley Ann Caesar (1938 -) is the gospel singer nicknamed the 'First Lady of Gospel Music'

Shit on Lock is slang for: having a situation under control

Shittin' Bricks is slang for: being extremely petrified, nervous, or upset

Shock and Awe is a US military doctrine utilizing the use of overwhelming power to paralyze an adversary's will to fight

Shogun: [征夷大将軍] *Sei-i Tai-Shogun* means: 'Barbarian-subduing Genralissimo'. This was the most sought after military rank in *Nippon* for over a thousand years. A Samurai named *Sakanoue no Tamuramaro [坂上田村麻呂] (758? – 811?)* was the first to assume this exalted position. Depicted as a "paragon of military virtues," according to historian, Dr. Alexander Francis Chamberlain, he was a "Negro." This warrior is venerated at *Kiyomizudera* [清水寺], which is the temple Sakanoue established in Kyoto City

Shook and Shook-Daddy are slang for:being scared; i.e. petrified

Shorty is slang for: either a child or a young lady

Shuckin' and Jivin' is slang referring to: deceit, mischief, or involving lies

Sitting Bull: Thatháŋka Íyotake (1834? – 1890) was a Hunkpapa-Lakota Sioux holy man who, in June of 1876, led a united coalition of American tribes in the *Black Hills* to massacre Gen. **George A. Custer** and his 7th

366

Calvary

Skeezer is '80s slang for: a girl who is known to be sexually promiscuous; i.e. a whore

Skunk: Perhaps the most fragrant strain of cannabis in the world, it is also known for its sweet flavor and pleasant high

Slap-boxing was a contest using open hands to penetrate an opponent's defense and smack him in the face

Slow Jams: In modern America, with the exception of the Latin dances (salsa, merengue, etc.), melanin-rich men and women rarely dance in each other's arms. However, back in the day, it was an essential segment of every party

Sneak is slang for: punching someone in the face when they aren't expecting it; i.e. a sucker-punch

Sole Survivor Policy: see DD 1315.15

Soror is Latin for: sister

SOCOM: US Special Operations Command (USSOCOM); i.e. the Special Forces

SOS is the abbreviation for: *Scientists of Sound.* They were deejay crew in my town.

Soul Train was created and hosted by Don Cornelius. The "hippest trip in America" aired in syndication from 1971 until 1993

Soul to Soul is a British music group comprised of: Jazzie B, Caron Wheeler, Simon Law, Daddae, and Nellee Hooper

Spades is a card game played in pairs. It is very popular in black and brown communities

Special Forces: US Special Operations Command (USSOCOM)

Spicoli: *Jeff Spicoli* is a character from the comedy film, *Fast Times at Ridgemont High,* played by Sean Penn. He is depicted as a 'surfer-dude' who enjoys smoking marijuana

Spike Lee: Shelton Jackson Lee (1957 -) is a film director well known for examining race relations

Spit-shine: A meticulous method for polishing boots which leaves the surface of the leather as reflective as a mirror

Spliff is slang for: a cone-shaped marijuana cigarette

Sports Center is a daily sports, news program on ESPN

Steady B: Warren Sabir McGlone (1969 -) is infamous for being an emcee who actually lived the life of a 'hustla' – not just rapped about it. *Steady B* is currently serving a life sentence for his part in the murder of a police officer during a botched bank robbery in 1996

Steatopygia means an extreme amount of fat on the buttocks region

Stevie Gee is a neighborhood emcee

Stick is a designated group of paratroopers jumping together from an aircraft during an Airborne mission

Stick Ball is a street version of baseball. This game was popular in US

367

cities because it only required a stick, a ball, and some space

Stogie is slang for: a cheap cigar

Straw Man: According to the Redemption Theory, the US government creates a fictitious person corresponding to each newborn citizen and pledges them as collateral to borrow money; i.e. foundation of slavery

Street Entrepreneurship is the ability to hustle or make money; sometimes by selling illegal merchandise

Super Six: This was the name of an actual posse in my hood. Comprised of six members, they were known for their various shades of sheepskin coats and stomping kids in the ground

Sun Tzu [孫武[(544?–496 BC) was a high-ranking Chinese general during the Zhou dynasty's Spring and Autumn Period

Survival of the Fittest: According to Wayne Chandler, Darwin's theory of evolution contradicts every ancient codex on how humans and animals evolved. Claiming it "lacks convincing evidence", Chandler also talks about a "pervasive genius" which encompassed the ancient world. He goes on to describe a time "when humans were truly advanced beings" and "walked in harmony with God and Nature" (pg. 215)

SWAT is an acronym for: Special Weapons and Tactics; it is an elite paramilitary unit that was created to combat 'radical' organizations like the Black Panthers

Sweating is slang for: obsessing over a person

Synagogue of Satan: Revelation 3:9 states: "Behold, I will make them of the synagogue of Satan, which say they are Jews, and are not, but do lie; behold, I will make them to come and worship before thy feet, and to know that I have loved thee"

S-2 is Military Intelligence; they collect data on enemy movement, strengths, and battlefield deployments

T – Z

T-10: The most common static line-deployed parachute used for combat, mass-assault, Airborne operations

TA-50: Table of Allowances is the standard issued gear; i.e. kevlar helmet, ruck sack, canteens, etc.

Taino-Arawak are the indigenous peoples of the Caribbean Isles

Takuan is the family name of Takuan Soho [沢庵宗彭] (1573-1645) He was a Zen monk, calligrapher, painter, poet, gardener, tea master, and author. His collected writings total six volumes and over 100 published poems, including his best known treatise, *The Unfettered Mind*. A central figure in the Rinzai School of Zen Buddhism, his list of accomplishments include being the inventor of the pickled, *daikon* radish that was named after him. At the moment before his death, it is said he painted the

Chinese character [夢] 'dream', laid down his brush, and died

Tall, Young, Legend in Leather is a title used by LL Cool J in his lyrics to describe himself

Tamahu: The ancient Egyptians spoke of a group of uncouth nomads that were described as having pale skin, red to blond hair, and blue eyes.

Tarzan is a *very* fictional character who rules the "African jungles" all by himself. This icon has been a tool for white supremacist imagery since the early-1900s

Tet Offensive: At 3 am on Jan. 31, 1968, North Vietnamese and Vietcong forces launched simultaneous attacks on South Vietnamese and American forces all throughout South Vietnam. The fighting, the heaviest of the Vietnam War, coincided with the Lunar New Year, or *Tet*. It was the military turning point in the war and a political and media disaster for the US

The Christ is a title for Jesus in the New Testament. It is Hebrew for 'Messiah'[מָשִׁיחַ], meaning: the Anointed One

The Clark Sisters are comprised of Jacky, Elbernita, Dorinda, Denise and Karen. They are credited as being pioneers in bringing gospel music to the mainstream

The Doors: Led by Jim Morrison, this rock group took its name from Aldous Huxley's book *The Doors of Perception*

The System is a government structure imposing biased inequality. The discrimination is viewed as 'normal', or even 'ethical', by the law / media simply because they are part and parcel of the very same infrastructure

The Winans are a family, gospel quartet from Detroit, Michigan. The members consist of four brothers: Marvin, Carvin, Michael, and Ronald

Thrasher is someone who listens to heavy-metal music; i.e. a metal-head or a headbanger.

Timbuktu: This city, in the West African nation of Mali, is just north of the River Niger. In its Golden Age, the city's extensive trade network along with the *University of Sankore Madrasah* were internationally famous

Timothy Francis Leary (1920 – 1996) was a psychologist known for his advocacy of psychedelic drugs

Titties is slang for: breasts; i.e. jugs, boobs, knockers, etc.

Toby: In a scene in *Roots, Kunta Kinte,* played by LeVar Burton, was whipped into accepting his slave name, Toby

Top is the officially recognized nickname for a US Army 1st Sergeant

Toussaint Louverture: Francois-Dominique Toussaint Louverture (1743 - 1803) led the rebellion at Saint Domingue, in 1791, which led to the Haitian Revolution. A military genius, not only did he outwit Napoleon on the battlefield, he helped found the independent state of Haiti – that to this day, is still being punished for defeating France

Townies: is a condescending term describing the local people; akin to hillbilly

Tramaine Davis (1951 -) is a well-known gospel singer

Triathlons are competitions consisting of a 2.4 mile swim, a 112-mile bicycle ride, and a 26.2-mile marathon

Trim is slang for: vagina

Trippin': Negative terminology meaning: to behave in an irritating way. Or, it means: using LSD

Trips is slang for: tabs of LSD

Tsunami [津波[refers to: tidal wave

Turned-out: is slang related to the sexual act. Usually negative, it can mean raping someone; or satisfying a person to the point they're sexual orientation is altered; i.e. from heterosexual to homosexual

UCMJ is the abbreviation for: Universal Code of Military Justice. It is the military's list of laws and statutes

Ultra Man [ウルトラマン] first aired in 1966, and is still a popular Japanese television series amongst children

Uncle Sam is a popular nickname for the 'US' government

Uncle Tom is the title character in Harriet Beecher Stowe's 1852 novel, *Uncle Tom's Cabin;* it is also an epithet for a person who is slavish and excessively subservient to the ruling class

Underage is a reference to persons who are below the legal age limit to procure or consume alcohol

Undercover Brother is a reference to a movie starring comedian, Eddie Griffin (see bibliography)

Underground Railroad: A secret network of routes and safe houses used by people in the 19th century to escape slavery in the Americas

Unit Colors is the flag identifying the brigade, battalion, company, etc. This practice of marking the location of the commander originated in ancient Egypt

Up North is street terminology for: prison; i.e. up state

Uprock is a soulful type of street-dance consisting of foot shuffles, spins, and freestyle movements

UPS: United Parcel Service is a US-based, global package, shipping company

Up-State is street terminology for: prison; i.e. up north

US Military Installations: The NATO watch committee reveals that the US operates between 700-800 bases in at least 63 countries. There are over 90 in Japan alone

Vapors means: being high in a chemically-poisoned way; this phrase was made famous by Biz Markie in a 1988 song

Vatos is *Calo* slang for 'dude'

Vaya con Dios: In Spanish, this phrase means: to go with God

Venus was the goddess of love and beauty in ancient Rome. She is also known as *Aphrodite*

370

Vick is street terminology for: robbing or stealing

Video Music Box: Created in 1983 by Ralph McDaniels, it was the first TV show to give mainstream exposure to Hip Hop

Visine is a brand of eye drops that constricts the eye's superficial blood vessels; i.e. "it gets the red out"

Vogue: was a dance imitating super-model poses. Developed in NYC gay clubs, it was later popularized by *Madonna*

WKDU is a Philadelphia college-radio station at Drexel University *(see Master Jay)*

Wack is slang for: something uncool; i.e. corny

Wench is a derogatory word for: an unvirtuous woman; i.e. a bitch or slut

West Point: The preeminent four-year military academy located in West Point, New York

When the Saints go Marching in is a famous gospel hymn often played by Jazz musicians

Whiteboy is a derogatory term meaning: fearful, having no rhythm, or any trait associated with melanin-deficiency

White Devil: Wallace Fard Muhammad was one of the co-founders of the Nation of Islam (NOI). He taught the original humans were melanated and that Caucasians were 'artificial, white devils' created on the Greek island of *Patmos,* by a mad scientist named *Yakub*

White Lie is a diplomatic or well-intentioned untruth; a fib

Who's Zoomin' Who? This phrase means: turning the tables on someone. It was popularized by a 1985 song by Aretha Franklin

Wild Styles is a reference to: the 1983 motion picture produced by Charlie Ahearn

Wile E: Referring to the Warner Brothers character, *Wile E. Coyote*

William Franklin Graham, Jr. (1918 -) is a Christian evangelist, ordained as a southern Baptist minister

Willie Lynch: Allegedly, in 1712, a British slave owner named Willie Lynch delivered a speech in Virginia detailing tactics to pit the indigenous tribes against one another; i.e. the secret to controlling the majority population

"Willie" Wilver Dornell Stargell (1940 – 2001), nicknamed 'Pops', was a left fielder on the Pittsburgh Pirates for 21 years

Wop: the name of a popular dance in the 1980s

Ye are Gods: Psalm 82:6: *I said, 'You are gods, sons of the Most High, all of you';* John 10:34: *Jesus answered them, 'Is it not written in your law, I said, ye are gods?'*

Yeshua [יְהוֹשֻׁעַ]: This was a common spelling in many translations amongst Jews of the Second Temple period

Yin-Yang: In Chinese cosmology, *Yin* represents female energy while *Yang* expresses the masculine principle

Yoni [योनि] is a Sanskrit word meaning: vagina or womb; symbolic of the goddess, *Shakti*

Young Boy means: younger kid. However, this label can also be a term of endearment, or an insult toward an actual peer

Your Arms Too Short to Box with God is a Broadway musical based on the biblical book of *Matthew*

Youse is a phrase meaning 'you guys' which is commonly used by people of Italian descent in the New Jersey / New York area

Zacchaeus: According to the Gospel of Luke, he was a tax collector in Jericho; his name means 'pure and righteous one'

Zested is slang for: being intoxicated or getting high

Zooted: the state of being overly intoxicated; i.e. fucked-up

Numbers

007 is the codename of author Ian Fleming's legendary MI6 agent, *James Bond*

144,000: In Christianity, this number represents the sum of God's people going to heaven

7-Eleven is the world's largest chain of convenience stores

808: A 3-way speaker system utilizing 5 drivers mounted in a bass-reflex enclosure

Bibliography

Articles

Bishop, J. (1988, Aug. 26). To fend off the sun, researchers are using body's own chemistry. The Wall Street Journal. Retrieved from ProQuest databases.

Chamberlain, A. (1911, Apr) The contribution of the negro to human civilization. Journal of Race Development 1(1). Retrieved from https://archive.org/details/jstor-29737886.

King, R. (1986). Black dot, the black seed of humanity. Ureaus, The Journal of Unconscious Life, 2(1). Los Angeles, California: Aquarian Spiritual Center.

Sirota, D. (2011, March 16). How your taxpayer dollars subsidize pro-war movies and block anti-war movies. The Huffington Post. Retrieved from http://www.huffingtonpost.com/david-sirota/how-your-taxpayer-dollars_b_836574.html.

Blog

The Remix with MsBlue. (2010, October 15). "The psycho-sexual war against black girls!" Bro Umar Johnson [Audio file] Retrieved from http://www.blogtalkradio.com/theremix/2010/10/16/the-psycho-sexual-war-against-black-girls-bro-umar-johnson

Books

Ashby, M. (2005). *The Egyptian Book of the Dead: The Book of Coming Forth by Day*. Atlanta: Sema Institute.

Barnes, C. (1988). *Melanin: The Chemical Key to Black Greatness*. Houston, Texas: Lushena Publishing.

Browder, A. (1989). *From the Browder File, 22 Essays on the African-American Experience.* Washington DC: Institute of Karmic Guidance Publishing.

Bruce, R. (2009). *Astral Dynamics: The Complete Book of Out-of-Body Experiences.* Newburyport, Massachusetts: Hampton Roads Publishing.

Chandler, W. (1999). *Ancient Future: The Teachings and Prophetic Wisdom of the Seven Hermetic Laws of Ancient Egypt.* Baltimore, Maryland: Black Classic Press

Howard, R., Sprague De Camp, L., & Carter, L. (1968). *Conan.* New York: Ace Books.

Kingseed, C. (2006). *Old Glory Stories: American Combat Leadership in World War II.* Maryland: Naval Institute Press.

Muhammad, E. (1965). *Message to the Blackman in America.* Arizona: Secretarius MEMPS Publications.

Rashidi, R. (1985). *African Presence in Early Asia.* Rutgers – The State University of NJ, Piscataway, NJ: Transaction Publishers.

Standley, F. (1989). *Conversations with James Baldwin.* Mississippi: University Press of Mississippi.

Whitaker, R. (1979). *Shibumi.* New York: Crown Publishers.

Music

Baker, A. (1985-1986). Been so long [Recorded by Anita Baker] *Rapture* [Vinyl]. California: Elektra Records. (1986)

Baker, A. (1985). Sweet love [Recorded by Anita Baker] *Rapture* [Vinyl]. California: Elektra Records. (1986)

Barrier, E., Griffen, W. (1986). Eric B. is president [Recorded by Eric B. & Rakim] *Paid in Full* [Vinyl]. New York: 4th & B'way/Island. (1986)

Blackmon, L., Jenkins, T. (1986). Word up! [Recorded by Cameo] *Word up!* [Vinyl]. New York: Atlanta Artist. (1986)

Cameo (1983-1984). She's strange [Recorded by Cameo] *She's Strange* [Vinyl]. Casablanca. (January 16, 1984)

Chandler, J. Bell, F., & McDonald, C. (1981). Silly [Recorded by Denise Williams] *Silly* (single) [Vinyl]. Pennsylvania: Columbia/ARC. (1981)

Dewese, M. (1986). Go see the doctor [Recorded by Kool Moe Dee]. *Go See the Doctor* [Vinyl]. New York: Jive. (1986)

Dixon, M., Murphy, D., Dechalus, L., Withrow, K., Brickell, E., Houser, J., Bush, J., & Aly, A. (1989 -1990). Slow down [Recorded by Brand Nubians] *One for All* [Vinyl]. United States: Elektra Records. (1990)

Edwards, B., Rodgers, N. (1978). Le freak [Recorded by Chic] *Le Freak/Savior Faire* [Vinyl]. Atlantic. (January 1978)

Edwards, B., Rodgers, N. (1978). We are family [Recorded by Sister Sledge] *Easier to Love* [Vinyl]. Cotillion. (1979)

Elam, K., Martin, C. (1990). Just to get a rep [Recorded by Gang Starr] *Step in the Arena* [Vinyl]. New York: Chrysalis/ EMI Records. (1991)

Fekaris, D., Perren, F. (1978). Shake your groove thing [Recorded by Peaches & Herb] *2 Hot* [Vinyl]. Polydor. (1978)

Fequiere, S., Campbell, J., Reeves, F., & Bailey, M. (1985). Roxanne roxanne [Recorded by UTFO]. *UTFO* [Vinyl]. New Jersey: Select Records. (1985)

Gamble K., Huff, L. (1978). Use ta be my girl [Recorded by The O'Jays]. *So Full of Love* [Vinyl]. Philadelphia: Philadelphia International (1977-1988)

Gamble, K, Huff, L., Jackson, A. (1972). Foe the love of money [Recorded by The O'Jays] *Ship Ahoy* [Vinyl]. Philadelphia: Philadelphia International Records. (1973)

Ginyard, R., Bryce, R., Riley, T., & Brown, J. (1988). It takes two [Recorded by Rob Base and DJ E-Z Rock]. *It takes two* [Vinyl]. New York: Profile. (1988)

Green, R., Aleem, T., Aleem. T. (1984). Cosmic blast [Recorded by Captain Rock]. *Captain Rock* [Vinyl]. New York: NIA. (1984)

Greene, S. (1984).Let the music play [Recorded by Shannon]. *Let the Music Play* [Vinyl]. New York: Mirage. (February 1, 1984)

Griffey, D., Sylvers, L. (1978). It's all the way live [Recorded by Lakeside]. *Shot of Love* [Vinyl]. California: Solar Records. (1978)

Hancock, H., Laswell, B., & Beinhorn, M. (1983). Rockit [Recorded by Herbie Hancock]. *Future Shock* [vinyl]. (August 1983)

Hanson, A., Davis, E., Mantronik, K. (1986). Hungry for your love [Recorded by Hanson & Davis] *I'll Take You On/Hungry For Your Love/Hold On To Yesterday EP* [Vinyl]. Fresh Records. (1986)

Hardy, A (1986-1988) Vapors [Recorded by Biz Markie]. *Goin' Off* [Vinyl]. New York: Cold Chillin' Records. (1988)

Hardy, N.S., McDaniels, Jr., Simmons, J., & Smith. (1983). Sucker M.C.'s (Krush Groove 1)[Recorded by Run-D.M.C.] *Run-D.M.C.* [Vinyl]. Profile, Arista. (1984)

Hendrix, J. (1967). Purple haze [Recorded by The Jimi Hendrix Experience] *Are you experienced* [Vinyl]. United Kingdom: Track Records. (1967)

Hutchins, J., Fletcher, J., Carter, D. (1984). Friends [Recorded by Whodini] *Escape* [Vinyl]. Jive/Arista Records (October 17, 1984)

Jabara, P., Shaffer, P. (1979). It's raining men [Recorded by The Weather Girls] *Success* [Vinyl]. New York: Columbia. (1982)

Jackson, M. (1982). Beat it [Recorded by Michael Jackson] *Thriller* [Vinyl]. Epic. (November 30, 1982)

Jackson, M. (1982). Thriller [Recorded by Michael Jackson] *Thriller* [Vinyl]. Epic. (1982)

Johnson, H., Gill, P., O'Toole, M., Nash, B. (1983-1984). The World is my oyster [Recorded by Frankie Goes to Hollywood] *Welcome to the Pleasuredome* [Vinyl]. London: ZTT. (1984)

McCoy, V. (1975). The hustle [Recorded by Van McCoy & the Sould City Symphony]. *Disco Baby* [Vinyl]. New York: Avco Records. (1975)

Moltke, S. (1986). The bridge [Recorded by MC Shan] *Down by Law* [Vinyl]. New York: Cold Chillen/Warner Bros. Records. (1985)

Myers, D., Parrish, G., Dixon, T., & Ferrell, F. (1986-1987). The overweight lover's in the house [Recorded by Heavy D & the Boyz] *Living Large* [Vinyl]. New York: Uptown Records. (1987)

Pryor, R. (1975). That nigger's crazy [Recorded by Richard Pryor]. *That nigger's crazy* [Vinyl]. San Francisco: Warner Bros. Records. (1974)

Richie, L., McClary, T., Williams, M., King, W., La Pread, R., Orange, W., & Dean, C. (1980). Jesus is love [Recorded by The Commodores] *Heroes* [Vinyl]. United States: Motown Records. (1980)

Ridenhour, C., Sadler, E., Boxley, H., & Boxley, K. (1990). *Fear of a black planet* [CD]. United States: Def Jam / Columbia Records.

Ridenhour, C., Sadler, E., Boxley, H., & Boxley, K. (1989). Fight the power [Recorded by Public Enemy] *Fight the power* [Vinyl]. United States: Motown Records. (1989)

Robinson, J., Glover, M., & Robinson, S. (1982). Message II (Survival) [Recorded by Melle Mel & Duke Bootee of Grandmaster Flash & The Furious Five] *Message II (Survival)* [Vinyl]. England: Sugar Hill Records. (1982)

Simmons, J., McDaniels, D. (1983). Jam-master jay [Recorded by Run-D.M.C.] *Run-d.m.c.* [Vinyl]. United States: Profile / Arista Records. (1984)

Simmons, J., McDaniels, D. (1985). My adidas [Recorded by Run-D.M.C.] *Raising hell* [Vinyl]. United States: Profile / Arista Records. (1986)

Smith, C., Williams, Kaye, & Montnegro. (n.d.). Sucker DJ's (I Will Survive) [Recorded by Marley Marl] *Sucker DJ's (I Will Survive)* [Vinyl]. Party Time. (1983)

Smith, J. (1986-1987). I'm Bad [Recorded by LL Cool J] *Bigger and Deffer* [Vinyl]. New York: Def Jam, Columbia, CBS Records. (1987)

Smith, J., Jay, J., & Rubin, R. (1984). I Need a Beat [Recorded by LL Cool J] *Radio* [Vinyl]. New York: Def Jam/Columbia/ CBS Records. (1985)

Tosh, P. (1975). Legalize it [Recorded by Peter Tosh] *Legalize It* [Vinyl]. Jamaica: Columbia Records. (1976)

Williams, J. Mantronik, K. (1986). Cold Gettin' Dumb [Recorded by Just-Ice] *Back to the Old School* [Vinyl]. Fresh/Sleeping Bag Records. (1986)

Withers, B., Salter, W., & MacDonald, R. (1981). Just the Two of Us [Recorded by Grover Washington & Bill Withers] *Just the Two of us (B-side: Make Me a Memory)* [Vinyl]. Elektra. (1981)

Movies

Beckerman, S., Feitshans, B. (Producer), & Milius, J. (Director). (1984). *Red dawn* [Motion picture]. United States: MGM/UA Entertainment Co.

Ben-Ami, Y., Carver, S. (Producer), & Carver, S. (Director). (1983). *Lone wolf Mcquade* [Motion picture]. United States: Orion Pictures.

Bregman, M. (Producer), & De Palma, B. (Director). (1983). *Scarface* [Motion picture]. United States: Universal Pictures.

Canton, N., Gale, B. (Producers), Zemeckis, R. (Director). (1985). *Back to the future* [Motion picture]. United States: Universal Pictures.

Chartoff, R., Winkler, I. (Producer). Avildsen, J. (Director). (1976). *Rocky* [Motion picture]. United States: United Artists.

Curtis, K., Harris, T., Ross, D. (Producer), & Murray, D. (Director). (1970). *The cross and the switchblade* [Motion picture]. United States: 20th Century Fox.

Donner, R., Silver, J. (Producers), Donner, R. (Director). (1987). *Lethal weapon* [Motion picture]. United States: Warner Bros. Pictures.

Feitshans, B., Kassar, M., Vajna, A. (Producer), & Kotcheff, T. (Director). (1982). *First blood* [Motion picture]. United States: Orion Pictures.

Fox, T., Henderson, G. (Producers), O'Bannon, D. (Director). (1985). *The Return of the living dead* [Motion picture]. United States: Orion Pictures.

Gordon, L., Silver, J., Davis, J. (Producer), & McTiernan, J. (Director). (1987). *Predator* [Motion picture]. United States: 20th Century Fox.

Grazer, B. (Producer). (2002). *Undercover brother* [Motion picture]. United States: Universal Pictures.

Kennedy, K., Jones, Q., Marshall, F., Spielberg, S. (Producer), Spielberg, S. (Director). (1985). *The color purple* [Motion picture]. United States: Warner Bros. Pictures.

Kopelson, A. (Producer), & Stone, O. (Writer/Director). (1986). *Platoon* [Motion picture]. United States: Orion Pictures.

Lee, S. (Producer/Writer/Director). (1989). *Do the right thing* [Motion picture]. United States: 40 Acres and a Mule Filmworks.

Lester, D., Miller, D., Rappaport, M. (Producer), & Shelton, R. (Director). (1992). *white men can't jump* [Motion Picture]. United States: 20th Century Fox.

Linson, A., Azoff, I., (Producer), & Heckerling, A. (Director). (1982). *fast times at ridgemont high* [Motion picture]. United States: Universal Studios.

Nasheed, T. (Director). (2011). *Hidden colors 1* [Motion picture]. United States: King Flex Entertainment.

Nasheed, T. (Director). (2012). *Hidden colors 2* [Motion picture]. United States: King Flex Entertainment.

Nicolaides, S. (Producer). Singleton, J. (Writer/Director). (1991). *Boyz n the hood* [Motion picture]. United States: Columbia Pictures.

Puttnam, D. (Producer), Hudson, H. (Director). (1981). *Chariots of fire* [Motion picture]. United Kingdom: The Ladd Company.

Raymond, C. (Producer), & Wei, L. (Writer/Director). (1972). *Fist of fury* [Motion picture]. Hong Kong: Golden Harvest Miramax.

Roddenberry, G. (Producer), Wise, R. (Director). (1979). *Star trek: The Motion Picture* [Motion picture]. United States: Paramount Pictures.

Shapiro, A. (Producer), Shapiro, A. (Writer/Director). (1978). *Scared straight!* [Motion picture]. United States: Golden West Television.

Silver, J. (Producer), & Lester, M. (Director). (1985). *Commando* [Motion picture]. United States: 20th Century Fox.

Simpson, D., Bruckheimer, J. (Producer), & Scott, T. (Director). (1986). *Top gun* [Motion picture]. United States: Paramount Pictures.

Solo, R. (Producer), Hopper, D. (Director). (1988). *Colors* [Motion picture]. United States: Orion Pictures.

Spielberg, S., Marshall, F. (Producers), Hooper, T. (Director). (1982). *Poltergeist* [Motion picture]. United States: Metro-Goldwyn-Mayer.

Wachs, R., Wayans, K. (Producers), & Townsend, R. (Director). (1987). *Eddie Murphy raw* [Motion picture]. United States: Paramount Picutres.

Television

Barbera, J., Hanna, W. (Producer). (1977). *Captain caveman and the teen angels* [Television series]. United States: Hanna-Barbera Productions.

Barbera, J., Hanna, W. (Producer). (1980). *Richie Rich* [Television series]. United States: ABC.

Bass, J., Rankin, A. (1974). *The year without a santa claus* [Television animation]. ABC.

Carsey, M., Werner, T., Kukoff, B., Leahy, J. (Producers). (1984). *The Cosby show* [Television series]. United States: Viacom Enterprises; Paramount Domestic Television; Carsey-Werner Distribution.

Cornelius, D. (Producer). (1971). *Soul train* [Television series]. United States: Tribune Entertainment.

Correll, C., Gosden, F. (Creators). (1951). *The Amos 'n' Andy show* [Television series]. United States: WMAQ AM.

Davis, A. (Director). (1947). *The goofy gophers* [Television series]. United States: Warner Bros. Pictures.

Dozier, W., Horwitz, H. (Producer). (1966). *Batman* [Television series]. United States: Greenway Productions/20th Century Fox Television

Freston, T., Pittman, R. (Founders). (1980). *MTV: Music television* [Television series]. United States: Viacom Media Networks.

Healy, T. (Creator). (1925). *The three stooges* [Television series]. United States: Columbia Pictures Corporation.

Levitt, G. (Creator). (1977). *Fantasy island* [Television series]. United States: ABC.

Margulies, S. (Producer). (Jan. 23, 1977 – Jan. 30, 1977). *Roots* [Television miniseries]. United States: ABC.

McDaniels, R. (Creator). (1983). *Video music box* [Television series]. United States: WNYE-TV.

Michaels, L. (Producer). (1975). *Saturday night live* [Television series]. United States: Broadway Video.

Monte, E., Evans, M. (Creators). (1974). *Good times* [Telvision series]. United States: CBS.

Peppiatt, F., Aylesworth, J., Brillstein, B. (Creators). (1969). *Hee haw* [Television series]. United States: CBS-TV.

Ruby, J., Spears, K. (Creators). (1976). *Jabberjaw* [Television series]. United States: Hanna-Barbera Productions.

Takamoto, I., Lovy, A. (Producer). (1973). *Inch high private eye* [Television series]. United States: NBC.

Terry, P. (Creator). (1942). *Mighty mouse* [Television series]. United States: 20th Century Fox.

Tsuburaya, E. (Creator). (1966). *Ultraman* [Television series]. Japan: TBS.

Walsh, J. (Creator). (1979-). *SportsCenter* [Sports news program]. United States: ESPN.

www.ingramcontent.com/pod-product-compliance
Lightning Source LLC
Chambersburg PA
CBHW061549120626
46550CB00004B/1425